Accent and Listening Assessment

Language Testing and Evaluation

Series editors: Rüdiger Grotjahn
and Günther Sigott

Volume 21

Frankfurt am Main · Berlin · Bern · Bruxelles · New York · Oxford · Wien

Luke Harding

Accent and Listening Assessment

A Validation Study of the Use of Speakers with
L2 Accents on an Academic English Listening Test

PETER LANG
Internationaler Verlag der Wissenschaften

Bibliographic Information published by the Deutsche Nationalbibliothek
The Deutsche Nationalbibliothek lists this publication in the Deutsche Nationalbibliografie; detailed bibliographic data is available in the internet at http://dnb.d-nb.de.

Cover Design:
Olaf Glöckler, Atelier Platen, Friedberg

ISSN 1612-815X
ISBN 978-3-631-60939-2
© Peter Lang GmbH
Internationaler Verlag der Wissenschaften
Frankfurt am Main 2011
All rights reserved.

All parts of this publication are protected by copyright. Any utilisation outside the strict limits of the copyright law, without the permission of the publisher, is forbidden and liable to prosecution. This applies in particular to reproductions, translations, microfilming, and storage and processing in electronic retrieval systems.

www.peterlang.de

Acknowledgements

This book is a revised version of my PhD thesis, which was submitted to the University of Melbourne in 2008. This publication is supported by a grant from the Research and Research Training Committee, Faculty of Arts, The University of Melbourne.

I would like to thank my supervisor Professor Gillian Wigglesworth for her unwavering support from the very beginning of the project, and my associate supervisor Dr Carsten Roever for helping shape various key parts of the thesis. I would also like to acknowledge the assistance of Associate Professor Janet Fletcher who was an associate supervisor during my first two years.

In addition to my supervisory team, I would particularly like to thank the staff of the Language Testing Research Centre: Associate Professor Cathie Elder and Dr Ute Knoch, for advice and constant encouragement, as well as Kerry Ryan for providing friendship and a life-line to the working world. I am very grateful to Professor Tim McNamara for his generosity in taking time on numerous occasions to discuss the ideas in this thesis, and to Dr Paul Gruba for his advice on verbal report methods.

Many colleagues and fellow PhD students assisted in various ways throughout the course of my candidature. Among them, Susy Macqueen has been a wonderful friend and support since the Masters program. Jerry Cross has also helped me to understand where this thesis was going at various points. Thanks, too, to Dr Debbie Loakes, Joshua Clothier, Kathryn Hill, Craig McArthur and members of the School of Languages Listening Group.

I am very grateful to a number of experts across different fields who agreed to meet with me to discuss my research: Professor Alan Davies, Dr John Field, Dr Tony Lynch, Dr Susan Nissan, Professor Tracey Derwing and Professor Suresh Canagarajah.

This thesis could not have been completed without the help of the many participants – both speakers and listeners – who provided their time, but who must remain anonymous. I would also like to thank a number of people who were of great assistance during the process of data collection: Nancy Reid, Anita Gray, Tracey Schilder, Janina Tucker, Nick Philippou, Chris Burgess, Dale Shapter-Lau, Neralie Hoadley, Yoko Quinn (and colleagues), Barry Turner and Miranda Lai.

Finally I would like to thank my friends and family – who endured a lot of thesis talk over those years – for their unfailing encouragement. My brother Matthew's advice in the final stages was extremely valuable, and I may still have been writing were it not for him. Most of all, though, I would like to express my deepest gratitude to my wife Rachael who patiently and lovingly supported me in every way throughout my PhD. This book is dedicated to her.

Table of contents

Acknowledgements 5
Table of contents 6
List of Tables 11
List of Figures 15

Chapter 1:   Introduction 17
  1.1   The challenge of EIL for language testing 17
  1.2   Conceptualising accent 18
  1.3   The orthodox approach to accent in listening test design ... 20
  1.4   A rationale for diverse accents in EAP listening assessment ... 25
    1.4.1   Authenticity and the TLU domain 25
    1.4.2   Construct representation of EAP listening ability 26
    1.4.3   Test consequences 27
  1.5   Problem statement and aim 28
  1.6   Outline of the book 28

Chapter 2:   Literature Review 31
  2.1   Listening to L2 accents: a cognitive perspective 31
    2.1.1   Intelligibility and the listening comprehension process ... 31
    2.1.2   Listening costs associated with L2 speech 34
    2.1.3   The accent-intelligibility distinction 37
    2.1.4   Intelligibility as listener-speaker related 40
    2.1.5   Familiarity and shared-L1 effects in L2 listening research ... 44
  2.2   Listening to L2 accents: a social perspective 50
    2.2.1   Attitudes towards accent and accented speakers 50
    2.2.2   Attitudes and comprehension 52
  2.3   A preliminary study of test-taker perceptions 53
  2.4   Summary 56

Chapter 3:   Research design 58

3.1	Stages of research	58
3.2	Stage one	58
3.3	Stage two	61
3.4	Stage three	65

Chapter 4: Construction of test materials ... 66

4.1	The UTESL listening sub-test	66
4.1.1	Background	66
4.1.2	Listening subtest: format and specifications	66
4.1.3	Description of selected materials	67
4.2	Speaker selection	69
4.2.1	Aims	69
4.2.2	Methods	69
4.2.3	Results	76
4.2.4	Representativeness of selected speakers	80
4.3	Construction of a diverse-accents UTESL (DA-UTESL)	81

Chapter 5: Differential Item Functioning ... 82

5.1	Research questions	82
5.2	Methodological considerations	83
5.2.1	An overview of differential item functioning (DIF)	83
5.2.2	Selection of DIF procedures in the current study	85
5.2.3	DIF as part of a broad methodology	87
5.3	Methods	88
5.3.1	Participants	88
5.3.2	Instruments	90
5.3.3	Data collection procedure	92
5.3.4	Scoring	93
5.4	Preliminary analyses	94
5.4.1	Test and item analysis	94

	5.4.2	Language Experience Questionnaire analysis 101
	5.4.3	Between-groups performance 106
5.5		DIF detection procedures 111
	5.5.1	Overview of analytical procedures 111
	5.5.2	Matching groups 112
	5.5.3	Calculating DIF 115
5.6		DIF in Sleep (Kaori – Japanese accent) 118
	5.6.1	Shared-L1 analysis results 118
	5.6.2	Familiarity analysis results 119
5.7		DIF in The Oldest Old (Jun – Mandarin Chinese accent) 120
	5.7.1	Shared-L1 analysis 120
	5.7.2	Familiarity analysis 121
5.8		Evidence of accent-related DIF 123
	5.8.1	Analysis of exemplar items in Sleep 124
	5.8.2	Analysis of exemplar items in the Oldest Old 128
5.9		Discussion 144
	5.9.1	Summary of main findings 144
	5.9.2	Hypothetical conditions for accent-related DIF 145
	5.9.3	Limitations of the study 148
Chapter 6:		**Attitudes towards speakers** 150
6.1		Research questions 150
6.2		Methodological considerations 151
	6.2.1	An overview of the speaker evaluation approach 151
	6.2.2	The use of the speaker evaluation approach in the current study 153
6.3		Methods 154
	6.3.1	Participants 154
	6.3.2	Instruments 154
	6.3.3	Data collection procedure 157

6.4	Results for all traits	158
6.5	Data reduction	159
6.6	Results for lecturer competence	162
6.6.1	All listeners	162
6.6.2	L1 groups	164
6.7	Results for social attractiveness	167
6.7.1	All listeners	167
6.7.2	L1 groups	168
6.8	Attitudes and test performance	171
6.8.1	Performance with Henry (Australian English accent)	171
6.8.2	Performance with Kaori (Japanese accent)	172
6.8.3	Performance with Jun (Mandarin Chinese accent)	173
6.9	Discussion	175
6.9.1	Attitudes and acceptability	175
6.9.2	Attitudes and test performance	177
6.9.3	Limitations of the approach	178
Chapter 7:	**Verbal reports**	**180**
7.1	Research questions	180
7.2	Methodological considerations	181
7.2.1	An overview of verbal report methods	181
7.2.2	The use of verbal reports in the current study	184
7.3	Methods	188
7.3.1	Participants	188
7.3.2	Instruments	191
7.3.3	Procedure	192
7.4	Initial analysis	194
7.4.1	Coding	194
7.4.2	An overview of the data	195

7.5	The nature of accent-related difficulty	199
7.5.1	Misperception/inability to recognise key phonetic information	199
7.5.2	Processing cost	206
7.5.3	Comments on speaker clarity	208
7.6	The nature of "online" attitudinal response	208
7.6.1	Negative evaluations and affective response	208
7.6.2	Positive evaluations and acceptability	212
7.6.3	Attitude and performance	213
7.7	Post hoc comments	215
7.7.1	Retrospective identification of Kaori and Jun	215
7.7.2	Perceptions of general acceptability and fairness	216
7.8	Summary	222
Chapter 8:	**Summary and implications**	**225**
8.1	Summary	225
8.1.1	Review of approach and methods	225
8.1.2	Key findings from three studies	226
8.1.3	Contribution to the field	227
8.2	Three models for the use of speakers with L2 accents in listening assessment	228
8.2.1	The weak ELF approach	229
8.2.2	The strong ELF approach	231
8.2.3	The local Englishes approach	233
8.3	Suggestions for further research	235
8.4	Concluding remarks	236
References		**238**
Appendix A		**260**
Appendix B		**264**
Appendix C		**270**

Appendix D 271
Appendix E 276
Appendix F 285
Appendix G 286
Appendix H 289

List of Tables

Table 4-1: Details of three UTESL listening sub-tests 68
Table 4-2: Task types by sub-test 68
Table 4-3: Initial pool of speakers 70
Table 4-4: Order of stimuli 72
Table 4-5: Rater characteristics 74
Table 4-6: Transcription task scoring examples 75
Table 4-7: Mean transcription error scores by speaker 77
Table 4-8: Mean comprehensibility ratings by speaker 78
Table 4-9: Mean accent ratings by speaker 79
Table 4-10: Accent identification for selected speakers 80
Table 5-1: Participants by first language (L1) 88
Table 5-2: Participants by nationality 89
Table 5-3: Length of residence by L1 group 90
Table 5-4: Test topic-related majors by L1 group 90
Table 5-5: Mean raw score by test version 95
Table 5-6: Range of raw scores by test version 95
Table 5-7: Reliability and SEM by test version 95
Table 5-8: Correlations between test versions 96
Table 5-9: Summary of item statistics for Food Technology 96
Table 5-10: Item statistics for Food Technology 97
Table 5-11: Summary of item statistics for Sleep 98

Table 5-12: Summary item statistics for The Oldest Old 98
Table 5-13: Item statistics for Sleep 99
Table 5-14: Item statistics for The Oldest Old 100
Table 5-15: Mean familiarity self-ratings by accent 101
Table 5-16: Self-ratings of familiarity with Japanese accent by Japanese L1 status 102
Table 5-17: Self-ratings of familiarity with Chinese accent by Mandarin Chinese L1 status 103
Table 5-18: Summary of contact scores by accent 104
Table 5-19: Descriptive statistics for familiarity with Japanese accent by familiarity group 106
Table 5-20: Descriptive statistics for familiarity with Chinese accent by familiarity group 106
Table 5-21: Mean performance on Food Technology and Sleep by Japanese L1 status (z score conversion) 107
Table 5-22: Mean performance on Food Technology and Sleep by JA familiarity group (z score conversion) 108
Table 5-23: Mean performance on Food Technology and The Oldest Old by Mandarin Chinese L1 status (z score conversion) 109
Table 5-24: Mean performance on Food Technology and The Oldest Old by CA familiarity group 110
Table 5-25: Score levels and sample sizes by Japanese L1 status 114
Table 5-26: Score levels and sample sizes by JA familiarity group 114
Table 5-27: Score levels and sample sizes by Mandarin Chinese L1 status ... 114
Table 5-28: Score levels and sample sizes by CA familiarity group 114
Table 5-29: Number of DIF items detected in Sleep by method (shared-L1 analysis) 118

Table 5-30: Overview of flagged items in Sleep and DIF indices (shared-L1 analysis) 118
Table 5-31: Number of items detected in Sleep by method (familiarity analysis) 119
Table 5-32: Overview of flagged items in Sleep and DIF indices (familiarity analysis) 120
Table 5-33: Number of DIF items detected in The Oldest Old by method (shared-L1 analysis) 120
Table 5-34: Overview of flagged items in The Oldest Old and DIF indices (shared-L1 analysis) 121
Table 5-35: Number of DIF items detected in The Oldest Old by method (familiarity analysis) 122
Table 5-36: Overview of flagged items in The Oldest Old and DIF indices (familiarity analysis) 122
Table 5-37: Correct response with "revive" by Japanese L1 status 125
Table 5-38: Correct response with "revive" by JA familiarity group 125
Table 5-39: Sleep item 2 response type by Japanese L1 status 125
Table 5-40: Sleep item 2 response type by JA familiarity group..................... 125
Table 5-41: Sleep item 27 response type by Japanese L1 status 127
Table 5-42: Sleep item 27 response type by JA familiarity group................... 127
Table 5-43: The Oldest Old item 1 response type by Mandarin Chinese L1 status 129
Table 5-44: The Oldest Old item 1 response type by CA familiarity group 129
Table 5-45: Range of incorrect number responses by Mandarin Chinese L1 status 130
Table 5-46: The Oldest Old item 3 response type by Mandarin Chinese L1 status 132
Table 5-47: The Oldest Old item 3 response type by CA familiarity group 132

Table 5-48: The Oldest Old item 8 response type by Mandarin Chinese L1 status 134

Table 5-49: The Oldest Old item 8 response type by CA familiarity group 134

Table 5-50: The Oldest Old item 17 response type by Mandarin Chinese L1 status 136

Table 5-51: The Oldest Old item 17 response type by CA familiarity group .. 136

Table 5-52: The Oldest Old item 23 response type by Mandarin Chinese L1 status 139

Table 5-53: The Oldest Old item 23 response type by CA familiarity group .. 139

Table 5-54: Approximations of "environmental" by Other L1 listeners 140

Table 5-55: The Oldest Old item 25 response type by Mandarin Chinese L1 status 142

Table 5-56: The Oldest Old item 25 response type by CA familiarity group .. 143

Table 6-1: Mean evaluations on all items by speaker 158

Table 6-2: Total variance explained 160

Table 6-3: Rotated factor matrix 161

Table 6-4: Total variance explained (affective response item removed) 161

Table 6-5: Rotated factor matrix (affective response item removed) 162

Table 6-6: Cronbach's α reliability coefficients for the items comprising each factor 162

Table 6-7: Descriptive statistics of lecturer competence by speaker 163

Table 6-8: Pairwise comparisons of speakers on lecturer competence 163

Table 6-9: Overview of the four L1 groups 164

Table 6-10: Mean lecturer competence scores by speaker and L1 group 165

Table 6-11: Attitudes towards each speaker by L1 group 166

Table 6-12: Descriptive statistics of social attractiveness scores by speaker... 167

Table 6-13: Pairwise comparisons of speakers on social attractiveness 167

Table 6-14: Mean social attractiveness scores by speaker and L1 group 168

Table 6-15: Multiple pairwise comparisons by L1 group 170
Table 7-1: Identifications of speakers' accents 216

List of Figures

Figure 3-1: Stages of research 60
Figure 3-2: Research design in three studies 64
Figure 4-1: Means on each measure by speaker 79
Figure 4-2: Two forms of the diverse-accents UTESL 81
Figure 5-1: Familiarity with Japanese accent by Japanese L1 status 102
Figure 5-2: Familiarity with Chinese accent by Mandarin Chinese L1 status . 103
Figure 5-3: Performance on Food Technology and Sleep by Japanese L1 status 107
Figure 5-4: Performance on Food Technology and Sleep by JA familiarity group 108
Figure 5-5: Performance on Food Technology and the Oldest Old by Mandarin Chinese L1 status 109
Figure 5-6: Performance on Food Technology and the Oldest Old by CA familiarity group 110
Figure 5-7: An overview of DIF detection procedures 111
Figure 5-8: Focal and reference groups on matching criterion by score level . 115
Figure 5-9: Custom table generated for calculation of standardised p difference 116
Figure 5-10: Details of Sleep item 2 124
Figure 5-11: Details of Sleep item 27 126
Figure 5-12: Details of the Oldest Old item 1 128
Figure 5-13: Details of the Oldest Old item 3 131
Figure 5-14: Details of the Oldest Old item 8 133
Figure 5-15: Details of the Oldest Old item 17 135

Figure 5-16: Details of the Oldest Old item 23 138
Figure 5-17: Details of the Oldest Old item 25 141
Figure 5-18: A hypothetical model of conditions for accent-related DIF 147
Figure 6-1: Speaker evaluation task scales 156
Figure 6-2: Screeplot 160
Figure 6-3: Mean lecturer competence scores by speaker 164
Figure 6-4: Mean lecturer competence score by speaker and L1 group 166
Figure 6-5: Mean social attractiveness scores by speaker 168
Figure 6-6: Mean social attractiveness score by speaker and L1 group 169
Figure 6-7: Relationship between lecturer competence evaluation and FT total score 171
Figure 6-8: Relationship between social attractiveness evaluation and FT total score 172
Figure 6-9: Relationship between lecturer competence evaluation and SL total score 173
Figure 6-10: Relationship between social attractiveness evaluation and SL total score 173
Figure 6-11: Relationship between lecturer competence evaluation and OO total score 174
Figure 6-12: Relationship between social attractiveness evaluation and OO total score 174
Figure 7-1: Verbal report procedure 187
Figure 7-2: SPAREs and AIRD on the Sleep test by listener 196
Figure 7-3: SPAREs and AIRD on the Oldest Old test by listener 197

Chapter 1: Introduction

This chapter situates the research within current philosophical and practical debates in the field of language testing. It begins by discussing the broad issues for language testing raised through the emergence of English as an International Language (EIL), before focusing on the particular challenges presented by speaker accent. The next section then discusses the underpinnings of what is termed the "orthodox approach" to accents in listening assessment, locating the basis of this orthodoxy in a set of concerns which may be translated as potential threats to validity. Following this, a theoretical rationale for diverse accents in EAP listening tests is presented, which builds a case for the broader representation of accent on the premises of authenticity, construct representation and consequences. Having established this context, the problem statement and aim of the research is presented followed by a discussion of the conceptual approach taken in this book. Finally, an outline of each chapter is provided.

1.1 The challenge of EIL for language testing

Over the past two decades, sociolinguistic research has documented that English is being indigenised and legitimised in outer-circle contexts (Bambgose, 1992; Chisanga & Kamwangamalu, 1997; Higgins, 2003; Kachru, 1983) and is increasingly being appropriated as a *lingua franca* in expanding-circle contexts (Lowenberg, 2002; Mauranen, 2003; Seidlhofer, 2005). These developments have thrown into question traditional understandings of the ownership of English, and with them the dichotomy of "native" and "non-native" speakers (see Widdowson, 1994). In their place, a number of new ways of theorising the use of English in global contexts have emerged – World Englishes, Global English and English as a Lingua Franca among others.

The new perspectives afforded by such developments have presented considerable challenges to language testing, where debate has surfaced from both within and outside the field calling for change in assessment practices. This debate has generally focused on whose language norms should take primacy in assessment standards (see Davies, Hamp-Lyons and Kemp, 2003). Lowenberg (2002), for example, critiques what he terms "the prevailing wisdom" in language testing, that "the appropriate norms for Standard English usage around the world are those that are accepted and followed by educated native speakers" (p.431). Lowenberg argues that in outer- and expanding-circle contexts, proficiency tests based on inner-circle norms may lack validity as they ignore the sociolinguistic reality of the candidates' language use (see also Brown & Lumley, 1998). Similarly, Jenkins (2006) asks for test examination boards to embrace "NNS-led change" (p.48), and to modify assessment criteria in light of empirical, corpus-based evidence of new and emerging norms found in Seidlhofer's (2001) Vienna-Oxford International Corpus of English, Mauranen's (2003) Corpus of Academic English, and her own model of ELF pronunciation, the Lingua Franca Core (Jenkins, 2000).

More recently, Canagarajah (2006) has argued that language testing must embrace the heterogeneity of language use in post-modern societies, and in so doing, reconceptualises the place of English as an International Language (EIL) in assessment practice. Drawing on Hall's (1997) notion of "postmodern globalization", Canagarajah describes the characteristics of contemporary societies thus:

- The interaction between communities is multilateral—that is, international involvement at diverse levels is needed in today's economic and production enterprises.
- National boundaries have become porous—people, goods, and ideas flow easily between borders.
- Languages, communities, and cultures have become hybrid, shaped by this fluid flow of social and economic relationships.

(Canagarajah, 2006, p.231)

Canagarajah argues that the implication of this shift for language testing is that designing assessment based solely on "local norms", whether they be inner-, outer- or expanding circle local varieties, is no longer tenable. The porousness of borders, and the subsequent hybridity of social domains has led to the need for speakers of English to be able to negotiate their way through varieties of English, and subsequently, a need for language testing to acknowledge these complexities of language use, and to attempt to model these in assessment.

1.2 Conceptualising accent

One such complexity is accent variation. It is generally accepted that "accent" refers to different varieties of pronunciation (Hughes & Trudgill, 1996)[1]. In this sense, accent is distinct from "dialect", where dialect includes lexical, syntactic, discourse and pragmatic variation as well as variation in pronunciation. Strevens (1983) notes that because variation typically occurs in "accent + dialect pairs" (p.89), these terms have often been confused. However he points out that Standard English as a dialect has no particular accent pairing, and thus may be spoken "with an unrestricted choice of accent" (p.88). For example, a newsreader may read from an autocue in a lexically or syntactically standardised code, though with pronunciation features characteristic of their accent.

---

1   This is not to be confused with other closely related definitions of "accent" which relate to either the placing of word stress, or to diacritics placed over letters or words.

Accent may manifest both at the segmental and suprasegmental levels of pronunciation (Wells, 1982), including variation in vowel and consonant realisations, stress patterns and intonation. Accents also serve as indexical markers of social or regional identity. Patterns of pronunciation associated with socially powerful groups are typically granted prestige, and in some cases are accepted as "standard" accents – such as the case of Received Pronunciation (RP) in English. Standard accents are often treated as the unmarked form ("no accent"), while speakers of non-standard varieties are labelled "accented". However it is fundamental to establish, firstly, that all speakers of all languages have an accent, and that those notions of "no accent" and "accented" are social constructs (Esling, 1998; Lippi-Green, 1997).

Traditionally, a common distinction has been made in accent-related research between non-native or second language (L2) pronunciation – often referred to as "foreign accent" – and "accent", which is applied exclusively to native-speaker variation[2]. To illustrate, Wells (1982, p.1), a leading authority on accents of English, defines "accent" as:

> A pattern of pronunciation used by a speaker for whom English is the native language or, more generally, by the community or social grouping to which he or she belongs.

"Foreign accent" is described separately as:

> Pronunciation patterns seen as typical of the speech of those for who English is not the native language; patterns which may be expected to reflect many of the phonological and phonetic characteristics of their mother tongue.
> (Wells, 1982, p.1)

Wells' (1982) characterisation of "foreign" accent as the result of first-language transfer alone suggests that such accents are not viewed as socially or linguisti-

---

2   It is acknowledged that the terms "native" and "non-native" have been critiqued within Applied Linguistics (see Brutt-Griffler & Samimy, 2001; Davies, 2003; Kramsch, 1993). In this thesis, the use of terminology follows Jenkins (2000) in preferring the more neutral terms "L1 accent" or "L1 variety" primarily to refer to English accents of the Inner Circle (e.g., Australian or British varieties), as well as the accents of speakers in Outer Circle contexts who speak English as a first language (e.g., L1 speakers of Singapore English), and "L2 accent" or "L2 variety" primarily to refer to English accents of the Expanding Circle (e.g., Japanese or Chinese varieties) as well as the accents of those in Outer Circle contexts who speak English as a second language (e.g., Cantonese L1 speakers of English in Hong Kong). The term "L2 accent", then, may be seen as roughly synonymous with the terms "non-native accent" or "foreign accent", which are regularly used in literature from wider fields. Distinctions such as native/non-native, however, will be used throughout the thesis in the discussion of literature in which those terms hold particular currency.

cally systematic in their own right. This is characteristic of much research on L2 speech, in which non-native-like variation has generally been classified as "error" (e.g., Anderson-Hsieh, Johnson & Koehler, 1992). Substantial evidence exists that listeners – generally native speakers – can regularly distinguish non-native accents from native varieties (see Flege, 1984; Flege & Fletcher, 1992; Flege, Munro & McKay, 1995). Moreover, the degree of detected foreign accent has been shown to correlate positively with the presence of certain non-native-like segmental and suprasegmental features (see for example Magen, 1998), suggesting that listeners judge strength of accent according to the number of times speakers deviate from native-like pronunciation norms.

However the extent to which such L2 variation can be considered "error" is increasingly being challenged with empirical findings. For example, while the English of Cantonese L1 speakers in Hong Kong had long been considered an interlanguage, with the attendant notion that its characteristic pronunciation was due, in part, to common transfer errors, a series of studies attempting to describe the phonology of Hong Kong English (HKE) have concluded that there exists a HKE accent which is systematic, and not reducible to Cantonese L1 transfer alone (Hung, 2000, Peng & Setter, 2000).

While the case of Hong Kong English fits Kachru's characterisation of outer-circle Englishes as "norm-developing", there still remains resistance to recognising the systematicity of English accents in expanding-circle contexts. Crystal (1995, p.364), for example, explains that, "the question of whether autonomous norms can develop in a foreign language situation (such as Japan) remains unresolved." This lack of consensus has led some to conclude that L2 varieties should not be used as models for language learning (see Quirk, 1982). Recently, however, Jenkins (2002) has critiqued this point of view, shifting the issue from one of accent to intelligibility. Arguing that "a native-like accent is not necessary for intelligibility in EIL" (p.207), Jenkins posits that an L2 accent in itself "does not equal incorrectness" (p.206) provided the variation does not affect the "core" phonological features crucial for intelligibility[3]. In such cases, where intelligibility has been demonstrated to be secure, and salient features of accent remain, Jenkins (2000) maintains that L2 accents should be considered equivalent to native speaker regional accents.

1.3 The orthodox approach to accent in listening test design

Within this wider debate, the issue of accent norms in listening assessment has recently emerged as an area of inquiry. In the *TOEFL 2000 Listening Framework*, which reported on the revised TOEFL – eventually taking the form of TOEFL iBT – speaker accent was flagged as an important variable in listening

---

3   These are discussed in Section 2.2.1.

comprehension, and the prospect of "non-standard" accent use on TOEFL was raised in the form of a research agenda where the authors stated: "the theoretical, practical, and psychometric impact of the use of accents other than standard North American accents will be investigated" (Bejar, Douglas, Jamieson, Nissan & Turner, p.17). In response, two ETS-commissioned research studies, conducted by Major, Fitzmaurice, Bunta & Balasubramanian (2002; 2005), emerged in which the effect of speaker accent on listening test scores was explored for both L2 and non-standard L1 accents.

Llurda (2004) has noted that the existence of such a research program signals a shift in language testing towards EIL concerns, acknowledging both, "the existence of the huge number of non-native English speakers and the need to incorporate their voices into mainstream English language teaching and language testing" (Llurda, 2004, p.315). However, mainstream language testing still maintains, in practice, an approach to speaker accent that may be characterised as "orthodox". Large-scale tests of academic English such as TOEFL and IELTS, in their most recent incarnations, appear to acknowledge the changing communicative needs of candidates through their approach to speaker accent in listening assessment, however the range of speaker accents remains restricted to inner-circle varieties. In the TOEFL iBT, for example, innovations to the listening section have included the representation of "a range of global accents" (see www.ets.org/toefl). Yet this range extends from North American to British and Australian accents, and these "new" accents will only be heard on one part of the listening section (mini-lectures), and may or may not appear on any given listening test (ETS, 2005).

IELTS makes similar claims regarding their approach to international communication. The 2007 *IELTS Handbook* states that the range of accents utilised in the listening paper "reflects the international usage of IELTS", however it is also clearly stated that these accents are "native-speaker" varieties (IELTS, 2007, p.6). In practice, candidates sitting IELTS may encounter British, Australian, North American or New Zealand varieties (see Cambridge ESOL, 2008). According to Taylor (2006), the guiding principle behind the IELTS approach has been, "that the test should represent those English varieties used in the contexts in which IELTS test-takers are likely to find themselves, i.e. the 'dominant host languages'" (p.56). Taylor argues that the question of speaker accent, then, relates to "validity and 'fitness of purpose'" (p.56). However, a counter-argument can be made, based on Canagarajah's notion of the increasing hybridity of social domains, for conceptualizing greater diversity even within the parameters of "dominant host languages". One clear example is the heterogeneity of accent varieties within the domain of academic English in metropolitan Australia. In this sense, tests which do not model diversity – the sociolinguistic reality of many inner-circle contexts – may be criticised as falling short in "fitness of purpose".

Apart from the question of "fitness of purpose", however, the orthodox approach to speaker accent may also be understood as stemming from caution among test developers over a range of issues relating to intelligibility, measurement and acceptability among stakeholders. Buck's (2001) *Assessing Listening* – a widely-cited, standard text – provides a useful source for identifying some of these specific concerns. In a section entitled "Finding suitable speakers", Buck outlines several considerations that provide constructive guidance in the recording of oral stimuli. Buck is progressive in his general outlook, noting that speaker selection "depends entirely on the purpose of the text, and the context in which it is used" (2001, p.162); and he is open to the use of L2 accents, for example, in tests of English for international communication. However in a passage on general considerations in the selection of speakers, a number of concerns surrounding the use of L2 accents and other non-standard varieties are illuminated by several caveats and cautions:

> In some cases, there may be no standard English speakers available, and then the test developer may have to make a difficult decision: whether it is appropriate to use speakers with a strong regional accent, or even non-native speakers. The answer depends entirely on the purpose of the test, and the context in which it is used. English is a world language, which comes in many different versions, and is used in many different situations. Often a little variety will be a good thing: a mild Australian or Scottish accent may be quite appropriate on a general proficiency test, even if test-takers have not heard these accents before. However, a strong accent would be a problem. For a test of English in Japan, a high-ability Japanese speaker of English may be quite acceptable. In India, where English is used as a native language, a speaker of Indian English may be preferable. To a considerable extent, it depends on what test users are prepared to accept. From a measurement perspective, the most important thing when using an unfamiliar accent is that it is equally unfamiliar to all.
> (Buck, 2001, p.162)

Initially, it can be inferred from this passage that the default, safe position for language testers is to use speakers with standard accents; this is clear in the proposition that to choose to do otherwise would be a "difficult decision". We can then locate in this passage three main reasons why the use of non-standard accented speech is considered a difficult, and perhaps risky, decision:

1. Strongly accented speech on a listening test would be problematic:
   "However, a strong accent would be a problem"
2. Using an accent that is familiar to some test-takers and not others may affect the measurement qualities of the test:
   "From a measurement perspective, the most important thing when using an unfamiliar accent is that it is equally unfamiliar to all."

3. Test takers may find certain accents unacceptable:
   "To a considerable extent, it depends on what test users are prepared to accept"

The first of these points – that a strongly accented speaker would be problematic – relates to the broader concern over intelligibility, and ultimately a listener's ability to understand a spoken text. The concern for intelligibility leads Buck to caution elsewhere in his book that in a listening test, "accent is a very important variable ... [that] can cause problems and may disrupt the whole listening comprehension process" (p.35). That this is an orthodox belief within language testing is highlighted by the similar view expressed in Weir's *Language testing and validation*: "it is sometimes suggested that the stronger the accent, the lower the listeners' comprehension" (2005, p.81). While the concern over strength of accent does not make direct mention of L2 accents but to "strong" accents more broadly, non-native (or "foreign") accents are typically distinguished as stronger than native speaker varieties in research using global accent ratings (for overview, see Jesney, 2004). Yet while non-native accents, in particular, have long been associated with a range of communicative "costs" (e.g. Flege, 1988; Anderson-Hsieh and Koehler, 1988), more recent research suggests that strength of accent is not an accurate predictor of intelligibility.

The second concern – that the use of an accent that is familiar to some and not others may affect the measurement qualities of the test – relates directly to construct validity and the potential for test bias. This concern is premised on research which suggests that a second language listener who is familiar with a speaker's accent will comprehend that speaker more easily than other listeners who are unfamiliar with the accent. In summarising a range of research on this issue, Flowerdew (1994), for example, has stated this position on accent and listening comprehension thus:

> The research into the effect of accent on listening comprehension is quite clear cut in supporting the commonsense view that unfamiliar accents cause difficulty in comprehension ... the concept of familiarity extends to the question of the comprehensibility of local vs. standard accents of English, local accents proving to be more comprehensible ... If non-native speakers have least difficulty with familiar accents, then, other things being equal, those lecturers who are likely to be most easily comprehended will be from the students' own language background. Next most comprehensible are likely to be those lecturers with the accent closest to the model learners have been exposed to in their studies and in society at large.
>
> (Flowerdew, 1994, pp.24-25)

From this, it may be extrapolated that in a listening test whose candidates represent diverse L1 backgrounds, there is potential for some test-takers to be advantaged over others if they are highly familiar with, or in fact share, a speaker's accent. In addition, those listeners who are not familiar with an accent, and who therefore find it more difficult to understand than other test-takers, may be disadvantaged.

This potential threat of a shared-accent advantage to the validity of inferences made from test scores – for example, in a situation where a Japanese speaker is heard on a test by listeners from diverse L1 backgrounds, some of whom are Japanese – is clearly articulated by Major et al. (2002, p.174) who state that: "accented language may affect the listening comprehension of ESL listeners differently depending on their native languages. Such effects would constitute test bias, which would be considered evidence against the test's construct validity." An own-accent bias would be comparable to a gender bias given that it would be dependent on an unchangeable characteristic: a listeners' L1. On the other hand, a familiarity advantage – for example, in a situation where some listeners, regardless of their L1 background, have had extensive experience with a Japanese accent compared with others – raises the potential of a different type of threat to test fairness: lack of access. On this point, Taylor (2006) notes that, "demands of validity and reliability mean that a test must include as wide and as appropriate a range of content as possible but without significantly disadvantaging any particular candidate group ... while some test-takers will have considerable exposure to certain varieties, other test-takers will not" (p.57).

The third concern – that test-takers may find certain varieties of accent unacceptable – is related to the concept of "test appeal" which is discussed by Bachman and Palmer (1996) as relating to authenticity. Acceptability of accents is likely to be dependent both on the context in which a test is taken, and the particular use for which a test is designed. Taylor (2006) notes that although many applied linguists have a progressive stance in the debate over appropriate norms and models, "we should not ignore or override the attitudes and perceptions of learners themselves" (p.52). Research has suggested that learners prefer standard accents over non-standard accents (e.g., Jenkins, 2007), and that second-language listeners are particularly critical of their own accent (Fayer & Krasinski, 1987). However, Harding (2008) found that learner attitudes towards non-standard accents in the specific context of listening assessment were varied, and that in certain cases the use of L2 accents was viewed as a positive addition because it provided a "real-life" listening situation.

Related to the issue of acceptability of speakers' accents, though not specifically addressed in Buck's passage, is the concern that attitudes towards accented speakers could interfere with comprehension, and may arguably result in construct-irrelevant variance at the score level. Lindemann (2002), for example, has found that listeners who hold negative attitudes towards L2 accented speech are more likely to "reject the burden" of communication, claiming that a speaker is unintelligible or incomprehensible, and problematise the listening process.

Given this range of concerns it is, perhaps, unsurprising that test developers have not embraced the representation of diverse accents on listening assessment. Yet although an orthodox approach persists, there are certain testing contexts where a compelling argument may be made for greater accent variety. One such context is the assessment of English for Academic Purposes (EAP). In the academic domains of multicultural inner-circle countries, students are likely to encounter a variety of accents not only among other students, but also among lecturers, tutors and teaching assistants (see Kirkpatrick, 2007a, p.187). In such contexts, there is a strong rationale for a broader range of accents in listening assessment that extends beyond issues of representation, and touches on aspects of authenticity, construct modelling and ethics that are central to validity. The next section will set out this rationale for diverse speaker accents in the specific context of English for Academic Purposes (EAP) listening assessment, which is the focus of this book.

1.4 A rationale for diverse accents in EAP listening assessment

1.4.1 Authenticity and the TLU domain

Driving much of the current interest in the use of diverse accented speakers is a concern for authenticity in listening input. For example, as a rationale for their own study, Major et al. (2002, p.174) state that "if a test of listening comprehension is to reflect the authentic language of important listening contexts at the university, it should include accented English." As the previous section argued, language norms (in this case, pronunciation) can vary across and within domains of target-language use in inner-, outer- and expanding-circle countries. This is particularly the case for the TLU domain of academic English in metropolitan inner-circle contexts.

Evidence of such accent diversity in inner-circle academic settings can be found in a number of sources. For example, in the Michigan Corpus of Academic Spoken English (MICASE) – a corpus of academic language sampled at the University of Michigan – 122 of the 1,571 speakers within the corpus are L2 speakers of English. These speakers represent 36 different first-language backgrounds, with accents ranging from Armenian, to Mandarin Chinese, to Swahili. In describing a "medium-sized university" in New Zealand, Ogier (2005) reports survey results showing that of 1054 lecturers employed between 1994-2003, 138 spoke English as a second language. The student body of many tertiary institutions in English-speaking countries has also become increasingly internationalised. For instance, in 2007 there were 177,760 international students enrolled in Australian universities, with China, India, Malaysia, Hong Kong and Indonesia the most prominent countries of origin (AEI, 2008).

A wider representation of accents, then, would theoretically result in listening tests that more realistically reflect speech variation in these heterogeneous target language use (TLU) situations. The type of authenticity that may be achieved through the broadening of accents is, however, a "weak" authenticity in itself. There is an argument to suggest that wider accent representation in oral stimuli would not, in fact, result in greater authenticity as such, but only in the increased "genuineness" of listening texts (Buck, 2001). Widdowson (1978) states that texts taken from the TLU domain are genuine, but they are only authentic if the way in which the test-takers deal with them also corresponds to the TLU domain. Yet, a distinction can be drawn between the authentic academic listening tasks (which would replicate the communicative demands of, say, a lecture), and authentic academic listening texts (which replicate authentic features of texts in 'real-life' domains, such as speaker's accent). Nevertheless, whether it is construed as enhanced authenticity, or increased genuineness, evidence suggests that greater variability among speaker accents would more accurately reflect the type of speech variability found in the domain of academic institutions, and in the day-to-day lives of test-takers in metropolitan, ESL situations.

1.4.2 Construct representation of EAP listening ability

While authenticity may be a reasonable rationale for broadening accent when considered alone, it is at the same time a necessary condition for a more compelling argument: the broader representation of accented speech on listening tests would enable the testing of a more accurate model of the construct of academic listening proficiency. Research on academic listening typically identifies accented speech as a potential source of difficulty (Bilbow, 1989; Brindley, 1998; Brindley & Slatyer, 1998; Flowerdew, 1994; Hasan, 2000; Kennedy, 1978). However, in an early taxonomy of abilities required for academic listening, Richards (1983, p.230) listed "ability to follow lecture despite differences in accent and speed" as a necessary academic listening skill. The implications of Richards' (1983) observation for the design of academic listening tests have not been directly addressed in subsequent discussions of the L2 listening construct (for example, Buck, 2001; Dunkel, Henning & Chaudron, 1993; Rost, 1990), which offer more generalist understandings of listening comprehension. This is, perhaps, symptomatic of a lack of discussion of the specific construct of academic listening (Read, 2002).

Recently, however, Richards' (1983) view has gained indirect support from advocates of an EIL-based model of "intercultural communicative competence". For example, Alptekin (2002, p.63) states that language learners in cross-cultural settings should be equipped with "an awareness of difference, and with strategies for coping with such difference." As it has already been demonstrated that modern academic institutions are cross-cultural "sites", Alptekin's (2002) idea could also be applied to academic listening situations. Canagarajah (2006) puts forward a similar argument suggesting that what is now required is "an additional level of assessment to examine one's proficiency in negotiating diverse varieties of English." Part of this additional level of proficiency involves adaptation to new varieties:

> One should be able to inductively process the underlying system in the varieties one encounters in social interactions. One should draw on intuitive skills to develop relative communicative competence in new varieties according to one's needs. Therefore, tests should examine a candidate's ability to discern the structure, pattern, or rules from the available data of a given language.
> (Canagarajah, 2006, p.6)

While these views may seem progressive, they are not incommensurable with previous models of communicative competence. Being "aware" of variation is related to the sub-competency "sociolinguistic competence" proposed by Canale and Swain (1980), and reiterated by Bachman (1990). Coping with, or adapting to, variation can be related to the sub-competency "strategic competence", as proposed by Canale and Swain (1980), and expanded on by Bachman (1990). Following McNamara (1996), these elements of strategic competence can also be seen as components of "ability for use" – the ability to perform communicative tasks introduced by Hymes (1972). Certainly, learning to adapt, or "tune in", to someone else's accent is an important aspect of communicative performance in listening. This aspect of the construct may only be modelled through the introduction of diverse accented speakers.

1.4.3 Test consequences

Shohamy (2004) has written that, following Messick's (1989) views on the consequential validity of tests, "language testers have begun to view language tests not as isolated events, but rather as connected to psychological, social, and political variables that have effects on curriculum, ethicality, social class, politics, and language knowledge" (pp. 72-73). "Washback" is one such implication; defined as "the effect of testing on instruction" (Davies *et al.*, 1999). It is worth considering the effect that using inner-circle, native-speaker accents on major high-stakes listening tests is having on pedagogical decisions in the wider ESL/EFL community such as the design of course-books, the creation of other tests within language programs (such as placement tests and achievement tests), attitudes towards teachers with non-standard accents, and, at the extreme, the hiring of language teachers (see Lippi-Green, 1997).

1.5 Problem statement and aim

Sections 1.2 and 1.3 have shown that while there are compelling arguments that justify the representation of diverse accents – including L2 accents – on EAP listening assessment, language testing has tended to take an orthodox, native-speaker approach to accents which may be understood as stemming from a range of concerns over intelligibility, threats to construct validity and acceptability. While the orthodox approach persists, to date little empirical research on accent and listening comprehension has been conducted within the specific context of language testing to address these concerns. Where such research has been conducted – most notably on the question of test bias in Major et al. (2002) – findings have been inconclusive due to limitations in the study design, and further research has been called for. Thus, to a large degree concerns over fairness, validity and acceptability to candidates are still conjectural.

Against this background, the primary aim of this research is to investigate the use of speakers with L2 accents on an EAP listening test within the framework of a validation study. To this end, the research will address the specific concerns articulated above with empirical evidence to evaluate the extent to which they represent threats to validity. Secondly, an attempt will be made to establish under what conditions, and through what preparatory measures, an EAP test featuring speakers with L2 accents may be feasible.

1.6 Outline of the book

This book is organised into eight chapters. The structure and content of each chapter is summarised below:

Chapter 1 – The research context

This chapter has situated the research within the context of debates on the impact of EIL on language testing. A theoretical rationale for diverse speaker accents on listening assessment has been presented, and the basis of the orthodox approach to accent has been "unpacked" and discussed. A set of concerns have emerged which potentially threaten the practicality and validity of a listening test with diverse accented speakers. A problem statement and aim have been articulated, and an outline of the book is presented.

Chapter 2 – Literature Review

Chapter 2 explores the veracity of the concerns outlined in Chapter 1 in greater depth through a review of literature related to accent, intelligibility, attitudes and listening comprehension. Research findings related to listening to L2 accents are explored firstly from a cognitive perspective, and then from a social perspective. A summary of a preliminary study of test-taker perceptions of the use of L2 accents in listening assessment is also provided. The chapter concludes by re-evaluating the set of concerns identified in Chapter 1.

Chapter 3 – Research design

Chapter 3 presents the overarching design and approach of the research, which attempts to incorporate elements of Kane's approach to validation within a mixed methods triangulation research design. In the first section an overview of the three stages of the study is presented. In the following three sections, each stage is discussed separately, with an emphasis on the major, second stage which includes three linked empirical studies.

Chapter 4 – Construction of test materials

In Chapter 4, the instrument used throughout this book – the University Test of English as a Second Language (UTESL) – is first described with a focus on its purpose, current use, and specifications. Secondly, the method of speaker selection to construct a diverse-accents UTESL forms an embedded study within the chapter. This section details the rigorous process by which three diverse accented speakers of comparable, high levels of intelligibility were selected from an initial pool of nine.

Chapter 5 – Differential item functioning

Chapter 5 presents the findings of study one which explored the potential for listeners who share a speaker's L1 background, or who are highly familiarity with a speaker's accent, to be advantaged on a listening test featuring that speaker. The methodological approach – differential item functioning (DIF) – is explained in detail, following which the statistical results of the study are presented. Finally, an analysis of candidate responses is undertaken to uncover evidence of accent-related DIF.

Chapter 6 – Attitudes towards speakers

Chapter 6 presents the findings of study two which measured listeners' attitudes towards speakers used on the diverse-accents UTESL with a view to drawing conclusions about the acceptability of speakers, and the relationship between attitudes and test performance. The methodological approach is presented in detail, after which listener attitudes are analysed by speaker and by listener L1 background. Relationships between evaluations of speakers and performance on a test featuring that speaker are also explored.

29

Chapter 7 – Verbal reports

Chapter 7 presents the findings of study three which sought to triangulate and extend upon the findings of studies one and two by investigating test-taker behaviour throughout the test "event" using verbal report methods. The chapter begins with an overview of methodological considerations concerning verbal reports. Then, data from 8 test-takers is analysed and discussed with reference to the nature of accent-related listening difficulty, "online" attitudinal response and test-taker perceptions of general acceptability and fairness.

Chapter 8 – Summary and implications

Chapter 8 begins with a summary of the approach and methods used in the research, followed by a presentation of the key findings from the three studies and a discussion of their contribution to the field. Implications for test design are then suggested, with three different "models" proposed. Suggestions for further research are also provided, after which concluding remarks are made.

Chapter 2:   Literature Review

The introductory chapter has shown that while there are strong theoretical justifications for the use of speakers with L2 accents in academic listening assessment, there also remain serious concerns for test developers regarding: intelligibility; differential performance depending on listener L1 background or familiarity with accent; test-score variance related to attitude towards accent, and lack of acceptability among test-takers. The purpose of this chapter is to provide a deeper and more precise understanding of these concerns through a review of research on L2 accent and listening comprehension from a variety of fields.

The chapter is divided into three sections. Section 2.1 considers literature from a cognitive perspective which concerns listening to L2 accents. It begins by conceptualising the role of intelligibility in the listening comprehension process, before presenting an overview of listening "costs" associated with accented speech. This notion of listening costs is then critiqued through discussions of the distinction between "accentedness" and intelligibility, and the role of listener-related factors in determining intelligibility. Finally, an overview of research which has gauged shared-L1 and familiarity effects in L2 listening is presented. Section 2.2 considers related literature from a social perspective. The section looks firstly at attitudes towards accents and accented speakers with a focus on the attitudes of language learners towards other L2 accents including their own. It then turns to consider the relationship between attitudes and listening comprehension. Section 2.3 then provides a summary of the findings of a preliminary investigation of test-taker perceptions of a listening test featuring diverse accented speakers.

2.1 Listening to L2 accents: a cognitive perspective

2.1.1 Intelligibility and the listening comprehension process

Much of the research concerning the reception of L2 accents has been conducted with a focus on the construct of intelligibility. Before reviewing this research it is first necessary to understand what is meant by intelligibility, and also to delimit the construct. The term "intelligibility", in modern usage, generally means the ability to understand or to comprehend. Within applied linguistic and psycholinguistic research, however, the term has been used in a variety of specific ways. Field (2005, p.401), for example, defines intelligibility narrowly as "the extent to which the acoustic-phonetic content of the message is recognisable by a listener", thus characterising intelligibility as a measurable construct of speech perception. In a slightly broader definition, Smith and Nelson (1985) view intelligibility as "word/utterance recognition". Smith and Nelson (1985) provide a useful delineation between intelligibility, as concerned with the

31

accurate perception of incoming speech, and the higher order listening constructs of "comprehensibility" and "interpretability" in their three-level conceptualisation of understanding:

1. intelligibility   =   word/utterance recognition
2. comprehensibility =   word/utterance meaning (locutionary force)
3. interpretability   =   meaning behind word/utterance (illocutionary force)[4]

Under Field's (2005) and Smith and Nelson's (1985) definitions, intelligibility concerns form only, and is considered separately from matters of meaning. This conceptualisation has guided the methodological approaches of intelligibility studies, which have used perceptual accuracy, word recognition or transcription tasks. It is, however, difficult to separate the effects of higher levels of knowledge in measures of intelligibility. Even at the level of speech recognition, theories have tended to favour interactive models, in which top-down knowledge – for example, knowledge of lexis – are drawn upon in making phonemic decisions, such as in the TRACE model (McClelland & Elman, 1986); although it should be noted that such models are still the topic of intense debate (see Norris, McQueen & Cutler, 2000). Nevertheless, it seems reasonable to assume that certain methods of measuring intelligibility are more susceptible to the influence of higher order knowledge, such as the transcription tasks regularly used by Munro and Derwing in which listeners transcribe a given utterance which is then scored for accuracy. Field (2005) makes the valid point that, "Munro and Derwing's transcription task clearly embraces within intelligibility factors such as contextual transparency or syntactic and lexical knowledge" (pp.400-401). Indeed, Munro and Derwing themselves define intelligibility in broader terms as, "the extent to which an utterance is actually understood by a listener" (1995a, p.76), a definition more synonymous with the broader sense of comprehensibility (and even interpretability) in the Smith and Nelson (1985) model. Yet while transcription tasks might tap into higher order knowledge, they clearly measure form recognition more validly than they do understanding of meaning.

That intelligibility may be conceptualised and measured separately from higher levels of understanding, however, does not mean that these levels are not connected. Commenting on the Smith and Nelson (1985) framework, Field (2005) argues that intelligibility so conceived is a component of the broader construct of comprehensibility; by this he effectively argues that accurate

---

4   While this distinction between levels of understanding has informed a number of studies (Riney, Takagi & Inutsuka, 2005; Bambgose, 1998), there is still no consensus on the terms themselves. For example, Bambgose (1998) uses the single term "intelligibility" to represent all three levels of understanding.

recognition of the form of an utterance is one part of the general process of listening comprehension. Listening comprehension has been described as an "inferential process" in which the listener makes use of linguistic and non-linguistic knowledge to understand what they have heard (Rost, 2002). With regard to linguistic knowledge, the listening process involves the use of various types of knowledge including phonetic, phonological, prosodic, lexical, semantic, syntactic, and pragmatic (Buck, 2001; Flowerdew, 1994; Lynch, 1994). Non-linguistic knowledge, on the other hand, may include background knowledge of a given topic, knowledge of genre, and knowledge of the listening situation among others (Anderson & Lynch, 1988; Wu, 1998). These knowledge sources are activated in listening comprehension through bottom-up or top-down processes.

Throughout early research on second language listening, an assumption that listening was primarily a bottom-up process held sway (see Brown, 1990). This view can be seen as emanating from an information processing paradigm, such as that proposed by Clark and Clark (1977) which saw the perception of input as the first in a series of linear steps towards processing and understanding speech (for critique, see Rost, 1990; 1994). However this notion of a bottom-up comprehension model has been superseded by one which views listening as an interactive process, where knowledge types are drawn on in no established order, and where "top-down expectation-driven processing" and "bottom-up, data-driven processing" can co-occur (Anderson & Lynch, 1988; Lynch, 1994).

Although the general shift towards interactive views of the comprehension process has taken some emphasis off the importance of bottom-up processing skills, the nature of phonetic information provided within the speech signal, and its accurate perception, are still considered a vital component of the listening comprehension process for a number of reasons. Firstly, there may be certain contexts in which one type of processing is favoured over another. Vandergrift (2007), for example, notes that the type of processing that a listener will activate depends to a large extent on the nature of the task they are performing. By way of illustration he suggests that, "a listener who needs to verify a specific detail, for example, will engage in more bottom-up processing than a listener who is interested in comprehending the gist of a test" (p.193). This is an important observation in the context of listening assessment, where task variables function in mediating roles. Secondly, Field (2004) draws on Stanovich's (1980) "interactive-compensatory" mechanism – a theory developed in the context of L1 reading comprehension – to suggest that interaction in the comprehension process may be driven by confidence in the reliability of perceptual input. The interactive-compensatory mechanism would hold that the listener compensates with top-down strategies when information at the perceptual level is "deficient"; thus "restoring" parts of the text which have not been understood. Finally, the importance of perceptual information has also been highlighted by Brown (1990):

> The foreign learner needs to learn to control the phonological code of the target language sufficiently to be able to use the richness of cues at this level – with sufficient ease to provide a constrained input for the 'top-down' inference driven interpretation to be constructed. This is, after all, the raw data of language input – without this there *is* no linguistic message ... [italics hers]
> (p.151)

In this sense, an understanding of the effects of accent at the level of intelligibility is of vital importance in understanding the effects of accent on the listening comprehension process more generally.

To summarise, the definition of intelligibility taken up in this book is that provided by Smith and Nelson (1985): "word/utterance recognition". Following from this, research concerned with speech recognition within this literature review will be classified according to its method of measurement: those studies which have used measures such as word recognition tasks or transcription tasks are considered primarily intelligibility studies (even though the terminology used in such studies may be different). Other studies which concern higher levels of understanding are considered within the purview of comprehension. Also, within this book, listening comprehension is viewed an interactive process, during which listeners draw on a range of knowledge types and strategies to attempt to understand input. However, following Brown (1990), the importance of the "raw data" of linguistic input in aiding or constraining listening comprehension processes is acknowledged.

2.1.2 Listening costs associated with L2 speech

Psycholinguistic and speech perception research has tended to regard L2 speech as a source of variability in the speech signal which may have a deleterious effect on intelligibility (see Clarke & Garrett, 2004). The phonetic characteristics of non-native speech have been associated with greater numbers of misperceptions or misidentifications of segments or words, and this is particularly marked in studies which have investigated speech-in-noise. Lane (1963), for example, found that native listeners identified words spoken in Japanese, Serbian and Punjabi accents of English with around 36% less accuracy than when they heard a native speaker. Munro and Derwing (1995a) have also found that the utterances of Mandarin Chinese accented speakers were less intelligible for native listeners than were those of native speakers. This lower score was attributed to a greater number of misidentified words in the transcription of utterances spoken by Mandarin accented speakers.

The relationship between non-native pronunciations and misperception has also been discussed by Bond (2005; see also Bond, 1999), who notes that listeners may make two kinds of perceptual errors when confronted with a non-native accent. In the first, they may perceive a non-native speaker's realisation of a word or utterance "veridically" (as it sounds phonetically) and thus "recover something other than the intended utterance" (2005, p.298) resulting in the perception a different word from that uttered, or even a non-word. Bond gives an example from her data of a listener who hears a speaker with an Eastern European accent who, "produced a flap for the rhotic, as would be appropriate in her native language" (2005, p.298) leading the listener to mishear "barrel" as "bottle". In the second case, having noticed an accent, listeners may overcompensate using their own phonological expectations.

Misperceptions of this kind have the potential to cause serious breakdowns at other levels of understanding. Field (2003) points out that a perceptual error may alter a listener's interpretation of a whole utterance, giving the example of a second-language listener who mistakenly hears "I won't go to London" as "I want to go to London". In this case, a perceptual misidentification could affect the listener's understanding, not only of that single proposition, but of the discourse which follows. Rost (1990), however, argues that although mishearings are located at the phonemic level, they involve "hierarchical cues for perception" as well (Rost, 1990, p.52). Similarly, Tartter (1998, p.283) states, "at some point ... there must be interaction with information as to possible lexical items and consistency with the syntax and semantics of the input". In this sense, misperceptions may be viewed not only as symptoms of perceptual error, but of deficiencies in knowledge at other levels as well. They may be particularly salient, then, for second language listeners, as Peterson (2001, p.88) suggests: "with higher levels of language proficiency, the listener works more efficiently and is able to maintain activity on all levels simultaneously. At beginning proficiency levels, perceptual (bottom-up) operations require great amounts of conscious attention, so that little capacity remains for higher level operations."

Listening to L2 accented speech has also been shown to increase processing time for listeners. Munro and Derwing (1995b) investigated the effects of non-native accent on processing time by asking native US-English listeners to complete a sentence verification task (SVT) in which they had to judge the truth value of statements spoken in Mandarin Chinese accented English and American English. The results showed that listeners were able to process the American English accents significantly faster than the Mandarin Chinese accents. The findings also showed that there was a significant relationship between processing time and listeners' perceptions of comprehensibility, but not between processing time and a degree of accent rating. This indicated that a perception of increased difficulty is related to increased processing time while listening to accented speech, but that processing time is not necessarily related to perceived strength of the accent itself.

Schmid and Yeni-Komshian (1999) also found that processing time was greater for the comprehension of Spanish and Tamil-accented speech than for American English for NS listeners. Schmid and Yeni-Komshian used a "different paradigm" for investigating processing time from that used by Munro and Derwing (1995b) in which listeners were asked to detect mispronunciations in a stream of speech. These mispronunciations – based on modifying existing materials of the Speech Intelligibility in Noise (SPIN) test – all included word-initial position errors such as pronouncing "booth" as "vooth", or "bench" as "mench". The words were then presented within the SPIN test format, which includes high and low predictability sentences. Participants took part in a reaction time experiment in which they were asked to press a key when they heard a mispronunciation. Results revealed that listeners detected mispronunciations more accurately when listening to a native speaker, and also detected them more quickly than when they heard a non-native speaker. It was also observed that detection of mispronunciations became less accurate as strength of accent increased.

Perhaps owing to these perceptual and processing "costs", a general connection between accent and listening difficulty has emerged in studies of perceptions of comprehensibility (see Eisenstein, 1983; Llurda, 2005), or measurable comprehension performance. Relating to the latter, in an influential early study, Anderson-Hsieh and Koehler (1988) sought to investigate the effect of foreign accent (together with speaking rate) on native speaker comprehension. This study was conducted in the context of complaints from native speaker students about non-native speaker teaching assistants. They employed three speakers from a Chinese L1 background[5] and one native speaker of North American English to record a series of passages which were then transformed into a comprehension test instrument. A sample of 224 native speaker university students who took the test scored significantly higher on passages delivered by the native speaker. It was also shown that speaking rate interacted with "strength of accent" to decrease comprehension further for the Chinese speaker whose accent was rated the strongest.

The perception of accent-related difficulty has also emerged in studies of second language learners engaged in listening comprehension tasks or in real world communication. For example, Hasan (2000), asked speakers of Arabic studying English for Specific Purposes at Damascus University to indicate whether they found it difficult to achieve good understanding "when speakers speak with varied accents" (p.146). Around 25% of respondents indicated that

---

5   No further information is provided as to what Chinese language/dialect groups these speakers represented.

this was sometimes the case, and 70.3% that this was often or always the case. Speaker accent was also cited as a major source of difficulty in Goh's (1999) study of listener awareness and factors that influence comprehension. Goh conducted a diary study with 40 mainland Chinese ESL students in Singapore in which she asked them to record details of English language listening encounters over a period of two months. Of this group, 68% reported that their listening comprehension was affected by a speaker's accent at some point.

It is certainly theoretically plausible that serious breakdowns at the level of intelligibility may occur when listeners are unable to decode phonetic information at a phonemic or word level, or cannot process speech at an efficient rate. Recent research, however, has pointed to two areas of investigation which serve to critique the general assumption that an L2 accent is synonymous with such reductions in intelligibility. These are, firstly, studies which have drawn a distinction between features of L2 speech which contribute to perceptions of "accentedness" and features which affect intelligibility; and secondly, studies which have investigated the role of the listener in determining speech intelligibility. These lines of research are discussed in the sections below.

2.1.3 The accent-intelligibility distinction

Although L2 accents have been linked to reduced speaker intelligibility, and subsequent "costs" in comprehension, there has been less understanding of the specific features within non-native phonologies which add to, or detract from, intelligibility. In this vein, Munro (2008) notes that, "researchers have not often distinguished between those aspects of L2 speech that cause it to sound foreign and those that reduce its intelligibility" (p.197). Munro's push for such a focus stems from his involvement in an extensive program of research, with Derwing, which has provided empirical support for the notion that L2 accented speech does not necessarily equate with low intelligibility.

Munro and Derwing first flagged the idea of an accent/intelligibility distinction in their (1994) study of evaluations of foreign accent. In it they speculated that:

> It seems likely that ratings of accentedness would be very high where intelligibility is limited; however, there may be a crossover point at which intelligibility is secure but certain features of accent remain extremely salient.
>
> (Munro & Derwing, 1994, p.264)

This was followed by an important study (Munro & Derwing, 1995a) on the relationship between ratings of foreign accent, ratings of comprehensibility and measures of intelligibility for 10 native-speakers of Mandarin Chinese and 2 native-speakers of North American English. The findings of the study revealed that ratings of accentedness correlated significantly with counts of "errors" (deviations from native-like pronunciation norms) in the stimuli and also with "goodness of intonation" judgements. However there were significant correlations between accent ratings and intelligibility scores as measured by an orthographic transcription task for only 28% of the listeners. It was noted that even when listeners could transcribe a speaker unproblematically, they sometimes assigned these same speakers "moderate" or "heavy" accent ratings, leading the authors to conclude that "this finding demonstrates empirically that the presence of a strong foreign accent does not necessarily result in reduced intelligibility or comprehensibility" (p.90).

The findings of the (1995a) paper were supported in a follow-up study (Derwing and Munro, 1997) in which native-speakers of English listened to Cantonese, Japanese, Polish and Spanish L1 speakers of English. Again, while the dimensions of accent, comprehensibility and intelligibility were related, they were not equivalent, leading the researchers to state that, "the results provide additional evidence in support of the claim that, although some features of accent may be highly salient, they do not necessarily interfere with intelligibility. A clear implication of this finding is the need to disassociate "strength of accent" and "intelligibility" in language assessment instruments, which often confound these two dimensions" (Derwing & Munro, 1997, pp.11-12).[6]

Recent studies – particularly in the field of L2 pronunciation research – have attempted to gain a deeper understanding of which features of L2 speech do in fact affect intelligibility, and which do not. Findings from such studies have generally acknowledged the importance of suprasegmental features (intonation, stress and rhythm) over segmental features as contributors towards intelligibility (Derwing, Munro & Wiebe, 1998; Hahn, 2004; Field, 2005). This is not to say, however, that intelligibility can not be affected by non-standard segmental features. Zielinski's (2007) study found that, in the speech of three Vietnamese L1 speakers, non-standard segments were implicated in a half to two-thirds of instances of reduced intelligibility with each speaker in her data (where listeners were misled in the transcription of utterances). By contrast, non-standard syllable stress was implicated in only between 8 to 12 per cent of sites of reduced intelligibility. There was, however, a good deal of overlap (22 to 44 per cent) where intelligibility problems occurred where segments *and* suprasegmentals were non-standard.

All of the studies considered above have focused on the intelligibility of non-native accents for native speakers. This narrow conceptualisation of the native speaker as the "ideal" listener is a valid criticism of many intelligibility studies (see Rajadurai, 2007), making it difficult to generalise many of these findings to L2 listeners. A significant, rectifying contribution to this problem has

---

6   Munro (2008) argues that this conflation of strength of accent and intelligibility has been a long-standing problem in pronunciation criteria for speaking assessment.

been Jenkins' (2000) proposal of a "lingua franca core" (LFC) specifically for EIL intelligibility (NNS-NNS communication). Based on a study of intelligibility-related miscommunication in classroom contexts, Jenkins has proposed a set of pronunciation requirements which are crucial for intelligible pronunciation, containing a balance of segmental and suprasegmental features. These are set out in full below, because they form a useful framework for understanding perceptual errors among L2 listeners in later chapters of this book:

1. The consonantal inventory with the following provisos:
   - rhotic [ɻ] rather than other varieties of /r/
   - intervocalic /t/ rather than [ɾ]
   - most substitutions of /θ/, /ð/, and [ɫ] permissible
   - close approximations to core consonant sounds generally permissible
   - certain approximations not permissible (i.e. where there is a risk that they will be heard as a different consonant sound from that intended)
2. Phonetic requirements:
   - aspiration following the fortis plosives /p/, /t/, and /k/
   - fortis/lenis differential effect on preceding vowel length
3. Consonant clusters:
   - initial clusters not simplified
   - medial and final clusters simplified only according to L1 rules of elision
4. Vowel sounds:
   - maintenance of vowel length contrasts
   - L2 regional qualities permissible if consistent, by /ɜː/ to be preserved
5. Nuclear stress production and placement and division of speech stream into word groups.

(Jenkins, 2000, p.159)

Jenkins states that, "outside these areas, L2 variation should be regarded as regional accent variation akin to L1 regional variation" (p.159).

Notwithstanding debate over the relative contribution of segmental and suprasegmental features in speaker intelligibility, these lines of research, together with the key findings of Munro and Derwing regarding an accent/intelligibility distinction, suggest that the presence of non-native-like features in a speaker's phonology (and concomitant high ratings of "accentedness") should not necessarily be conflated with the assumption of reduced intelligibility. Such findings have useful consequences for the feasibility of using L2 accents in listening assessment as they signal the potential for selecting speakers to record test input who are demonstrated to be highly intelligible, but who maintain salient characteristics of their accent (in aspects of their phonology which do not impact on intelligibility).

2.1.4 Intelligibility as listener-speaker related

A second critique of the notion that L2 accented speech results in listening costs concerns the role of listener-related factors in determining intelligibility. It is clear from the definition of intelligibility provided at the outset of this chapter – word/utterance recognition – that a listener is necessarily involved in the methods which seek to measure intelligibility. Smith and Nelson (1985), in fact, flagged the potential for a listener-related influence when they wrote that intelligibility is "interactional between speaker and listener" (p.336). Recently, listener factors have come to be increasingly recognised as important variables in speech perception. As Hustad (2006, p.268) notes:

> Essential to the construct of intelligibility is (a) a speaker who produces an acoustic signal for the purposes of conveying linguistic content and (b) a listener who receives the signal and interprets the linguistic content ... Thus, both production-related variables associated with the speaker and perception-related variables associated with the listener play key roles in intelligibility.

The importance of listener factors, then, serves to make the construct of intelligibility more complex. As expressed by Bent and Bradlow (2003, p.1600), "speech that is of relatively low intelligibility for one group of listeners (e.g., non-native accented English for native listeners of English) may be highly intelligible for another group of listeners (e.g. non-native listeners of English)."

Familiarity

It has been demonstrated above that a range of production- (or speaker-) related variables may contribute to, or detract from, intelligibility. The range of listener-related factors is perhaps less well documented (see Pickering, 2006); however chief among them is listener experience or familiarity. One of the earliest studies to investigate the effects of listener familiarity on intelligibility was conducted by Gass and Varonis (1984). Gass and Varonis hypothesised that intelligibility (they use the terminology comprehensibility for their measurement of the same construct) was the result of an interaction which could be explained as containing the following factors:

$$C = p_\alpha + g_\beta + f1_\gamma + f2_\delta + f3_\varepsilon \ldots fl_\zeta + s_\eta$$

(Gass & Varonis, 1984, p.67)

Where: C = comprehensibility[7], p = pronunciation, g = grammar, f1 = familiarity with topic, f2 = familiarity with person, F3 = familiarity with speaker's native language, fl = fluency, s = social factors, and where the Greek letters represent

---

7   Read as "intelligibility". See note in paragraph above.

the weighting of each factor. In exploring this model, Gass and Varonis conducted an experiment to assess the impact of familiarity with topic, accent, person and non-native speech in general on intelligibility scores. In this study, two Japanese L1 speakers and two Arabic speakers recorded sets of sentences together with a longer passage. These were presented to 142 native English listeners who completed a series of transcription tasks in a complex study design in which different familiarity conditions were modelled. It was found that topic familiarity was greatly facilitative of intelligibility, and that familiarity with the other four factors generally aided intelligibility. Of principle importance to this study, it was demonstrated that short exposure to a particular accent aided intelligibility of a different speaker with the same accent.

There is theoretical support for such a familiarity effect from the field of cross-language speech perception (for overview, see Strange, 1995). Studies investigating speech perception in another language have generally shown that perceptual patterns change as exposure to a new language increases. Recently, perceptual adjustment to accented speech has also been found to follow exposure to a given accent through experience with either one or several talkers of that accent (see Bradlow & Bent, 2008; Clarke, 2000; 2003; Weil, 2001). These studies have emerged from new findings that challenge the theory of "normalization" in speech perception. To address the challenge within speech perception that the speech signal is not invariant, normalization holds that the listener strips away variability (believed to be noise) in the speech signal to arrive at underlying, "idealized forms" (Pisoni, 1997, p.18). Within research of this kind, foreign accent has typically been identified as one such source of "noise". However, Pisoni suggests that, rather than functioning as "noise", variability is in fact vital information in the perceptual process:

> What a listener learns about a talker's voice – the acoustic correlates of gender, dialect, speaking rate, and so forth – are encoded and subsequently used to facilitate a phonetic interpretation of the linguistic content of the message.
> (Pisoni, 1997, p.11)

Extending on Pisoni's (1997) findings on perceptual learning for single talkers, Clarke & Garrett (2004, p.3647) investigated whether processing speed would decrease for comprehension of a "foreign" accent after exposure to "only a few accented utterances." They hypothesised that brief amounts of speech would provide listeners with enough phonological regularities to be exploited in the perceptual decoding of an accent. Using reaction times as a measure of processing efficiency, Clarke and Garrett (2004) found that listeners were able to adapt to Spanish and Chinese accented speech with less than one minute of experience. Clarke and Garrett (2004) argue that their findings are consistent with the notion that "processing improves due to on-line perceptual learning of phonological patterns" (p.3656), however, they also stress that in "real world" listening scenarios, top-down knowledge of lexical, semantic, syntactic and situational context may also contribute to adaptation (p.3657). Similar findings have also been reported by Bradlow and Bent (2008) who found that after two days training, native listeners developed accent-dependent, talker-independent adaptation to a Chinese accent. They suggest that this finding provides "evidence for the basic phenomenon of native listener adaptation to foreign-accented speech" (p.726).

These findings can not easily be generalised to non-native listeners, as Strange (1995) suggests that L2 learners perceive speech in very different ways to native-speakers, and use different perceptual strategies. However, the notion that listeners can adapt to accented speech is what underlies the notion that familiarity aids intelligibility. What is unknown is whether such adaptation for L2 listeners could be as "rapid" as it appears to be for native speakers. It would be reasonable to assume, as Buck (2001) has suggested, that "it generally takes L2 learners much longer to adjust to a new accent than native speakers." However it may also be assumed that, if short term adaptation to a novel accent is possible, then long term exposure would also certainly aid intelligibility. In ELF situations, or in ESL classrooms, L2 learners may be exposed to certain accents over a period of time which would potentially enable greater intelligibility. Few studies have investigated the notion of long term familiarity in depth, probably because there is no clear way to gauge levels of familiarity with particular speakers over a long period. One such attempt was Matsuura, Chiba and Fujieda (1999), who investigated the effects of Japanese learners' regular exposure to American and Irish English as a function of their intelligibility of those varieties. However as research in the next section will show, long term familiarity is often theorised beforehand for certain listener groups, or raised post hoc in explanation of findings.

Shared-L1

Related to the notion that familiarity with a variety is an aiding factor in the intelligibility of a given accent, the possibility of a shared-L1 intelligibility advantage has also been explored. There is theoretical support for such an advantage from the field of cross-language speech perception (see Best, 1995; Strange, 1995). This support rests on the principle that L2 accents are primarily characterised by transfer from the L1, and that listeners who share a speaker's L1 will be intimately familiar with the phonology of that speaker's L2 accent; sharing a knowledge base which includes, "the system of consonants and vowel categories, phonotactics, stress patterns, and intonation as well as other features of the sound system" (Bent & Bradlow, 2003, p.1607). There is also support for this theory from a World Englishes perspective, which would accept an own-accent intelligibility advantage among listener-speaker pairs as evidence of common pronunciation norms in an emerging variety.

A spate of research from an intelligibility perspective has addressed the issue of a shared-L1 intelligibility advantage. Perhaps the most significant contribution in this area has been Bent and Bradlow's (2003) study. Bent and Bradlow conducted perception tests in which Chinese, Korean, native speaker and mixed-nationality groups heard Chinese, Korean and English accented speakers reading sentences in English. Results showed that native-speakers of English were most intelligible to native-speaker listeners. However, they also showed that for each of the non-native listener groups, a highly proficient non-native speaker from the same L1 background was equally as intelligible as a native-speaker. Bent and Bradlow labelled this phenomenon a "matched interlanguage intelligibility benefit" (p.1606). This label, though, is somewhat misleading in that it suggests some advantageous condition for shared-L1 talker-listener pairs, when in fact what was observed in most cases was only equivalent levels of intelligibility for native-speakers and highly proficient non-native speakers. However, they also found that a low proficiency Korean speaker was of a similar intelligibility for Korean listeners as the high proficiency Chinese speaker and the native speaker, lending more weight to their argument.

Bent and Bradlow also claim to have found a "mismatched interlanguage intelligibility benefit" (2003, p.1606) in their study through their observation that Chinese L1 listeners found the highly proficient Korean speaker significantly more intelligible than the native speaker. Bent and Bradlow suggest two explanations for this: shared knowledge of general strategies for perceiving and producing sounds among L2 learners; and possible similarities in the sound structures of languages such as Chinese and Korean. However the mismatched interlanguage intelligibility benefit has been challenged in a study conducted by Stibbard and Lee (2006), which was a partial replication of Bent and Bradlow (2003). Stibbard and Lee found what they termed a "mismatched interlanguage intelligibility detriment" (2006, p.440) in the form of lower intelligibility scores for non-native listeners who heard a low proficiency L2 speaker from a different language background. Their findings for high proficiency speakers were comparable to Bent and Bradlow's (2003) in that within each listener group there were no significant differences in intelligibility scores for high proficiency non-native speakers and native speakers. While in each of these studies a speaker-listener interaction effect was significant, the findings suggest that a shared-L1 effect may only be taking hold when listeners hear lower proficiency speakers.

Taking a slightly different stance, though with similar findings, Munro, Derwing and Morton (2006) advance the theory that a shared-L1 background has little impact on intelligibility. In their study, Munro et al. measured the intelligibility of Japanese, Cantonese, Polish and Spanish L1 speakers for listeners from Japanese, Cantonese, Mandarin and Canadian English language backgrounds. There was a significant speaker x listener interaction effect, although the effect size for speaker on its own was much larger. In post hoc analyses, the authors found that Japanese listeners found the Japanese speaker more intelligible than any of the other listener groups. However this effect did not hold when a Cantonese shared-L1 advantage was investigated. Munro et al. stress that this provides only weak evidence of a shared-L1 or familiarity effect, and hypothesise that the effect is so small that it is "readily outweighed by other factors" (2006, p.127).

The findings of these studies have several important implications for the conceptualisation of accent and intelligibility more broadly. Previously held views on the costs of L2 accents may be criticised as having been too narrowly focused, considering they have typically been conducted with the same type of participants, native English listeners, who would not have been familiar with non-native accents[8]. If intelligibility can be viewed as partly a function of listener experience or L1 background, then some of the costs associated with non-native accents – misperceptions and increased processing time – may be recast as related to listener factors. Certainly the metaphor of "familiarity" – the role of listener experience – has gained ground in listening comprehension research. Buck, for example, states that "an unfamiliar accent can make comprehension almost impossible for the listeners" (2001, p.35). Similarly, Rost states that "a hearer's initial contact with speakers of an unfamiliar dialect most often results in continuous mishearings until such systematic adjustments are made" (1990, p.56). However Munro (2008) is cautious, suggesting that research needs to investigate the relative contributions – or the weightings – of various speaker-related factors and listener-related factors in intelligibility studies. Findings such as those in Bent and Bradlow (2003) suggests that speaker and listener related factors contribute to intelligibility in complex and interacting ways.

2.1.5 Familiarity and shared-L1 effects in L2 listening research

The finding that listener experience or listener L1 background may impact on intelligibility provides support to those researchers who approach issues of pronunciation and intelligibility from a World Englishes or ELF perspective; who see in these findings evidence that the native speaker is neither the best judge of what is intelligible, nor the highest echelon of intelligibility themselves (see Rajadurai, 2007). At the same time, however, these findings raise concern for language testing in their implicit suggestion that listeners who are highly familiar with a given accent, or who share a speaker's L1, may have an intelligibility advantage over other listeners who are not familiar and who do not share an L1 background with a given speaker. This section will review research,

---

8   See Jenkins (2000) and Rajadurai (2007) for similar criticisms.

conducted within the field of English language teaching and assessment, which has explored familiarity or shared-L1 effects in second language listening.

Early research from an English language teaching (ELT) perspective which touched on familiarity or shared-L1 effects in listening was generally conducted with the aim of gauging the relative impact of different L2 varieties compared with native speaker varieties. In an early investigation of the intelligibility of three English accents, Brown (1968) reported that Twi and Ewe speaking students at the University of Ghana found their own accent more comprehensible than either Received Pronunciation (RP), or a different Ghanian variety. This finding was based on the results of 45 students who completed an aural perception test, which consisted of a phoneme discrimination task, a sentence stress task, and a rhythm and intonation task. Brown's (1968) study challenged a previously held view that local West-African accents would be less comprehensible than RP for Ghanaian students (see Strevens, 1956), and supported the notion that the most intelligible accent was not necessarily a standard, inner circle variety. However Brown conducted no significance tests on his findings. Another early study which found a shared-L1 advantage for listeners was conducted by Wilcox (1978). Wilcox found that Singaporean students comprehended their own accent most easily on multiple-choice and cloze tests compared with their performance under Australian, US and British English accent conditions. However like Brown (1968) he did not carry out statistical tests of significance on the test scores from which he drew his findings. Moreover, Wilcox treats his findings with trepidation for a number of other reasons including the validity of his self-constructed measures, test construction and test administration (1978, p.124).

A more recent study conducted by Yule, Wetzel and Kennedy (1990) showed contradictory results. Yule, Wetzel and Kennedy investigated whether there were differences in perceptual accuracy scores when Spanish, Vietnamese and Chinese learners were asked to identify English words spoken by themselves, by other same L1 learners, by learners with a different L1, or by native speakers. The authors observed that all listeners found their own speech most intelligible, and that for the Spanish and Vietnamese listeners there were no significant differences across the other three conditions. However they did find a higher rate of perceptual accuracy among Chinese L1 listeners when listening to Chinese L1 speakers compared with native speakers. Yule, Wetzel and Kennedy (1990) suggest that this unique finding for the Chinese listener group may be attributable to their predominantly EFL-based language learning experience, compared to the other listener groups, who had primarily received English language instruction in an ESL context. In other words, the Chinese listeners found their own accent most intelligible because that was the variety with which they were most familiar.

Three important studies, however, appear to have laid the foundations for current beliefs concerning familiarity and shared-L1 effects in listening comprehension. The first of these is a widely cited study conducted by Smith and Bisazza (1982). In this study, the authors compared the scores of participants from Japan, Taiwan, Thailand, Hong Kong, India, the Philippines and the United States on a listening comprehension test featuring American, Indian and Japanese accents. Smith and Bisazza (1982) found that across all listeners, the American accent was significantly the most comprehensible variety, followed by the Japanese accent and the Indian accent. Individually, the Japanese listener group scored most highly with their own accent, however the Indian listener group found the American variety more comprehensible than their own. The finding for the Indian listeners, however, should be treated with caution, as the speaker was a native-speaker of Hindi whereas only two of the listeners (from a group of 30) were native Hindi speakers, and they had all had greater exposure to American English than to the Uttar-Pradesh variety of English used by the Indian speaker. Smith and Bisazza (1982) conclude that the key variable in the comprehensibility of English varieties is the listener's prior exposure to that variety, as listeners in all of the countries tested would have had high levels of experience with American English.

In response to Smith and Bisazza (1982), Ortmeyer and Boyle (1985) performed a study in Hong Kong on native Chinese speakers' comprehension of American, British and two speakers of Chinese ("clear" and unclear") accented speech, as measured by a standard, multiple-choice listening test and a dictation test. The listener group was also divided into three different proficiency levels: low, medium and high. Ortmeyer and Boyle (1985) found that for the standard listening test, the only significant difference in scores was between the American accent (the highest mean score) and the "unclear" Chinese accent (the lowest mean score). On the dictation test, although there were no significant differences between the scores for American and British accents and no significant differences between scores for both Chinese accents, there were significant differences between American and British varieties with both Chinese accents. Moreover, the differences between American/British and Chinese accents were more pronounced in the scores of the low proficiency group. Ortmeyer and Boyle's (1985) findings for the standard listening test seem to support the notion that familiar varieties, which are also highly intelligible, will be equally as comprehensible for non-native listeners as standard, native speaker varieties. However, this study also highlights that the effects of accent and intelligibility may become more or less prominent depending on the testing method. In a dictation test, which is primarily a test of perception and parsing, any bottom-up listening problems that a listener encounters would directly affect their response on the task. However, in a multiple-choice test, higher order listening skills may be activated, taking the emphasis away from the perceptual skills. In this sense, a dictation test would be more susceptible to variation in speaker intelligibility than a comprehension test.

Recent research by Tauroza and Luk (1997) adds weight to the hypothesis that comprehension is aided by familiarity with an accent which may not necessarily be one's own. Tauroza and Luk (1997) staged a partial replication of Ortmeyer and Boyle's (1985) study. Their subjects were 66 Hong Kong secondary school students (aged 14-16), who were all L1 Cantonese speakers. These participants were divided into their regular class groups, who were deemed to be of roughly equal listening ability in English according to a recently administered listening test.[9] Half of the listeners were presented with a passage recorded in RP by an English native speaker, the other half heard the same passage recorded by a native speaker of Cantonese with a Hong Kong English accent. Listeners were then required to write a summary of the passage (by recall), after which they answered 14 multiple choice items. T-tests showed no significant differences between each group on each measure, and so Tauroza and Luk (1997) concluded that their findings did not support an own-accent advantage in L2 listening, and that a familiar accent (in this case, RP) is equally as comprehensible as one's own.

Tauroza and Luk's (1997) findings form a significant contribution to the literature, and so it is worth noting some of the shortcomings of their analysis. Firstly, given their own concerns regarding the proficiency of their groups, their findings might have achieved greater validity had they assigned participants to groups using their test score as a guide. Secondly, they provide no reliability coefficient for the multiple choice test they designed for the study, and so we have no way of evaluating its quality as an instrument to measure listening comprehension. Finally, little information is given on the method by which the summary task was scored.

Nevertheless, Tauroza and Luk make a very useful point in their discussion, arguing that the sociolinguistic *milieu* of a language learning context may explain why some listeners find their own accent the most comprehensible and others do not, and may also explain some of the divergent findings in previous studies. Comparing their results with those of Smith and Bisazza (1982), they note that Hong Kong-based learners of English would have considerably more exposure to native-English speakers in the wider community than had the Japan-based learners in the early 1980s. For those Japanese learners at that time, a Japanese accent may have been the accent with which they had had the most regular experience. Tauroza and Luk (1997) conclude that: "L2 learners will find English spoken with familiar accents easier to comprehend than unfamiliar accents and differences between L2 learners' comprehension of own and model

---

9   Tauroza and Luk (1997) acknowledge that although the classes had equivalent mean scores on the test, the distribution of scores for each class indicated that one class had a higher proportion of "better" students than the other.

accents will merely reflect differences in the listener's familiarity with those accents." (p.64)

The Major et al. studies

Turning to the specific field of language testing, two studies of pertinence to the current research are the twin investigations conducted by Major et al. (2002; 2005). These studies were commissioned by the US-based Educational Testing Service (ETS) with the aim of collecting empirical data on the effect of non-native accent and dialect on listening test scores. In the first of these studies, Major et al. (2002) investigated the potential for a shared-L1 effect on scores for TOEFL mini-talks. They constructed a "Listening Comprehension Trial Test" – using the listening section of the "old" TOEFL PBT – in which mini-talk lectures were delivered in English by native speakers of Chinese, Japanese, Korean and Spanish backgrounds. These were then administered to a cohort of listeners who shared the same L1 backgrounds. A repeated-measures ANOVA showed a significant interaction effect between speaker and listener L1 background. Post hoc analyses showed that Spanish NS learners were advantaged by listening to a NS of their own language, but the Chinese L1 group were disadvantaged by listening to a Chinese-accented speaker. This led Major *et al.* (2002) to state the following: "do listeners perform significantly better on a listening test when the speaker shares the same language? The answer to this question was not a clear yes or no but, rather, sometimes" (p.185). They went on to conclude that based on their results, "a listening test including nonnative varieties in the interest of authenticity may create test bias, thereby posing a threat to construct validity" (p.188).

However, a number of limitations exist in the methodology of this study. Firstly, and most importantly, as the researchers themselves admit, the results of the study are affected by the possible incomparable difficulty of the tasks used to assess comprehension. The design of the study – although attempting to counter-balance task effects – meant that each L1 listener group heard different lectures and answered different questions to the other groups when hearing a given speaker, thus the differences in test scores compared across speakers could be attributable to differences in item difficulty rather than any accent effect. Secondly, the design of the study addresses the issue of "bias" only indirectly. The term "bias" in language testing literature is generally defined in relation to an item or test where candidates of equal ability, but from different groups, have an unequal chance of getting an item correct, or of attaining the same test score (see Angoff, 1993). In this sense, it is necessary to investigate a bias effect with a focus on between-groups differences. Major et al. find an interaction effect between speaker and L1 listener group, but only explain their findings by within-groups comparisons; the comparisons of different speaker effects within each listener group. These patterns certainly suggest that listener groups varied in their responses, but they do not give clear evidence of test bias.

Major *et al.*'s (2005) second study is less relevant to the current study as it focused on comprehension of standard (Standard US English), regional (Southern US English), ethnic (African-American Vernacular English) and international dialects (Australian English and Indian English). Using results from a similarly structured methodology to their first study, though without a focus on any particular L1 groups, Major et al. found that a population of ESL listeners scored lower on comprehension tasks when listening to ethnic and international dialects of English compared with standard American English and a regional (Southern) dialect of English. However this result is perhaps unsurprising given that the non-native listeners involved in the study (Chinese, Japanese, German, Russian and "other") had all lived within the western states of the US for up to one year, and thus would have had the greatest amount of exposure to the Standard and Southern varieties. Again, Major et al. conclude that their findings show that caution should be exercised, particularly in the sense that "using ethnic and international dialects of English in listening comprehension tests, such as TOEFL, is likely to disadvantage test takers" (p.64).

The limitations of the first Major *et al.* (2002) study mean that there is still no conclusive evidence to support claims that wider accent representation on a listening test would result in bias towards particular L1 groups. The findings presented in the Major et al. (2005) paper do not address the question of bias at all, but rather suggest that unfamiliar accent increases difficulty generally. Aside from these limitations, the Major et al. studies provide only a macro-level view of the potential effects of accent in listening assessment. The specific context of language testing provides scope for a micro-level understanding of the effects of accent through analysis at the item level. Such an analysis would also be able to draw on more sophisticated techniques for detecting bias in tests – those from the family of differential item functioning (DIF) approaches. As well as providing an item level view, DIF procedures provide the advantage of diminishing the problem of unequal difficulty across tasks or tests by first matching candidates on ability, and then conducting between-group analyses on individual test items. These methods are discussed in detail in Chapter 5. The next section now turns to a consideration of relevant literature which has been conducted from a social perspective.

2.2 Listening to L2 accents: a social perspective

While the research presented above falls within a psycholinguistic or cognitive paradigm, accent has also been investigated from sociolinguistic and social-psychological perspectives. It has already been established that accent serves as a marker of regional or social identity, and listeners respond to accents in ways which may not only be explained through processing metaphors, but through an understanding of attitudes towards accent varieties, and their role in the comprehension process.

2.2.1 Attitudes towards accent and accented speakers

A long tradition of language attitudes research has shown that accent is a powerful social marker that conveys indexical information to a listener (see, for example, Brennan & Brennan, 1981; Giles & Sassoon, 1983). Speaker evaluation studies support the view that listeners tend to hold positive attitudes towards standard accents and negative attitudes towards non-standard accents of English on particular traits. For example, Ryan, Hewstone and Giles (1984) found that speakers with standard accents were rated more highly on traits such as intelligence and competence than speakers with non-standard accents. Studies in which native-speakers have evaluated various non-native speaker accents have consistently found that non-native speakers are given negative ratings for traits such as solidarity and status (Ryan & Sebastian, 1980; Gill, 1994; Cargile, 1997). However, Cargile and Giles (1998) have also shown that the attitudinal responses of native listeners to L2 accents are not always predictably negative for L2 accents that are seen as "prestigious" and associated with intelligence and wealth such as Japanese.

While many studies of language attitudes have been conducted using the judgments of native speakers only, a growing body of research has examined learners' attitudes towards various non-native varieties. These studies have often utilised a "verbal guise" method, whereby listeners hear a range of voices, and rate the speakers on semantic differential scales containing a list of adjectival attributes. Listeners' attitudes towards speakers, and in some cases towards varieties, are inferred from the strength of these ratings. Two main trends have emerged from this research. Firstly, learners tend to have more positive attitudes towards standard native-speaker accents such as General American (GA) or Received Pronunciation (RP) than other accents in educational contexts. Secondly, learners may hold negative attitudes towards their own variety of accent.

In one of the earliest studies to examine learner attitudes towards L2 speech, Fayer and Krasinski (1987) found that Spanish L1 listeners were more critical of Puerto Rican-Spanish speakers than were native English listeners. This difference was particularly marked on dimensions of "distraction" and "annoyance", which Fayer and Krasinski collapsed within the concept of "irritation". They proposed two theories to explain why NNS are more irritated when listening to other NNS: because tolerance increases with proficiency, and because they are "embarrassed by their compatriots' struggles with the non-native language" (p.321). The linguistic features which were found to irritate most were pronunciation and hesitation, lending weight to the notion that accent and fluency are salient features in speaker evaluations.

The preference for native varieties among non-native speakers has also been recorded in Jenkins (2007) survey of ELF accent attitudes. Jenkins administered a questionnaire to 326 respondents in inner-, outer- and expanding-circle contexts which elicited attitudes towards speech varieties relating to a labelled map of the world. Jenkins' findings showed that native varieties – specifically UK English, US English and Australian English were considered, overall, the most correct, the most acceptable, the most pleasant and the most familiar compared with Swedish, Brazilian, German, Spanish, Chinese, Indian and Japanese accents of English. She also observed qualitative differences in the language used to describe certain accents. For instance, the US English accent was often believed to be "easy to understand", the UK English accent "traditional" or "proper" and the Australian English accent "half-way" between British and American English. By contrast, many of the non-native accents were described in negative terms with many varieties characterised as difficult to understand. Her findings thus revealed a clear and consistent pattern in which native varieties were preferred, and non-native varieties were not. However Jenkins' method may be critiqued on the grounds that participants were not presented with stimuli, and so they did not have a specific auditory image in mind. Their responses, therefore, may not have been indicative of their reactions when actually listening to speakers of these varieties.

Within a Japanese EFL context, Matsuura, Chiba and Yamamoto (1994) found that Japanese college students evaluated an American English accent more positively than they did Malay, Chinese Malay, Bangladeshi, Micronesian, Hong Kong or Sri Lankan accents. The study found that the proficiency level of the listener did not correlate with differences in attitudes, but evidence was shown of a link between listeners who had strong instrumental motivation or expressed respect for indigenized varieties of English, and a smaller difference in attitudes towards native and non-native accents. A follow-up study found that Japanese listeners rated familiar accents more positively than unfamiliar accents on an attitudinal rating scale, except for Japanese-accented English, which was rated negatively (Chiba, Matsuura & Yamamoto, 1995). The authors suggested that "'Japanese English' has a negative connotation in Japan, where English is a foreign language and the targeted model has been a native variety" (Chiba et al., 1995, p.84). The results of these studies connect with findings that language learners often want to sound more like native speakers (Derwing, 2003).

However, Chiba et al.'s (1995) findings also demonstrate that language attitudes are influenced by the "linguistic landscape", or the sociolinguistic milieu of the rating context (see Dailey, Giles & Jansma, 2005).

These findings were reflected, to some degree, in Dalton-Puffer et al.'s (1997) study of attitudes towards L2 pronunciation in Austria. Dalton-Puffer et al. (1997) asked 132 students of English (most of whom were German L1 speakers) to rate the speech of two British English native-speakers, one American English native-speaker and two Austrian non-native speakers on a range of adjectival attributes reflecting status and solidarity attributes. Listeners were told that the rating was being conducted to find suitable speakers for a published audio-book. Findings showed that the most positive ratings across all attributes were given to one of the British English speakers who spoke with an RP accent. The two other native speakers were rated next most positively, followed by the two Austrian L2 speakers. Dalton-Puffer et al. concluded that "Advanced Austrian EFL learners display negative attitudes towards their own non-native accent of English" (p.126).

However recent findings published by McKenzie (2008) suggest that attitudinal reactions to speakers from the same language background may be more complex. McKenzie conducted a verbal guise experiment (see Chapter 6) in which 558 Japanese native speakers rated the speech samples of the following varieties: Glasgow standard English, "heavily accented" Japanese English, Southern US English, moderately accented Japanese English, Midwest US English, and Glasgow vernacular. Ratings were provided on a scale in which items loaded onto two components: competence and social attractiveness. McKenzie found that the Japanese listeners rated all four native varieties highest on the competence trait, but, surprisingly, they rated the heavily accented Japanese speaker highest on the social attractiveness trait. McKenzie suggests that the strong Japanese accent may represent a "salient marker of in-group identity" among the Japanese students.

2.2.2 Attitudes and comprehension

While it is clear that learners may hold negative attitudes towards other L2 accents, and particularly their own, it is less obvious whether variance in attitudes translates to increased or decreased comprehension during listening tasks. Research has shown that when listeners hold negative attitudes towards non-native speakers, those listeners may resist collaborating in conversation to achieve understanding (Lindemann, 2002; Lippi-Green, 1997). Stereotyping of the communication skills of particular speakers can lead listeners to "expect" communication to fail. For example, Rubin (1992) played the same lecture given by an American native speaker to two groups of listeners, but visually prompted one group with a visual image of an Asian lecturer, and the other group with an image of a Caucasian lecturer. The group who believed they were listening to an Asian lecturer scored lower on a cloze test, and rated foreign accent as stronger than the other group. Thus, Rubin (1992) concluded that comprehension was related to listeners' expectations about accent.

This relationship between a listener's receptivity towards a speaker and their stereotyped expectations of that speaker's intelligibility can be connected to Norton's (1997) work on language, identity and ownership of language. Drawing on Bourdieu (1977), Norton critiques a common assumption about the conditions for communication that "those who listen regard those who speak as worthy to speak" (1997, p.411); listeners may instead "resist" a given speaker. Lindemann's (2002) findings support Norton's critique. In her study, Lindemann (2002) paired American English native speakers with Korean native speakers, and asked them to complete a task together in English. Through a conversation analysis, Lindemann (2002) found that some of the American English NS, who had previously been assessed as having negative attitudes towards Koreans on a questionnaire, used conversational strategies to "problematise" their partners' utterances, or to "avoid" them. Lindemann (2002, p.419) suggests that the relationship between attitude and comprehension, then, is "mediated by the native speaker's choice of strategies." In this sense, listeners may "reject the burden" of listening to non-native speakers.

These studies have investigated listeners' reactions to visual prompts or to speakers themselves within interaction. Fewer studies, though, have investigated the relationship between attitudes towards accented speech and comprehension based on the speech signal alone. Without visual cues, the relationship between attitudes toward accent and comprehension is problematised. It may be that negative attitudes towards an accent are a result of lowered intelligibility, rather than *vice versa*. In support of this idea, Bresnahan, Ohashi, Nebashi, Liu & Shearman (2002) found that, for American English native speakers, a highly intelligible "foreign" accent resulted in not only more positive attitudes, but also in more positive affective responses than for an accent that was deemed unintelligible. They concluded that the intelligibility of an accent has an effect on the emotional response of the listener. This emotional response is symptomatic of a resistance towards "out-group" members (see Tajfel & Turner, 1986), who are marked as such by the "strength" of their accent, measured by its dissimilarity from the accent of the "in group" (see also Cargile & Giles, 1997).

2.3 A preliminary study of test-taker perceptions

In a preliminary investigation, Harding (2008) conducted a qualitative study of test-taker perceptions of a listening test featuring speakers of diverse English accents. This study was intended to address a gap in literature relating to learners views of many of the concerns outlined in the sections above. Drawing on materials from *TOEFL® Test Preparation Kit* (ETS, 2000), a listening test was constructed with speakers representing four L1 backgrounds: Australian English, Mandarin Chinese, Japanese and Bengali. The test, together with a questionnaire designed to elicit participants' accent preferences, was then administered to 44 ESL learners from a range of first language backgrounds. Test-taker perceptions were explored through four *post hoc* focus groups with learners at different proficiency levels, as well as three one-on-one interviews with highly proficient participants. The goal of the focus groups and interviews was to elicit test-taker perceptions on three relevant issues: accent-related listening difficulty, a shared-L1 advantage in comprehension, and test fairness.

Findings showed, firstly, that test-takers generally perceived speaker accent as a source of difficulty in the test. However, perceptions of accent-related difficulty appeared to be more salient among higher proficiency test-takers; the test-takers of lowest proficiency tended to express difficulty with other elements of the task demands such as speech rate and level of vocabulary. This was shown to be consistent with Goh (1999) who observed that low ability test takers were less aware of accent as source of listening difficulty compared with high ability listeners. Focus group data also revealed that some lower proficiency learners perceived the Australian English speaker as most difficult to understand; a finding which was at odds with the rest of the participants who tended to single out the Australian English speaker as clear.

Secondly, when a shared-L1 accent was noted by participants, it was likely to be evaluated in a critical light rather than perceived as an advantage in comprehension. In the example below (taken from Harding, 2008, p.21) one of the test-takers from a Japanese L1 background characterised the Japanese accented speaker's pronunciation as distracting:

Kazumi: Japanese university student

Kazumi: And ... yeah the third speaker was, I think she's Japanese

Interviewer: Right .. yeah

Kazumi: And

Interviewer: Yes, you're correct actually

Kazumi: She: and she has Japanese accent and American accent

Interviewer: Uh huh

Kazumi: Quite strong

Interviewer: Uh huh

Kazumi: But I guess ... that I still got distracted by her like especially /r/ sound and it's I think it's common for Japanese speakers who, like who are very conscious about pronunciation they tend to focus on /r/ and /l/ sound

Interviewer: Mm mm

Kazumi: And because they're so conscious about /r/ and /l/ they tend to .. overdo it

Examples such as this suggested that attitudinal responses were strongly evoked when a shared L1 accent was noted, but no intelligibility "advantage" was necessarily felt. Other comments of this kind raised the notion that test-takers who are distracted by perceived errors in pronunciation and disfluency may lose "belief" in a speaker's assumed role (e.g., as a lecturer) on a listening test. This suggests a complex relationship, at least on the perceptual level, between attitudes towards speakers and level of engagement with the test, which could subsequently affect performance.

Finally, the general acceptability of using diverse accented speakers was explored through perceptions of test fairness. In the data, "fairness" was conceptualised in a number of distinct ways by the test-takers as:

fitness for purpose: the extent to which the test matched the candidates' current context
construct-relevance: the extent to which the comprehension of accented speech was deemed relevant to the test-takers' communicative needs
equal access: the possibility for test-takers to gain exposure to, or learn to listen to, an accent
equal advantage: the potential for an advantage if listener and speaker share an L1
fair conditions: the creation of reasonable conditions under which to test, specifically avoiding raising test anxiety

(Harding, 2008, p.28)[10]

Data showed that participants who commented on issues of access, equal advantage and fair conditions were somewhat unified in viewing the introduction of accented speech as potentially violating these aspects of test fairness. However a range of views emerged regarding fitness for purpose and construct-relevance which seemed to be based more on participants' own language learning goals, and their differing perceptions of the sociolinguistic demands of academic life in Australia. These findings suggested that learners distinguished between those accents which are seen as desirable in classroom contexts – the most intelligible or aesthetically attractive – and those which were perceived as necessary in a testing context – meeting the "real-life" communicative needs of the candidate.

---

10 It was noted that these test-taker-driven concerns closely reflected the five qualities proposed by Kunnan (2004) in his "Test Fairness framework": validity, absence of bias, access, administration and social consequences.

2.4 Summary

This review of literature has explored in greater detail the concerns first identified in the introduction. In the first section, it surveyed literature related to the concern over the intelligibility of L2 speech. Research showed that non-native accents have typically been associated with listening "costs". However two strands of research were discussed which served to critique the assumption that a non-native accent is synonymous with reductions in intelligibility. In the first of these, Munro and Derwing's notion of an accent/intelligibility distinction was discussed, together with current research on features of pronunciation which have been shown to aid, and detract from, intelligibility. In the second strain, research which has emphasised the co-construction of intelligibility between speaker and listener was discussed, with a focus on the role of experience with accent either through familiarity or through sharing a speaker's L1. This led into a survey of research which has gauged shared-L1 and familiarity effects in second language listening and listening assessment. The second section then provided an overview of research conducted from a social perspective. Firstly, attitudes towards accents and accented speakers were discussed, with a focus on the attitudes of second language learners. Following this, the relationship between attitudes and comprehension was considered. Finally, in the third section, a preliminary study of test-taker perceptions was summarised.

This review of research, allows for the refining of the concerns first identified in Chapter 1. Firstly, the literature presented above has direct implications for the concern over intelligibility. Given the accent/intelligibility distinction demonstrated by Munro and Derwing, it seems feasible that L2 speakers could be selected for a listening test whose accents are demonstrated to be highly-intelligible to a range of listeners, but who maintain characteristic features of their varieties. In other words, speaker-related features involved in intelligibility may be controlled to a certain extent across a range of diverse accented speakers.

However, the research from intelligibility studies concerning the role of the listener only serves to bolster the concern that listeners who share a speaker's L1 or are highly familiar with a speaker's accent may find a speaker more easily intelligible than other listeners. Findings for a shared-L1 advantage seem inconclusive and somewhat contradictory, although there is some evidence that an intimate knowledge of a speaker's L2 phonology may assist listeners, particularly when listening to speakers who are less proficient. At the same time, there is strong theoretical and empirical support that familiarity with an accent aids intelligibility, and that this benefit also manifests more broadly in comprehension. Less is known of the degree to which shared-L1 or familiarity effects may vary depending on characteristics of the speaker. From the evidence surveyed above, it seems reasonable to hypothesise that if a speaker reaches a certain threshold of general intelligibility, then variance attributable to listener factors would be less pronounced. Unfortunately only few studies which have investigated listener effects have attempted to choose speakers of comparable intelligibility.

Research also suggests that the concerns over acceptability and test score variance related to attitudes are not unfounded. L2 listeners commonly express less acceptance or negative attitudes towards other L2 varieties in both direct and indirect measures. In some cases, listeners seem to find their own accents particularly unacceptable, as evidenced in the preliminary study of test-taker perceptions, though this is certainly not always the case. Furthermore, there is some evidence – though this is less substantial – that listeners who hold negative attitudes towards a speaker's accent may perform worse on a listening test featuring that speaker. Although the link between attitudes and comprehension seem theoretically plausible for face-to-face interaction, though, it is less clear how such an effect would hold in the particular context of a monologic listening test.

Thus we may conclude that even if the concern for the intelligibility of non-native accents (or even for strong accents) is unfounded, and may be nullified through the careful selection of speakers, the other concerns remain:

1. Test-takers who share a speaker's L1 may potentially be advantaged over others in a listening test featuring that speaker
2. Test-takers who are highly familiar with a particular L2 accent may potentially be advantaged over others on a listening test featuring a speaker of that variety
3. Test-takers may hold negative attitudes towards speakers with L2 accents and find their use in listening assessment unacceptable
4. Attitudes towards accented speakers may influence listening test performance

The literature review has demonstrated that for each of these concerns there are considerable gaps in knowledge surrounding the conditions under which certain effects may occur. Furthermore, none of these concerns has yet been adequately addressed from within a language testing-specific context. Thus, although these concerns may drive an orthodox approach to the use of accents in language testing, they are still in many ways hypothetical. These concerns, then, form the basis for empirical enquiry in this book. Their integration into a framework for research is discussed in the next chapter.

Chapter 3: Research design

This chapter is divided into four sections. Section 3.1 presents an overview of the stages of research including a visual representation of the overarching research design. The first stage – the construction of test materials – is considered in detail in Section 3.2. Then, Section 3.3 describes the three main empirical studies of the research, and provides a discussion of the conceptual approach underlying the design. Finally, Section 3.4 describes the final stage, at which implications are drawn from the converged findings of the three studies.

3.1 Stages of research

The basic premise of this book is that, while the use of diverse accented speakers on EAP listening tests is justified by a strong theoretical rationale, a number of serious concerns regarding construct and face validity remain. As such the current study sought to investigate the use of speakers with diverse accents on an EAP listening test through the framework of a validation study. This necessarily involved three stages of research:

- Firstly, the construction of a listening test instrument with diverse accented speakers with which to conduct the research;
- Secondly, the undertaking of three research studies designed to address the potential threats to validity which were identified in Chapter 1, and refined in the literature review;
- Thirdly, the interpretation of findings from the research studies conducted in stage two, and their implications for questions of validity and future test development.

An overview of each stage of research is shown in Figure 3-1. Each stage will be described in more detail in the following sections of this chapter.

3.2 Stage one

Stage one of the project involved the construction of a listening test instrument with diverse accented speakers with which to conduct the validation research. The test selected was the UTESL (University Test of English as a Second Language) listening sub-test. In the sense that the research was designed to investigate the use of diverse accented speakers on EAP listening assessment broadly, the UTESL was conceptualised as an "instrumental case" – an exemplar of a general EAP proficiency test. However the UTESL also serves particular purposes, and has unique characteristics. Thus stage one involved developing a detailed description of the UTESL, including: the background of the test, its intended purpose, the specifications of the listening sub-test, and the characteristics of texts and tasks.

Stage one also involved a rigorous process of speaker selection to identify highly intelligible speakers of diverse accents who would record test materials. The principle reason why a speaker selection process was deemed necessary was to allay the concern, expressed in Chapter 1 and explored in Chapter 2, that non-native speech would be less intelligible, and could "disrupt the whole listening process" (Buck, 2001, p.35). A speaker selection process was also the recommendation of a previous investigation in which the researcher found that accented speakers, chosen impressionistically, often did not represent a level of "performance quality" (in their reading of scripted material) that test-takers appear to expect in a test of academic English (Harding 2008). Recommendations for further research were suggested:

> Future research should aim, if possible, to attempt to select accented speakers of a high level of intelligibility and perceived comprehensibility ... The aim of such a process would be to ensure that the intelligibility and comprehensibility of speakers, regardless of their accent, was shown to approximate that of speakers who may routinely be used for operational EAP listening tests.
>
> (Harding, 2008, p.29)

Although other studies on accent and listening comprehension had included speaker selection processes (see Major et al., 2002; 2005), these were usually based on a strength of accent rating, rather than an empirical determination of general intelligibility. A rigorous speaker selection process which aimed to identify diverse accented speakers with similarly high levels of general intelligibility – rather than low levels of accentedness – was considered an essential step in the construction of authentic, usable test materials.

For these reasons, a system of speaker selection was devised, with methods based on the series of intelligibility, comprehensibility and accentedness experiments that have been carried out by Munro and Derwing (see Munro & Derwing, 1995a, Derwing & Munro, 1997, Munro et al., 2006).

Figure 3-1: Stages of research

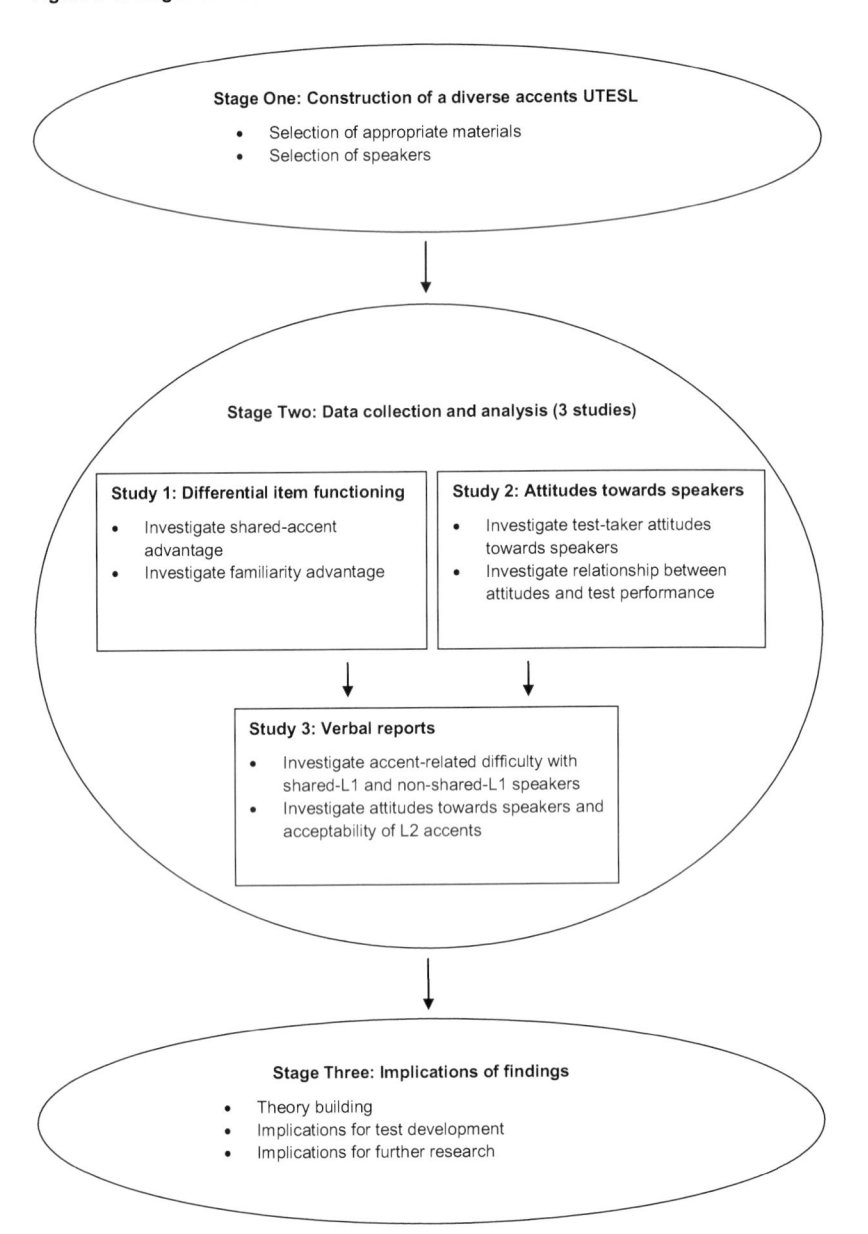

Stage One: Construction of a diverse accents UTESL
- Selection of appropriate materials
- Selection of speakers

Stage Two: Data collection and analysis (3 studies)

Study 1: Differential item functioning
- Investigate shared-accent advantage
- Investigate familiarity advantage

Study 2: Attitudes towards speakers
- Investigate test-taker attitudes towards speakers
- Investigate relationship between attitudes and test performance

Study 3: Verbal reports
- Investigate accent-related difficulty with shared-L1 and non-shared-L1 speakers
- Investigate attitudes towards speakers and acceptability of L2 accents

Stage Three: Implications of findings
- Theory building
- Implications for test development
- Implications for further research

3.3 Stage two

Stage two comprised the bulk of the research project, consisting of three separate, though linked, studies designed to address the potential threats to validity which emerged in Chapters 1 and 2, namely:

- The potential for a shared-L1 advantage
- The potential for an accent-familiarity advantage
- The potential for negative test appeal stemming from negative attitudes towards speakers with L2 accents
- Construct irrelevant variance related to attitudes towards accented speakers

Conceptualising validation

The approach to validation in the research represents the adoption of elements of Kane's (1992; 2006) argument-based approach. According to Kane (2006), test validation requires two distinct arguments. The first of these is the "interpretive argument", which Kane describes as "[specifying] the proposed interpretations and uses of test results by laying out the network of inferences and assumptions leading from the observed performances to the conclusions and decisions based on the performances" (2006, p.23). This argument, in fact, takes the form of a series of statements about the proposed interpretations and uses of test scores, which are framed in informal, presumptive reasoning. In this sense, constructing an interpretive argument is a method through which the underlying reasoning of test score interpretations is made explicit, and so made open to evaluation. The second argument – the "validity argument" – is the process by which the interpretive argument is then evaluated.

The identification of specific threats or concerns is of principle importance to Kane's approach as he states, "the argument-based approach to validation adopts the interpretive argument as the framework for collecting and presenting validity evidence and seeks to provide convincing evidence for its inferences and assumptions, especially its most questionable assumptions" (1992, p.527). This notion of "questionable assumptions" echoes more recent work by Fulcher and Davidson (2007) who suggest that the weakest part of a validity argument should be identified and investigated.

In the context of the current study, the set of four concerns presented above, brought about by the introduction of speakers with L2 accents, may be viewed as potentially weakening the interpretive claims of the existing UTESL listening sub-test. In order, then, to design a research plan to provide convincing validity evidence to address these concerns, the potential threats to validity were transformed into a set of four "questionable assumptions", similar to a set of hypotheses:

Assumption 1: Test-takers of otherwise equivalent ability will not perform differentially on an EAP listening test featuring a highly- intelligible speaker with an L2 accent, irrespective of whether or not they share the speaker's L1.

Assumption 2: Test-takers of otherwise equivalent ability will not perform differentially on an EAP listening test featuring a highly- intelligible speaker with an L2 accent, irrespective of whether or not they are highly familiar with the speaker's accent.

Assumption 3: Test-takers will not, overall, hold negative attitudes towards highly-intelligible speakers with L2 accents used on an EAP listening test.

Assumption 4: Test-taker attitudes towards diverse accented speakers will not affect their performance on a listening test featuring that speaker.

The studies designed to address these questionable assumptions are described below.

Mixed methods in a validation study

Kane suggests that with regard to research methods used in a validation study, an argument-based approach is,

> highly tolerant. It does not preclude the development of any kind of interpretation or the use of any data collection technique. It does not identify any kind of validity evidence as being generally preferable to any other kind of validity evidence.
>
> (1992, p.534)

In this sense, Kane's (1992) approach fits, to a certain extent, the arguments put forward by advocates of mixed-methods research (see Creswell & Plano Clark, 2007; Johnson & Onwuegbuzie, 2004). Mixed-methods research has emerged in recent years as a viable "third-way" in the quantitative/qualitative paradigm debate. Theorists of a mixed-methods approach have drawn a link between this approach and the philosophical worldview of pragmatism, which has its roots in the work of Charles Sanders Peirce, William James, John Dewey, George Herbert Mead and Arthur F. Bentley and later in the neo-pragmatists (see Maxcy, 2003). The central tenet of the approach – the "Pragmatic Maxim" – was expressed by Peirce thus:

> Consider what effects, that might conceivably have practical bearings, we conceive the object of our conception to have. Then, our conception of these effects is the whole of our conception of the object.
>
> (Peirce 1878: 146)

This maxim has been applied to the process of inquiry in the sense articulated by Tashakkori and Teddlie (1998) in that the best method is the one that is most effective (see also Maxcy, 2003). The research question, then, becomes "of primary importance – more important than either the method or the philosophical worldview that underlies the method" (Creswell & Plano Clark, 2007, p.26; see also Teddlie & Tashakkori, 2003). This argument for the primacy of the research question reflects Kane's argument for the acceptability of "any kind of evidence" that supports or refutes the interpretive argument.

For the current study, it was decided that the most useful research design within which to address the questionable assumptions would be to follow a "triangulation convergence" approach as described by Creswell and Plano Clark (2007). Triangulation is described by Cresswell and Plano Clark (2007) as the most common approach to mixed-methods, its purpose being to "obtain different but complementary data on the same topic" (Morse, 1991, p.122). Creswell and Plano Clark (2007) distinguish between four different types of triangulation design: the convergence model, the data transformation model, the validating quantitative data model, and the multilevel model. The triangulation convergence is the more traditional approach, described thus:

> In this model, the researcher collects and analyzes quantitative and qualitative data separately on the same phenomenon and then the different results are converged (by comparing and contrasting the different results) during the interpretation. Researchers use this model when they want to compare results, validate, confirm, or corroborate quantitative results with qualitative findings. The purpose of this model is to end up with valid and well-substantiated conclusions about a single phenomenon.
>
> (Cresswell & Plano Clark, 2007, pp.64-65)

A research design was conceptualised in which the four questionable assumptions would be addressed primarily through two quantitative investigations, the findings of which would be triangulated with a third, smaller-scale qualitative study. In this design, the quantitative results are granted more weight in the final convergence of results.

Practically, the research design involved expanding each of the questionable assumptions to a set of research questions[11], and then selecting the most appropriate and feasible methods to address those research questions. The result was a research design incorporating three linked empirical studies:

---

11 Each set of expanded research questions is presented in the chapters to follow.

Study one: Questionable assumptions 1 and 2 were addressed within study one which utilised differential item functioning detection methods and an analysis of test takers' written responses on the answer paper. This study is presented in Chapter 5.

Study two: Questionable assumptions 3 and 4 were addressed in study two which gauged attitudes towards speakers using the speaker evaluation method, and investigated their relationship with test performance. This study is presented in Chapter 6.

Study three: A third qualitative study – using verbal report methods – focused on the nature of accent-related difficulty among shared-L1 and non-shared-L1 speakers, their attitudes towards speakers and their general perceptions of acceptability and fairness. This study is presented in Chapter 7.

An overview of the three study research design is provided in Figure 3-2 which shows each study, the assumptions addressed, the type of data utilised and the analytical methods performed.

Figure 3-2: Research design in three studies

Study	Assumption addressed	Data	Analysis
Study One: Differential item functioning (Chapter 5)	Assumptions 1 and 2	• Test score data on 3 diverse-accents UTESL listening tests • Responses to language experience questionnaire	• Item analysis (CTT) • Analysis of variance • DIF analyses • Response analysis
Study Two: Attitudes towards speakers (Chapter 6)	Assumptions 3 and 4	• Responses to speaker evaluation task (verbal guise) • Test score data on 3 diverse-accents UTESL listening tests • Responses to language experience questionnaire	• Factor analysis • Analysis of variance • Regression analysis
Study Three: Verbal reports (Chapter 7)	Triangulation of findings from study one and study two	• Verbal report protocols on 2 modified diverse-accents UTESL listening tests • Post-hoc one-on-one interviews • Responses to a modified language experience questionnaire	• Qualitative analysis of verbal report protocols and post-hoc interview data

3.4 Stage three

In stage three of the study, findings from all strands were converged. This allowed for implications to be drawn for the development of listening tests featuring speakers with L2 accent varieties.

Chapter 4: Construction of test materials

4.1 The UTESL listening sub-test

4.1.1 Background

The primary instrument in this investigation is the listening sub-test of the University Test of English as a Second Language (UTESL). UTESL is a three-skills (reading, writing, listening) EAP test developed at the University of Melbourne's Language Testing Research Centre. In the past, UTESL has been used for a range of closely related purposes in medium-stakes contexts. It has been used as a measure of EAP proficiency by various faculties in Australian universities, and is taken by international students from non-English speaking backgrounds as part of a broader selection process for course entry. It has also been used by a number of tertiary institutions to assess the English proficiency of non-English speaking background students applying for admission to advanced English for Academic Purpose courses. For this purpose, it provides a means whereby tertiary institutions can make decisions about the amount and type of English language support an applicant is likely to need. Essentially, the UTESL represents a standard, reliable EAP proficiency instrument with which to gather evidence concerning the questionable assumptions set out in the previous chapter.

4.1.2 Listening subtest: format and specifications

The listening sub-test of UTESL – the focus of this research – consists of one lecture on a general academic topic. The lecture is divided into four parts, and candidates are required to listen and answer a series of items across a range of task-types. Candidates are provided with a pre-listening introductory reading passage to familiarise themselves with the topic of the lecture. They are also given time before and after each section of the test to preview questions, and to complete their answers. Candidates are encouraged to complete tasks as they listen to the lecture. The sub-test is approximately 30 minutes in length, and usually contains between 30 and 40 items.

The specifications for the UTESL listening sub-test identify four key components of listening ability that are tapped by items:

- Locate and recall specific or key information
- Reorganise information from the lecture to complete a graph, chart or diagram
- Summarise main points
- Distinguish between main points and supporting detail

On a more micro scale, UTESL measures a listener's ability to:

- Understand phonological features
- Understand grammatical concepts
- Understand discourse markers
- Understand syntactic structure
- Understand grammatical cohesion
- Understand lexis

There is a wide range of task types used in each version of UTESL. These are:

- Short-answer questions
- Sentence completion
- Listing
- Gap-fill
- Summary writing
- Multiple choice questions
- True/False questions
- Completing lecture notes
- Labeling a diagram
- Chart/flowchart completion
- Matching

Lectures on UTESL are general, academic topics that have been written in-house, and recorded professionally. In the past, speakers on UTESL listening sub-tests have invariably been native speakers, emblematic perhaps of the orthodox approach discussed in Chapter 1.

UTESL was chosen as the primary instrument of analysis in this investigation for a number of reasons. Firstly, as it has fulfilled a number of roles, UTESL can be conceptualised as an archetypal EAP listening test. Secondly, it is a low/medium-stakes assessment, and so access to materials, permission to modify materials, and permission to administer materials in experimental trials was easier to obtain. Thirdly, research findings generated in this investigation have the potential to be taken-up and used in the development of future UTESL materials given the researcher's professional association with the Language Testing Research Centre.

4.1.3 Description of selected materials

Access was granted to any of the UTESL tests that had been in operational use over the past ten years. Three tests were selected; each to be recorded by one of the selected speakers. These tests will be referred to as the Oldest Old (OO),

Sleep (SL), and Food Technology (FT) throughout the book. The Oldest Old features a lecture on the specific health issues of the very old (those over 95); Sleep features a lecture on reasons for sleep, the organisation of sleep, and some common sleep disorders; Food technology features a lecture on profitability in the food processing industry. The reasons for selecting these topics were that they were sufficiently different from each other in topic, and also that they had proved useful and reliable tests in past administrations.[12]

Although each test was designed to the same specifications described in the section above, they differed in several ways. A more detailed description of each test is presented below:

Table 4-1: Details of three UTESL listening sub-tests

	Oldest Old	Sleep	Food Technology
Number of words (script):	1676	2118	1417
Number of questions/tasks:	22	28	17
Number of items:	31	40	37
Mean items/task:	1.4	1.4	2.2
Mean items/section:	7.75	10	9.25

Each test also differed with regard to the representation of particular task types. Table 4-2 shows the spread of task types across each of the selected tests – it is noteworthy that short-answer questions are predominant in the Oldest Old, sentence completion in sleep, and listing in the Food Technology test.

Table 4-2: Task types by sub-test

Item type	The Oldest Old	Sleep	Food Technology
Gap-fill	4	2	0
Dictation	0	1	0
Information transfer	2	5	2
Listing	1	5	7
Matching	0	1	0
Multiple choice	0	1	1
Short answer question	9	3	4
True/false	0	0	0
Sentence completion	6	10	3

---

12 These UTESL materials are still confidential, and as such they could not be displayed as appendices to this book. Specific items will be shown or described as required.

4.2 Speaker selection

4.2.1 Aims

The selection of speakers for the recording of test materials in diverse accents required a rigorous approach to ensure both adequate performance quality, and a high level intelligibility comparable between speakers. The general aim of the procedures described below was to provide a range of information upon which the selection of speakers could be based.[13] The specific aims of the process were to select speakers according to the following criteria:

1. That speakers have high intelligibility
2. That speakers are not perceived to be unreasonably difficult to understand
3. That speakers have accents which are identifiably L2 varieties

4.2.2 Methods

Speakers

Nine speakers of three accents – Japanese-English, Mandarin Chinese-English and Australian-English – were selected to record excerpts of oral stimuli drawn from UTESL listening sub-test scripts (see next section for discussion of stimuli selection). The rationale for choosing speakers of these particular accents was partly to represent two significant accent groups found in Melbourne, and partly for the practical reasons of access to speakers, and eventually, to shared-accent listeners.

The University of Melbourne was canvassed to identify speakers who would be appropriate for the study. A pre-requisite for the Japanese and Chinese speakers was that they had lived in their native country until at least eighteen years of age, so that their English speech was more likely to retain features of a Japanese or Mandarin Chinese accent (see Piske, MacKay & Flege, 2001). A second pre-requisite was that speakers be studying for, or have attained, a post-graduate qualification. This was to ensure an accurate reflection of the educational level of instructional speakers in an academic setting. While gender of

---

[13] It is stressed that the process of speaker selection outlined here does not claim that intelligibility or comprehensibility scores represent speakers' general ability to make themselves understood in real-world communication. Rather, the process described is more accurately a measure of performance quality in the reading of a prepared lecture. Thus, because of the specific nature of monologic recorded speech, many of the valid criticisms that have been levelled at experimental intelligibility studies – chiefly, that they ignore the role of the interlocutor and context in measuring intelligibility – do not relate to this process of speaker selection (for an overview of critiques, see Rajadurai, 2007).

speaker has been shown to influence intelligibility (Bradlow, Toretta & Pisoni, 1996), it was considered somewhat impractical to select only-male or only-female speakers because in "real" listening test situations, speakers of both genders are regularly represented. Nevertheless, gender within each accent variety was kept constant. The details of each of the nine speakers are provided in Table 4-3.

Table 4-3: Initial pool of speakers

Name	Gender	Age	Nationality	L1(s)	LoR
Mark	Male	30	Australian	English	30 years
Chris	Male	37	Australian	English	34 years*
Henry	Male	32	Australian	English	29 years*
Yuko	Female	> 21	Japanese	Japanese	7 months
Aiko	Female	> 25	Japanese	Japanese	3 years
Kaori	Female	> 30	Japanese	Japanese	10 years
Jun	Female	> 25	Chinese	Mandarin Chinese	1.5 years
Zhi	Female	> 21	Taiwanese	Mandarin Chinese & Taiwanese	2 months
Hui	Female	> 21	Chinese	Mandarin Chinese	3.5 years

[LoR = length of residence in Australia; * = overseas for three years]

Intelligibility, comprehensibility and accent (ICA) rating task

Following Munro and Derwing (1995a; also Derwing & Munro, 1997; Munro et al., 2006), a set of tasks were designed to measure intelligibility while also eliciting ratings of comprehensibility and accentedness. This set (ICA rating task) consisted of a collection of recorded stimuli, and a booklet of response tasks.

Stimuli selection and recording

A set of stimuli in the form of 27 independent clauses (three per speaker) were excerpted from four UTESL scripts by the researcher. This method of stimuli selection contrasts with other psycholinguistic studies which have used stimuli previously designed for the evaluation of intelligibility in speech pathology situations such as the Revised Bamford-Kowal-Bench Standard Sentence Test (used in Bradlow & Bent, 2002), and the Revised Speech Perception in Noise Test (or SPIN-R, used in Clarke & Garrett, 2004). The primary benefit of using such tests is that they have already been trialled to control for lexical difficulty which could confound with a measure of intelligibility (see also Francis &

Nusbaum, 1999). However, the major drawback of using such tests in this study is that the stimulus sentences are very basic (e.g. "The ball is bouncing very high"; "Father forgot the bread")[14], and not representative of the task that speakers are being selected to eventually perform. As such, any inference of intelligibility drawn from performance on these stimuli would not be generalisable to a speaker's subsequent performance reading UTESL scripts. The method of excerpting stimuli from pre-existing scripts compares with that employed by Gass and Varonis (1984), who had speakers read sentences "of similar length". It also provides more control over stimuli than the method used by Munro et al. (2006), where extemporaneous speech was excerpted with, "no particular criteria for selection, except that each sample had to constitute a syntactically complete phrase in order not to confuse the listeners" (p.116).

Care was taken to ensure that these stimuli were approximately equivalent in lexical difficulty. A sample of 31 independent clauses from four UTESL scripts was selected by the researcher. This selection was based on two initial criteria: that the selections be no more than twelve words in length and that the level of vocabulary be, impressionistically, of a level within the range of an upper-intermediate level ESL student. The initial set was then trialled with an Australian English speaker reading each prompt, and four participants (two native listeners and two non-native listeners) asked to transcribe each utterance. Based on common errors between these listeners, four sentences were discarded, leaving a set of 27 oral prompts. These 27 oral prompts were divided into three groups based on number of syllables: a "short" group (8-11 syllables); a "medium" group (12-13 syllables); and a "long" group (14-17 syllables). Each speaker was then randomly assigned one sentence from each of these groups. Finally, the order of speakers was randomised to create the final recording; Table 4-4 shows the speakers and prompts in order.

Speakers were recorded on mini-disk using a desktop microphone. The recordings were made in a quiet room set aside for research purposes. Speakers were asked to record all stimuli (not only their assigned three), so that it would be possible to make changes to assigned sentences if problems arose. Each speaker read through each sentence in the presence of the researcher, who noted any ellipses. If necessary, particular sentences were re-recorded to exactly match the written prompt. The mini-disk files were then uploaded to a computer, and edited using Sound Studio 2.0.7 to make the set of 27 prompts shown in Table 4-4. Instructions and pauses were also added specific to each response task (see Data collection procedure).

---

14 These examples are taken from Bamford and Wilson (1979)

Table 4-4: Order of stimuli

Order #	Speaker	Stimuli	Syllable group
1	Mark	by this I mean people who are aged over ninety five	Long
2	Zhi	let's look at the bar graph to illustrate the point	Medium
3	Hui	there is enormous profit to be made from them	Medium
4	Chris	people want more information and choice in the food they eat	Long
5	Yuko	the theory compares the body to a machine	Medium
6	Jun	each cycle will last between ninety and one hundred minutes	Long
7	Kaori	look at what has happened to the hamburger	Short
8	Aiko	this would obviously damage the environment	Short
9	Chris	people have the right to know what they are eating	Medium
10	Mark	different governments are responding in different ways	Medium
11	Hui	this number is expected to double over the next 50 years	Long
12	Jun	they can be classified in two groups	Short
13	Henry	they're still able to live in their own home	Short
14	Jun	the results can be very serious indeed	Medium
15	Kaori	during sleep new information may be stored in the brain	Long
16	Zhi	the arguments usually focus on three main issues	Long
17	Henry	they cost very little to buy in the first place	Medium
18	Kaori	this sounds like a very positive development	Medium
19	Zhi	let's look in detail at these stages	Short
20	Hui	soft drinks are a good example	Short
21	Yuko	it is both dynamic and also highly organized	Long
22	Aiko	and these figures are expected to keep on rising	Medium
23	Yuko	early human beings found night-time difficult	Short
24	Henry	another variety of rice has been created	Long
25	Chris	they're also a risk to our health	Short
26	Mark	this involves changing people's eating habits	Short
27	Aiko	this is a common problem in developing countries	Long

Response tasks

The response tasks included (1) a brief questionnaire on raters' biographical details, daily language contact and accent experience, (2) an orthographic transcription task, (3) a comprehensibility rating task, (4) an accent rating task, and (5) a forced choice accent identification task (see Appendix A).

Orthographic transcription tasks involve word-for-word dictation of oral stimuli. The use of these tasks to measure intelligibility is supported by Munro and Derwing (1995a), who define intelligibility as "the extent to which an utterance is actually understood by a listener" (p.76), and advocate orthographic transcription as a means of measuring this construct. This follows other studies in which transcription tasks are commonly used as a measure of speaker intelligibility (e.g. Brodkey, 1972; Bent & Bradlow, 2003; Stibbard & Lee, 2006). Although the definition of intelligibility within this book is that proposed by Smith and Nelson (1985): "the recognition of a word/utterance" (see Chapter 2 for discussion), this second definition, which is premised on the notion that the recognition of a word/utterance is a necessary, though not a sufficient, condition for understanding, does not affect the justification for using an orthographic transcription task to measure intelligibility. In fact, the rationale for a transcription task is strengthened if Smith and Nelson's (1985) definition of intelligibility is accepted, because this type of task is scored on correct transcription alone, and is therefore a measure of form recognition in its purest sense.

Munro and Derwing (1995a) also provided a model for choosing nine-point comprehensibility and accentedness rating scales. Although scales of various degrees have been used to measure comprehensibility (e.g. seven-point scales in Matsuura et al., 1999), and accentedness (e.g. five-point scales in Anderson-Hsieh & Koelher, 1988; seven-point scales in Brennan & Brennan, 1981), the nine-point scale is recommended as a more sensitive measure which also avoids the ceiling effect of scales with fewer intervals (Southwood & Flege, 1999). The comprehensibility rating scale ranged from 1 = "easy to understand" to 9 = "extremely difficult to understand"; while the accent rating scaled ranged from 1 = "no accent" to 9 = "extremely strong accent". It was expected that, given the heterogeneous nature of the rating group, "no accent" would be interpreted differently among individuals, and the scale would be less stable.

Raters

20 raters from diverse linguistic backgrounds took part in the study. The rating group was heterogeneous, not only in their L1 backgrounds, but also in their overall experience with particular varieties, and in the frequency of their communication with speakers of other varieties on a day-to-day basis. The group consisted of 19 postgraduate students and one lecturer at an Australian university. 18 raters were taking a Master's level course on teaching pronuncia-

tion; 1 rater was undertaking a PhD in field linguistics, and 1 rater was a lecturer of phonetics. Therefore the rater group can be said to have had an unusual amount of experience with varieties of speech through their studies.

Despite this, however, the speaker selection trial attempted to address other criticisms that have been directed at intelligibility studies – chiefly that they are native-speaker-centric (Rajadurai, 2007). Thus, the pool of raters included diverse L1 background participants in an effort to address the problem that intelligibility is often only construed as what is easy for the native speaker to understand. In addition, the three speakers of Australian English were rated in exactly the same way as the speakers of Japanese and Mandarin Chinese – it was not assumed that these native speakers would be more intelligible, or that they would have "no accent". The demographics of raters is given in Table 4-5.

Table 4-5: Rater characteristics

Rater	L1	CoB	Gender	AE experience	JE experience	CE experience
1	Vietnamese	Vietnam	Female	extensive	some	some
2	Hokkien	Singapore	Male	extensive	some	extensive
3	English	USA	Male	extensive	extensive	some
4	Russian	Soviet Union	Male	extensive	some	some
5	English	Australia	Female	extensive	little/no	extensive
6	Japanese	Japan	Female	extensive	some	some
7	Vietnamese	Vietnam	Male	some	-	-
8	Thai	Thailand	Female	extensive	some	some
9	Japanese	Japan	Female	some	extensive	extensive
10	English	Australia	Female	extensive	some	some
11	English	Singapore	Female	extensive	extensive	some
12	English	Australia	Male	extensive	extensive	extensive
13	Chinese	China	Female	some	some	some
14	English	Australia	Female	extensive	some	some
15	English	England	Male	extensive	extensive	extensive
16	Arabic	Saudi Arabia	Male	little/no	little/no	little/no
17	Arabic	Saudi Arabia	Male	extensive	some	some
18	English	Australia	Female	extensive	extensive	extensive
19	English	England	Male	extensive	some	some
20	English	Australia	Female	extensive	some	little/no

Data collection procedure

Two listening sessions were held: the first with nineteen of the raters, and the second with an individual rater. The process was the same in both sessions. Raters were first briefed on the range of tasks, with particular emphasis on what was expected in the transcription task, and asked to fill in the questionnaire. They were then given three practice sentences to complete a transcription and use the rating scale. Following a brief discussion, raters were told that the main task would begin.

The stimuli were presented in two "passes". On the first pass, raters heard each sentence, and completed the transcription task and the comprehensibility rating. Raters were given 35 seconds to complete these two tasks for each sentence. A double-beep on the audio track after 25 seconds signalled that 10 seconds remained, and that listeners should give a comprehensibility rating if they had not already done so. The first pass took approximately 21 minutes to complete. On the second pass, raters were presented with the same set of sentences, but this time asked to perform the accent rating and accent identification. Because the time required to perform these tasks was shorter than for a transcription task, pauses were shortened to 20 seconds after each sentence. The second pass took approximately 14 minutes to complete.

Scoring of transcriptions

Transcriptions were scored using a total word phonemic match (TPM) scoring paradigm (see Hustad, 2006). Under this procedure, a transcribed word is counted as correct if it is an exact phonemic match of the target word; thus, homonyms are counted as correct, and misspellings are accepted if they approximate the phonemes of the spoken word. Examples from the data are provided below to illustrate these points:

Table 4-6: Transcription task scoring examples

Target word(s)	Transcribed word(s)	Scored as correct?
into	in two	Yes
they're	there	Yes
eating	eatting	Yes
beings	being	No
economical	ecomimical	No
detail	details	No

Missing words were scored as incorrect, while additional words were ignored. The number of words identified correctly was divided by the total number of words in the sentence and converted to a percentage to provide a transcription score for each sentence. The limitation of this scoring procedure, which is also used by Munro and Derwing (1995a), is that errors have greater weight the fewer words there are in a given utterance. For example, a single error in a seven word utterance would result in an intelligibility score of 86%, whereas a single error in an eight word utterance would result in an intelligibility score of 89%. On the other hand, longer utterances provide scope for a greater number of errors than short utterances. Given that the length of each sentence differed a maximum of three words under each length condition (short: 6-7; medium: 7-10; long: 8-11), and that the sentences were randomly assigned within each length condition, the method employed by Munro and Derwing (1995a) was seen as relatively unproblematic for the purposes of this study.

4.2.3 Results

The data yielded by the ICA task were analysed using SPSS 14.0. This data included (1) the orthographic transcription scores as a measure of intelligibility; (2) the comprehensibility ratings as a measure of "ease of understanding"; (3) the accent ratings as a measure of perceived accentedness; and (4) forced-choice responses to an accent identification task. Because the comprehensibility and accent ratings were given on a nine-point scale, and the intelligibility scores were expressed as percentages, the intelligibility scores were converted so that comparisons could be more easily made between the three measures. Firstly, because the nine-point scales yielded higher scores for less comprehensible or accented utterances, it was necessary to convert the intelligibility score to values which matched more difficult utterances with higher scores. This conversion was achieved through the calculation of an error score [100 − intelligibility score]. The error score was then multiplied by 0.09 to enable it to be mapped on to a nine-point scale. For example, an intelligibility score of 64% yielded an error score of 36, which was then mapped onto the 9 point scale as 3.24. This conversion is henceforth referred to as the "transcription error score" (TES). There was a perfect correlation of -1.0 for TES and raw intelligibility scores.

Reliability of ratings

Interrater reliability coefficients were calculated for the comprehensibility and accent ratings. These reliability statistics were intraclass correlations, derived from a two-way random model, and were a measure of consistency of agreement, rather than absolute agreement. The two-way random model was chosen as both the speakers and the raters can be treated as random samples from a larger population. Furthermore, as there was no rater training, the raters may have differed in the anchor points of their ratings; a situation that, according to McGraw and Wong (1996), necessitates a two-way model. There was a high inter-rater reliability both for comprehensibility ratings ($\alpha = 0.95$) and for accent ratings ($\alpha = 0.94$).

These high reliabilities are noteworthy for two reasons. Firstly, they indicate that the task itself was robust, and that the means derived from all ratings would be meaningful in the selection of speakers according to the criteria. Secondly, they indicate that the listening experiences of a group of diverse L1 background raters were, to some extent, similar. This second finding adds support to one of the key findings of Munro et al. (2006) who found "a notable degree of shared experience when listeners from diverse language backgrounds hear L2 speakers' utterances" (p.127).

Intelligibility, comprehensibility and accentedness scores

A mean TES was calculated for each speaker, and these are presented in Table 4-7. These scores show that Kaori was the most intelligible speaker, followed by Henry and Jun. A T-test showed that, overall, speakers received a lower mean TES with native listeners [$M = 0.46$, $SD = 0.23$] than with non-native listeners [$M = 2.18$, $SD = 0.41$; $t(9.58) = -4.13$, $p = .002$]. This is not surprising given that the nature of the task meant that it measured, to some extent, listening proficiency. Yet although the mean scores of speakers differed significantly between these groups, the relative order of speaker scores was very similar across the groups, with the three most intelligible speakers remaining Kaori, Henry and Jun in each analysis, followed by Chris and Mark, and with Yuko given the highest average TES by both groups.

Table 4-7: Mean transcription error scores by speaker

Speaker name	Speaker L1	Mean	Standard deviation
Kaori	Japanese	0.60	0.45
Henry	Australian English	0.65	0.48
Jun	Mandarin Chinese	0.70	0.13
Chris	Australian English	0.89	0.66
Mark	Australian English	1.09	0.69
Hui	Mandarin Chinese	1.52	1.15
Zhi	Mandarin Chinese	1.77	0.82
Aiko	Japanese	1.97	0.96
Yuko	Japanese	2.71	0.91

The comprehensibility ratings showed a slightly different speaker order. While Kaori and Jun were rated as the most easily comprehensible within their respective L1 groups, the three Australian English speakers received the top three rankings. This is illustrated in Table 4-8.

Table 4-8: Mean comprehensibility ratings by speaker

Speaker name	Speaker L1	Mean	Standard deviation
Chris	Australian English	2.13	0.44
Henry	Australian English	2.25	0.49
Mark	Australian English	2.48	1.03
Jun	Mandarin Chinese	2.71	0.07
Kaori	Japanese	2.77	1.09
Hui	Mandarin Chinese	3.78	1.89
Zhi	Mandarin Chinese	4.88	1.25
Aiko	Japanese	4.88	1.01
Yuko	Japanese	5.67	0.60

The mean TES and comprehensibility ratings for each sentence correlated highly [$r = .91$, $n = 27$, $p < .001$], indicating that each comprehensibility rating was a reasonably good indicator of the actual intelligibility of an utterance. This may be, in part, because during the task, listeners rated an utterance immediately after completing a transcription. As such, the comprehensibility rating may be as much a measure of confidence in the accuracy of the transcription as an independent assessment of "ease of understanding". Nevertheless, the presence of Jun and Kaori at fourth and fifth position in comprehensibility rankings reflect previous findings (Munro & Derwing, 1995a; Derwing & Munro, 1997) that listeners rate the speech of non-native speakers as more difficult to understand than it actually is according to their own intelligibility scores. Derwing and Munro (1997, p.12) suggest that, "the discrepancy between perceived comprehensibility ratings and transcription success suggests that some accented but fully intelligible utterances may require additional effort or processing time ... which leads listeners to rate them as more difficult."

The accent ratings reflected the order generated by the comprehensibility ratings more closely than that of the intelligibility measure. Again, the Australian English speakers were rated as having the 'least accented' utterances, followed by Jun and Kaori. However while the TES and comprehensibility means show a wide gap between Jun and Kaori and the other Japanese and Mandarin speakers, the accent ratings close this gap to some extent (see Table 4-9).

Table 4-9: Mean accent ratings by speaker

Speaker name	Speaker L1	Mean	Standard deviation
Henry	Australian English	2.68	0.19
Chris	Australian English	3.00	0.39
Mark	Australian English	3.30	0.10
Kaori	Japanese	4.32	0.48
Jun	Mandarin Chinese	4.34	0.30
Hui	Mandarin Chinese	4.79	0.61
Yuko	Japanese	5.83	0.58
Zhi	Mandarin Chinese	6.10	0.49
Aiko	Japanese	6.12	0.41

The accent ratings for each speaker utterance correlated moderately with the comprehensibility ratings for the same utterances [$r = .82$, n = 27, $p < .001$], but more weakly with the transcription error scores [$r = .62$, n = 27, $p = .001$]. As such, the accent ratings provide further evidence that accent (as perceived accentedness) and intelligibility are indeed separate, though related, dimensions of speech (see Munro, 2008). Comprehensibility ratings, while closely correlated with intelligibility, also reflect the contours of the accent ratings. The relationship between these three measures is illustrated in Figure 4-1.

Figure 4-1: Means on each measure by speaker

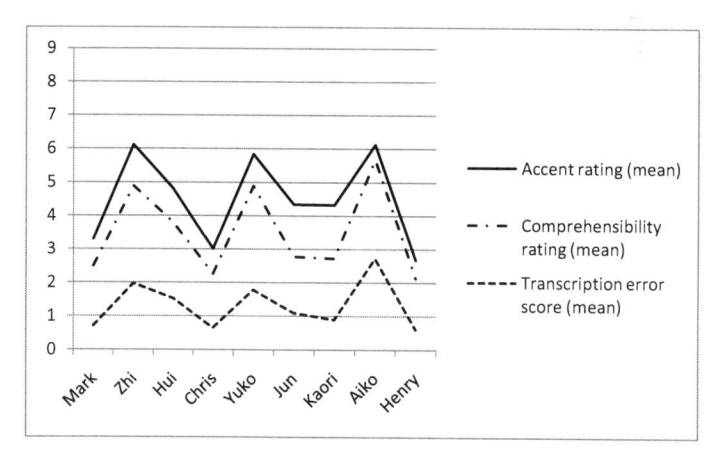

Having reached this point in the process, a decision was made to select Henry, Kaori and Jun as the three speakers based on the evidence elicited by the task. It was clear that Kaori, Jun and Henry were the representatives of their varieties most closely matched in intelligibility. While all three Australian English speakers were rated as highly comprehensible, the comprehensibility ratings for Jun and Kaori suggested that they were considered easiest to comprehend among their accent groups. These pieces of evidence addressed the requirement that the speakers be of a roughly equivalent intelligibility, and that they not be considered unduly difficult to understand.

4.2.4 Representativeness of selected speakers

From the accent rating figures, it is clear that the accents of Jun and Kaori were perceived to be stronger than those of the three Australian English speakers. This provides some evidence to suggest that Jun and Kaori were perceived to be speakers of other varieties, but does not indicate which accents they are perceived to be representative of. This issue was of particular importance given that both speakers, particularly Kaori, had resided in Australia for reasonably long periods of time. It was conceivable that Jun or Kaori had developed accents that were so near-native that to use their voices in the main study would have been counter-productive. In order to address this issue, the results of the accent identification task were analysed. While the responses to this task varied widely in accuracy across most speakers, the findings (see Table 4-10) illustrate that listeners rarely identified Jun's or Kaori's accents as one of the native-speaker varieties. On the other hand, Henry is systematically identified as an Australian English speaker.

Table 4-10: Accent identification for selected speakers

Speaker	AusE	BriE	AmE	ChE	KoE	IndE	JpE	DK
Jun (Mandarin Chinese)	3.33%	6.67%	1.67%	**36.67%**	11.67%	11.67%	16.67%	11.67%
Kaori (Japanese)	0%	5.0%	1.67%	36.67%	11.67%	1.67%	**26.67%**	16.67%
Henry (Australian English)	**71.66%**	18.33%	1.66%	1.66%	1.66%	0%	0%	5.0%

[AusE = Australian English; BriE = British English; AmE = American English; ChE = Chinese English; KoE = Korean English; IndE = Indian English; JpE = Japanese English; DK = don't know; (correct identifications bolded).]

These responses give support to the notion that, at the very least, Kaori and Jun were not perceived as having inner-circle English accents, and supports the claim that their accents were broadly identified as L2 varieties.

4.3 Construction of a diverse-accents UTESL (DA-UTESL)

The three selected speakers – Kaori, Jun and Henry – were invited to a soundproof recording studio to re-record the scripts of three existing UTESL tests on the topics of Sleep (Kaori), the Oldest Old (Jun), and Food Technology (Henry). All recordings required speakers to read from a script, and care was taken to ensure that all words present in the existing script were included in the new recordings. If lexical items or morphemes were clearly omitted, speakers would be asked to repeat a particular line or section. Speakers were also asked to repeat any sections where they stumbled over unfamiliar words or phrases and so lacked an authentic fluency. However, care was taken not to interfere with the characteristic features of speakers' pronunciation, nor to guide the speakers in rhythm or intonation.

A studio technician/professional audio producer was present during all recording sessions. Speech was captured using large diaphragm condenser microphones, and recorded with the Digidesign Pro Tools digital audio workstation. Raw recordings were burned to a CD as wav files, and these were then edited using Audacity – a digital sound editing software package – to insert pauses and instructions. The length of all pauses was identical to those in the original UTESL recordings of each individual test. Instructions were also copied verbatim, however all instructions were re-recorded in a common voice across each test to achieve consistency across the battery[15]. Two forms of the DA-UTESL Battery were created by re-arranging the order of tests; this allowed for the control of an order (and fatigue) effect during the data collection process. As one of the planned data collection trials would involve half of the total sample, it was decided to use two alternate forms, swapping the Japanese and Chinese accented speakers and keeping the Australian English speaker constant in the middle position. These two forms were edited in Audacity, exported to iTunes as wav files, and burned onto compact discs in an audio format. The two forms of the DA-UTESL are presented visually in Figure 4-2. These test materials – featuring Henry, Kaori and Jun – became the basis for the investigations which are presented in the next three chapters.

Figure 4-2: Two forms of the diverse-accents UTESL

	Test A	Test B	Test C
Form 1	Sleep (Kaori)	Food Technology (Henry)	Oldest Old (Jun)
Form 2	Oldest Old (Jun)	Food Technology (Henry)	Sleep (Kaori)

---

15 The instructions were delivered by the same Australian English-accented speaker who has recorded the instructions for past UTESL listening sub-tests.

Chapter 5: Differential Item Functioning

This chapter presents the findings of study one, in which three listening tests delivered in diverse accents of English (modified UTESL) were administered to a population of 212 ESL learners. The chapter is divided into nine sections. In section 5.1, a set of research questions, designed to address the first "questionable assumption", are presented. Section 5.2 provides a discussion of differential item functioning, first giving an overview of DIF, and then outlining the specific use of DIF detection in the current study, and providing a rationale for the procedures selected. Section 5.3 presents the methods used in collecting data, including a detailed description of the development of a "language experience questionnaire". Section 5.4 reports on preliminary analyses of test score and item data, results of the language experience questionnaire, and between groups comparisons at the score level. Section 5.5 then moves on to a description of procedures used in calculating DIF: matching groups at ability levels, and the calculation of DIF statistics. Sections 5.6 and 5.7 present the results of DIF analyses conducted on the Sleep test (Kaori – Japanese accent) and the Oldest Old test (Jun – Chinese accent) respectively. Section 5.8 then seeks to locate accent/intelligibility related causes of DIF in an effort to provide evidence that statistical DIF was related to the differential impact of speaker accent on focal and reference groups. Section 5.9 provides a summary of results, and a discussion of their relationship to previous research findings.

5.1 Research questions

Study one was designed to provide evidence either to support or to refute the following assumptions articulated in Chapter 3:

Assumption 1: Test-takers of otherwise equivalent ability will not perform differentially on an EAP listening test featuring a highly- intelligible speaker with an L2 accent, irrespective of whether or not they share the speaker's L1.

Assumption 2: Test-takers of otherwise equivalent ability will not perform differentially on an EAP listening test featuring a highly- intelligible speaker with an L2 accent, irrespective of whether or not they are highly familiar with the speaker's accent.

In light of the test materials that had been constructed (as discussed in the previous chapter), in order to guide the current study, these assumptions were broken down into a set of specific research questions:

Research Question 1:
a) Do Japanese L1 test-takers perform better than non-Japanese L1 test-takers on the UTESL featuring Kaori (Japanese accent)?
b) If so, is differential performance related to an intelligibility advantage?

Research Question 2:
a) Do test-takers who have high familiarity with a Japanese accent perform better than test-takers who have low familiarity with a Japanese accent on the UTESL featuring Kaori (Japanese accent)?
b) If so, is differential performance related to an intelligibility advantage?

Research Question 3:
a) Do Mandarin Chinese L1 test-takers perform better than non-Mandarin Chinese L1 test-takers on the UTESL featuring Jun (Mandarin Chinese accent)?
b) If so, is differential performance related to an intelligibility advantage?

Research Question 4:
a) Do test-takers who have high familiarity with a Chinese accent perform better than test-takers who have low familiarity with a Chinese accent on the UTESL featuring Jun (Mandarin Chinese accent)?
b) If so, is differential performance related to an intelligibility advantage?

5.2 Methodological considerations

Although a variety of statistical and qualitative methods are drawn on throughout this chapter to address the research questions, the detection of differential item functioning is of central importance. The point was made in the literature review that in the context of a test, the most detailed and rigorous way of establishing differential performance between groups is through the analytical methods of DIF. To date, however, there have been no studies which have applied the methods of DIF detection to the question of whether listeners will experience an advantage if they share a speaker's L1 or are highly familiar with it. This section will provide an overview of DIF, followed by a discussion of how DIF is utilized in the current study.

5.2.1 An overview of differential item functioning (DIF)

Differential item functioning is generally defined as existing when two groups of test-takers, who are otherwise matched in ability on a construct, have different probabilities of answering an item correctly (see Ferne & Rupp, 2007). A DIF finding, which in essence signifies the advantage of one group over another, may be attributed to the influence of construct-irrelevant variance on the studied item. Consequently DIF detection is often connected with the notion of "item bias". However, as McNamara and Roever (2006) point out, DIF is "a necessary but not sufficient condition for bias because a test item that functions differently for two groups might do so because it advantages one group in a construct-irrelevant way, but there might also be legitimate reasons for differential functioning" (p.83). In this sense, DIF detection is a first step, albeit an important one, in establishing an argument for bias.

The two important considerations involved in conducting DIF analyses are: identifying groups for comparison, and matching test-takers on ability levels. In the first, researchers conducting DIF analyses routinely separate test-takers into two groups based on *a priori* expectations of disadvantage. Thus test-takers may be grouped according to gender, race or in the case of language testing, L1 background. The groups are referred to as "reference" and "focal" groups. The focal group, usually the smaller, is often the group expected to be disadvantaged; however this is not always the case. In a broader sense, the focal group is the "group of interest", and the references group is the group with whom performance is being compared (Holland and Wainer, 1993, p.xv).

The matching of test-takers at ability levels is a crucial aspect of DIF detection because it is this step that allows for the detection of DIF rather than "impact". Impact can be understood as the difference between groups in average performance on a test or item. As Dorans and Holland state (1993, p.36) "impact is everywhere in test and item data because individuals differ with respect to the developed abilities measured by items and tests". For example, an analysis of scores on a language test scores may show that the average score for male learners was lower than for females. This may simply be because the language proficiency of that particular male cohort was lower than that of the female group. In other words, real differences between the groups existed. DIF procedures, on the other hand, calculate group differences in item performance after groups have been matched at ability levels on a measure of the construct under question. Most often, matching is performed using scores derived from performance on the test under investigation; this is known as "internal matching". However groups can also be matched using an "external criterion", a separate measure of the same ability/construct. By matching test-takers with regard to ability, DIF procedures ensure that test-takers at equal ability levels are compared. If groups which have been matched on ability differ in their chance of getting an item correct, this may signal that the item is testing something other than ability, i.e., a factor extraneous to the construct is affecting scores.

5.2.2 Selection of DIF procedures in the current study

Various procedures have been used to calculate DIF; Roever and McNamara (2006) classify them into four categories: analyses based on item difficulty, nonparametric approaches, item response theory (IRT) approaches, and "other" approaches (such as logistic regression). These approaches have emerged in a somewhat chronological order, with item difficulty approaches most often found in "early" DIF studies, and IRT and logistic regression the more current methods. Each "family" of approaches has different strengths and different assumptions. In selecting the appropriate DIF detection procedure for this study, it was firstly decided that multiple methods for DIF detection would be utilised. Ferne and Rupp (2007) comment that DIF studies within the field of language testing have only recently begun to utilize multiple DIF methods. Such variety of methods is warranted, they argue, given that studies have shown that certain methods may produce different results for the same items (see, for example, Kristjansson, Aylesworth & McDowell, 2005). It was also clear that 2- or 3-parameter IRT approaches would not be suitable, because they require that, ideally, sample sizes be over 1000 (see McNamara and Roever, 2006).

The two procedures considered appropriate methods for the current study were the standardization procedure (also known as conditional p value) and the Mantel-Haenszel procedure. Both are non-parametric procedures which match test-takers on ability level, and (importantly) allowed for matching to be performed using an external criterion (see Section 5.5.2). This selection reflects the approach taken by Roever (2007) in which both methods used together were found to be complementary, and useful for investigations with relatively small sample sizes[16]. A similar stance is taken by Hambleton (2006), who notes the advantages of these two procedures when dealing with limited numbers of test-takers: "with smaller samples, I prefer variations on the Mantel-Haenszel procedure and conditional P value comparisons" (p.186). A brief description of the strengths and limitations of each procedure is given below.

The standardization method

The standardization approach was proposed by Dorans (1989), and has been widely used in bias studies of SAT results in the United States. It is a nonparametric procedure that detects DIF by comparing differences in item estimates between groups at matched score levels (McNamara & Roever, 2006). It also uses a "weight" at each score level – most often based on the N-size of the focal group at each particular level – which determines how much influence the estimated difference at that score level will hold in the overall value for a given item. This value – the standardized p difference – is reported as a figure between

---

16   Roever's study involved 254 participants.

-1 and +1, from which magnitude of DIF may be inferred. The meanings associated with different values are presented in more detail in Section 5.5.

With the exception of Roever (2007), the standardization method has not been taken up as a common approach in DIF-related language testing studies, possibly because it does not have a significance test. However, the standardization approach is useful as part of a "suite" of DIF detection methods because it enables the researcher to map the performance of the reference and the focal group visually, and as such, provides a means by which non-uniform DIF may be identified. A disadvantage, and one with particular relevance to the current study, is that large samples are usually required to produce highly accurate results. This is principally because score levels should not be collapsed if possible. However, this may be balanced, to a certain extent, through careful "thick" matching procedures (see Donoghue & Allen, 1993).

The Mantel-Haenszel procedure

Within language testing, the most widely used approach in the literature has been the Mantel-Haenszel procedure, a nonparametric method which calculates the odds of a correct response for the reference and focal group through a contingency table stratified by score level. Mantel-Haenszel has been used to investigate differential performance between: males and females on the TOEFL (Ryan & Bachman, 1992); heritage speakers and non-heritage speakers on the reading and listening sections of the Australian Language Certificate (Elder, 1996); and Asian and European L1 background on a test of ESL pragmalinguistics (Roever, 2007) among others. It has been described as exhibiting "conceptual elegance" (McNamara & Roever, 2006, p.100), and is also less complicated and more practical to implement than the advanced IRT approaches. Although it is most useful in detecting DIF when sample sizes are substantial, Mantel-Haenszel requires much lower numbers than IRT approaches. Roever (2007) found that the Mantel-Haenszel procedure detected DIF somewhat more conservatively than the standardization procedure with a small sample (see also Muñiz et al., 2001). However Roever also noted that both procedures were in general agreement over items with "large DIF".

The chief drawback of the Mantel-Haenszel approach is that it is only able to detect uniform DIF. Uniform DIF occurs when either the reference group or the focal group are advantaged at all levels of the matching criterion. Conversely, non-uniform DIF (also known as "crossing DIF") would exist where one group is advantaged over a certain range of score levels, and then at a certain point along the score level continuum the other group becomes advantaged. This problem has seen increased use of the logistic regression procedure in the literature, which has been shown to be adept at identifying both uniform and non-uniform DIF (see Zumbo, 1999). However this is less problematic in the current study for two reasons. Firstly, there is no theoretical reason to believe that DIF related to a shared-L1 or familiarity advantage would be non-uniform. Secondly, non-uniform DIF may be identified in visual plots of item difficulty which are one of the benefits associated with the standardization method.

5.2.3 DIF as part of a broad methodology

DIF detection procedures are often employed as ends in themselves – i.e. for identifying, in a test development context, problematic items which may later be revised or discarded. In such contexts (e.g., high-stakes test development), decreased statistical power related to small samples is of serious concern because DIF items might not be correctly identified, or "good" items may be discarded. Alternatively, though, DIF approaches can be used within a broader methodology which is more interested in seeking an understanding of the underlying processes that lead to differential group performance. This approach has been identified as a feature of "third generation" DIF studies by Zumbo (2007), who writes:

> In this use DIF becomes a method to help understand the cognitive and/or psychological processes of item responding and test performance and investigating whether these processes are the same for different groups of individuals.
> (p.230)

In a study of this kind, the flagging of all potential DIF in a given test as part of a review process is not the chief goal. Rather, such a study would aim to use DIF approaches as a method to flag items which may, upon closer analysis, exhibit the particular group differences which have been hypothesised. DIF thus serves as one step in establishing that differences in group performance exist. The more revealing, explanatory analysis is conducted *post hoc* through a detailed study of that particular item.

The current study employs DIF detection in this way; as an important step in a broader methodology designed to locate evidence of a shared-L1 or familiarity advantage. In one sense, the use of DIF detection procedures is somewhat aligned with a "confirmatory" approach in which DIF detection procedures provide a method for testing a set of *a priori* hypotheses (see Abbott, 2007). However this study is interested not only in the statistical evidence of group differences in performance on items, but also in substantive evidence of a connection between those statistical observations and the phenomenon of an interaction between speaker accent and listener background. The study seeks both to collect and assess evidence of shared-L1 or familiarity effects, and to build theory based on this analysis.

5.3 Methods

5.3.1 Participants

213 participants from a range of Australian universities, English language centres and university pathway programs took part in the study. All participants spoke English as a second language, and represented a range of first-language (L1) backgrounds. Given the nature of the investigation, 70 test-takers from a Mandarin Chinese L1 background, and 60 from a Japanese L1 background were specifically recruited. The remaining 83 participants were drawn from a range of L1 groups. Korean was the most prominent among these other L1 background groups, however Spanish, Indonesian and Arabic were also well represented. All participants were international students, or foreign nationals working in Australia, and represented a wide range of nationalities. The demographics of the sample by L1 group, and by nationality, are shown in Tables 5-1 and 5-2 respectively.

Table 5-1: Participants by first language (L1)

L1	N	%
Chinese	70	32.9
Japanese	60	28.2
Korean	35	16.4
Spanish	13	6.1
Indonesian	10	4.7
Arabic	9	4.2
Vietnamese	4	1.9
Thai	4	1.9
French	3	1.4
Turkish	2	.9
Portuguese	1	.5
Hindi	1	.5
West Ambae language	1	.5
Total	213	100.0

Table 5-2: Participants by nationality

Nationality	N	%
Japanese	60	28.2
Chinese	48	22.5
South Korean	33	15.5
Taiwanese	20	9.4
Indonesian	11	5.2
Colombian	10	4.7
Vietnamese	4	1.9
Thai	4	1.9
United Arab Emirates	4	1.9
Saudi	4	1.9
French	3	1.4
Malaysian	3	1.4
Turkish	2	.9
Mexican	2	.9
Peruvian	1	.5
Portuguese	1	.5
Kuwaiti	1	.5
Indian	1	.5
Vanuatuan	1	.5
Total	213	100.0

At the time of data collection, all participants were residing and studying in Australia, and thus could be expected to have had some exposure to Australian English. The average length of residence (LoR) in Australia was 8 months, however reported LoR was not normally distributed; the median length of residence was five months, and the most common figures were two months (reported by 29 participants), seven months (reported by 23 participants) and three weeks (reported by 20 participants). Length of residence also varied across L1 groups. A comparison between the two largest L1 groups – Mandarin Chinese and Japanese – and an amalgamated "Other" L1 group showed that the Japanese L1 group had a much higher average LoR compared with the other two groups, who were fairly similar with each other (Table 5-3).

Table 5-3: Length of residence by L1 group

L1 group	N	Mean LoR (months)	Standard deviation
Mandarin Chinese L1	69	6.36	9.05
Japanese L1	60	15.04	23.11
Other L1	82	4.34	3.69
Missing data	2		

It should be noted, however, that the mode frequency for the Japanese L1 group was seven months – a figure comparable with the other two groups – and that the high mean reflects the fact that five Japanese L1 participants had been living in Australia for between five and nine years.

The average participant age was 24.5, and a majority of participants were female (65.3%). Most had studied at university or college level previously, although around 25% had not had any previous experience in higher education. Of those who had undertaken higher education, a survey of previous majors revealed a range of disciplines. A further analysis of this survey (Table 5-4) revealed that very few participants had undertaken majors which were closely matched to the topic of the tests: food science (Food Technology), behavioural science (Sleep) or health science (Sleep and Oldest Old).

Table 5-4: Test topic-related majors by L1 group

L1 group	Food science-related	Behavioural science-related	Health science-related
Mandarin Chinese L1	2	0	3
Japanese L1	2	0	1
Other L1	0	0	3

5.3.2 Instruments

Two instruments were utilised in this study: the diverse accents UTESL battery, and a "Language Experience Questionnaire". The construction of the diverse accents UTESL battery has been described in detail in Chapter 5; the development of the Language Experience Questionnaire is outlined below.

The Language Experience Questionnaire

A questionnaire was required to collect biographical data from research participants on a range of variables including first language, age, length of residence in Australia, and length of residence in other countries. This questionnaire also needed to gauge the familiarity of individuals with the three target accents, Australian, Japanese and Mandarin Chinese. No such instrument was found to exist in the research literature, the closest being the Language Contact Profile

(Freed, Dewey, Segalowitz & Halter, 2004) which was deemed not suitable for the purposes of the study. A questionnaire was therefore designed for the particular purposes of the study.

Initial considerations

As discussed in Chapter 2, researchers have defined the concept of "familiarity" or "experience" with accent in various ways. Tauroza and Luk (1997), for example, judged from the sociolinguistic environment of their Hong-Kong based participants that RP was a "familiar" accent. Implicit in this judgment is the notion that a familiar accent is one heard regularly, perhaps over a long period of time. Gass and Varonis (1984), on the other hand, conditioned listeners with controlled exposure to a given accent over a short amount of time. The current study was more interested in the kind of regular exposure that participants may have had to particular accents that is alluded to by Tauroza and Luk (1997). However, given that the participants in the study were from a variety of L1 backgrounds, that they were studying in a multi-lingual, ESL environment, and that they may have travelled, studied or worked in countries other than Australia, establishing familiarity through assumptions about the exposure of particular L1 groups to certain accents would have lacked validity.

It was decided that participants would be asked to self-report their familiarity with different accents. While self-report data have several limitations including the potential for conscious or unconscious error, self-report methodology is still used extensively in the fields of psychology, health and criminology. It has also been used widely within language learning research, particularly in investigations of strategy use (e.g. Cohen, 1998). In certain situations self-reports are the best, or indeed the only, way of accessing data, such as when patients are asked their medical history in a health context (Baldwin, 2000). Being dynamic and highly individualized, familiarity with, or exposure to, accent is a construct which fits into this category. However, in order to firmly establish the validity of the self-report, a series of "checks" were considered necessary in the questionnaire to specifically triangulate the familiarity measure.

Questionnaire structure

The first version of the Language Experience Questionnaire, designed with the considerations outlined above in mind, consisted of seven sections: section one eliciting general biographical information; section two eliciting self-reported familiarity with the target accents (Australian English, Chinese, Japanese); section three targeting specific experience with the accents of teachers; section four, experience with the accents of other students; section five, experience with accents at home; section six, experience with accents at work; and sections seven, experience with accents in the community. The rationale behind eliciting information on experience with accents across a number of domains (sections three to seven) was to attempt to triangulate the self-reported familiarity response in section two. In these latter sections, participants are asked to categorise their experience with a range of accents other than the three targets in order to collect information about participants who may have had exposure to a wide range of accents.

Trialling and revisions

Once the LEQ had been designed, the draft was trialled with a non-native speaker of English, who is also a researcher in the Applied Linguistics field with experience of developing questionnaires. In consultation with this individual, changes were made to the phrasing of some questions and instructions for the sake of clarity, and the list of accents was modified to reflect more appropriately the kinds of accents students studying in Melbourne would be likely to have encountered. The questionnaire was then trialled again with two non-native speakers who were postgraduate students in the field of Applied Linguistics. These students first completed the questionnaire, and then gave extensive feedback on the comprehensibility of questions and, more importantly, the efficacy of questions in eliciting accurate reflections of their actual experience with accents. Following this trial, the questionnaire was amended to address the concerns of these informants. The final questionnaire is presented in Appendix B.

5.3.3 Data collection procedure

The DA-UTESL was administered in a series of trials purposefully arranged for data collection for this project (i.e., these trials were not ordinary operational administrations of the UTESL). Administering the test in regular, operational administrations would have proven extremely difficult given the length of the test, and the need to test sufficient numbers of participants with Japanese and Mandarin Chinese L1 backgrounds. These trials were conducted between April and December 2007 at various language centres and universities in Melbourne. Each trial was conducted in the same format:

Step 1

Consent was first gained from all participants in accordance with the University of Melbourne Human Research Ethics guidelines, which stipulates that participants receive a plain language statement and sign a consent form before they can take part in a project.

Step 2

Participants received a booklet containing all tasks, tests and questionnaires arranged in the following order:

- Speaker Evaluation Task (see Chapter 6)
- Test A
- Test B
- Test C
- Language experience questionnaire

Participants were given a verbal outline of the order of proceedings for the session.

Step 3

After completing the Speaker Evaluation Task (described in Chapter 6), participants completed tests A, B and C. The tests were presented on CD with all instructions and pauses pre-recorded. A substantial rest break was taken between Test A and Test B in each of the trials.

Step 4

Following the completion of all three tests, the participants filled out the Language Experience Questionnaire.

Step 5

At the end of the session participants were given the opportunity to ask any questions about the research and were given a short debrief on the aims of the research and the way in which their data was to be used. Participants were also invited to request their scores on each of the three tests, which would be emailed back to them once all papers had been marked. Finally, participants received $20 payment for their participation.

5.3.4 Scoring

Scoring of each test was conducted in accordance with the existing marking guides for the UTESL listening sub-tests. The marking guides for all three tests had been refined, and used without problem, in all previous administrations of the tests. However, as most of the UTESL items have open-ended responses, such as short-answer questions or sentence completion tasks, the marking guide allows for alternative answers that match the semantic content of a model answer, and are therefore, to some extent, subjective. While marking, careful notes were kept concerning the range of answers that were deemed appropriate and those that were counted as wrong. In addition, the general rule of UTESL marking was enforced which stipulates that alternate or incorrect spellings are acceptable provided that they clearly signify a desired response (i.e., that they provide a phonemic match of the target word[s]), or that they do not signify an actual other word.

To ensure the reliability of the scoring procedure, two methods were employed. Firstly, a markers meeting was held with the researcher and a second trained-ESL rater. Before this meeting, 10% of the papers were double-marked, and markers were encouraged to note down any points at which they found it difficult to make a decision regarding the correctness of an answer based on the marking guide. During the meeting, scores were compared, and items that had been scored differently among markers were discussed with a view to refining the parameters of acceptable alternate answers by consensus. Following this meeting, the remaining papers were marked by the researcher against the marking guide, and in accordance with the parameters set out in the markers meeting. This is standard procedure for the marking of UTESL listening tests. Secondly, once marking had been completed, responses to open-ended items were entered into a spreadsheet with each candidate as a row, each item as a column, and the candidate's score on each item as an adjacent column. It was then possible to scan each column to review all candidate responses to each item, and to check for consistency in the acceptance of variant spellings and alternative answers. Although this was an unusually laborious procedure, and is not used in regular marking of UTESL listening, it was important for this study to ensure a high level of internal consistency in scoring, particularly because, as we will see below, a correct answer on many UTESL items often hinges on the identification, and adequate transcription, of key words.

5.4 Preliminary analyses

5.4.1 Test and item analysis

One Spanish L1 participant was removed from the analysis because it was noted that she had not completed the first full test in the booklet, and had left the testing session early. Therefore, the number of participants included in the full analysis was 212.

Test analysis

The mean score for each of the tests was calculated and is presented in Table 5-5.

Table 5-5: Mean raw score by test version

Test	Total score	Mean	SD
Food technology (Henry – Australian English accent)	37	17.28	6.95
Sleep (Kaori – Japanese accent)	38	17.47	7.31
Oldest Old (Jun – Mandarin Chinese accent)	31	10.18	5.66

Each of the tests appeared to be separating candidates adequately, with observed scores covering a wide range of possible scores:

Table 5-6: Range of raw scores by test version

Test	Total score	Minimum	Maximum
Food technology (Henry – Australian English accent)	37	3	34
Sleep (Kaori – Japanese accent)	38	3	35
Oldest Old (Jun – Mandarin Chinese accent)	31	1	28

Statistics showed that all tests were slightly positively skewed (FT = .475, SL = .346, OO = .744), and that, in terms of kurtosis, FT (-.513) and SL (-.572) were a little flatter, and OO (.107) somewhat more peaked in the distribution of scores. However these values were still within levels that would indicate a reasonably normal distribution (Bachman, 2004). Further inspection of histograms for each test confirmed that the data would be suitable for running parametric procedures; these histograms are included in Appendix C.

A reliability coefficient was calculated for each test using Cronbach's alpha, as well as a standard error of measurement (SEM) based on this reliability estimate. Table 5-7 shows that all three tests had acceptably high reliability coefficients, and reasonably low estimates of SEM:

Table 5-7: Reliability and SEM by test version

Test	N of items	alpha	SEM
Food technology (Henry – Australian English accent)	37	.892	2.28
Sleep (Kaori – Japanese accent)	38	.880	2.53
Oldest Old (Jun – Mandarin Chinese accent)	31	.872	2.03

Finally, the correlations between the raw test scores were investigated using Pearson's product-moment coefficient. The results showed that correlations between each combination of test were significant and strong (see Table 5-8).

Table 5-8: Correlations between test versions

Correlations	N	R	p
FT total score and SL total score	212	.853	<.001
SL total score and OO total score	212	.828	<.001
OO total score and FT total score	212	.825	<.001

Item analysis

A preliminary item analysis was also carried out using a Classical Test Theory (CTT) approach. These results are presented for each of the three tests below:

Food Technology (Henry – Australian English accent)

A summary of item statistics for the Food Technology test (Table 5-9) showed that the mean p value was .467, and that items were wide ranging in their difficulty indices:

Table 5-9: Summary of item statistics for Food Technology

N of Items	Mean	Minimum	Maximum	Range	Max/Min	Variance
37	.467	.104	.972	.868	9.364	.080

An inspection of individual item means (Table 5-10) showed that a number of items (1, 3, 6, 7, 8, 9, 11, 12) were relatively easy for the group, with p values over .85. However there were no items answered by all, and no items answered by none. An inspection of the item-total correlation, as a measure of item discrimination, showed that seven of these "easy" items were below the optimal level of .3, with item 11 discriminating particularly poorly at .059. Nevertheless, most of the remaining items appeared to discriminate well.

Table 5-10: Item statistics for Food Technology

Item	Mean	SD	Item-total correlation
FT item 1	.972	.166	.185
FT item 2	.637	.482	.332
FT item 3	.859	.349	.277
FT item 4	.226	.420	.520
FT item 5	.283	.452	.470
FT item 6	.873	.334	.354
FT item 7	.948	.222	.135
FT item 8	.892	.312	.172
FT item 9	.868	.339	.192
FT item 10	.613	.488	.526
FT item 11	.943	.232	.059
FT item 12	.958	.202	.156
FT item 13	.443	.498	.495
FT item 14	.354	.479	.640
FT item 15	.293	.456	.582
FT item 16	.481	.501	.569
FT item 17	.170	.376	.532
FT item 18	.373	.485	.366
FT item 19	.104	.306	.398
FT item 20	.486	.501	.520
FT item 21	.241	.428	.512
FT item 22	.656	.476	.369
FT item 23	.778	.416	.408
FT item 24	.118	.323	.398
FT item 25	.382	.487	.217
FT item 26	.377	.486	.528
FT item 27	.311	.464	.484
FT item 28	.274	.447	.430
FT item 29	.264	.442	.147
FT item 30	.415	.494	.487
FT item 31	.312	.464	.547
FT item 32	.113	.318	.363
FT item 33	.297	.458	.340
FT item 34	.160	.369	.386
FT item 35	.396	.490	.529
FT item 36	.189	.392	.548
FT item 37	.226	.420	.374

Sleep (Kaori – Japanese accent)

The summary statistics for the Sleep items (Table 5-11) showed that the mean p value (.460) was close to that of the Food Technology test. There was also a similar range of item difficulty; however the minimum and maximum p values were both somewhat lower than those on Food Technology.

Table 5-11: Summary of item statistics for Sleep

N of Items	Mean	Minimum	Maximum	Range	Max/Min	Variance
38	.460	.052	.877	.825	16.909	.050

An inspection of individual item means[17] (see Table 5-12) showed only one item with a p value over .85, which is in contrast with the high number of easy items on the FT test. Two of the items (5 and 39) were, in fact, very difficult for the sample population with means of less than .1. The item-total correlation coefficients showed a cluster of items (31, 32 and 33) which were discriminating relatively poorly below .2. On the test, these three items form a matching task, and the low discrimination may indicate a high level of guessing. Overall, though, the items appeared to discriminate well.

The Oldest Old (Jun – Mandarin Chinese accent)

The Oldest Old item summary statistics (Table 5-13) indicated that this test was more difficult than both Food Technology and Sleep. The mean item difficulty was low at .329, and the minimum and maximum p values were both less than those on the other two tests:

Table 5-12: Summary item statistics for The Oldest Old

N of Items	Mean	Minimum	Maximum	Range	Max/Min	Variance
31	.329	.024	.778	.755	33.000	.062

The individual item statistics (see Table 5-14) showed that eleven items had p values of less than .2, with seven of these (11, 13, 15, 21, 27, 29, 31) at less than .1. These figures indicate that around one-third of items were very difficult for the sample population. Nevertheless, these items appeared to discriminate well with only six items below .3 on the discrimination index.

---

17 Although there were 38 items on the Sleep test, the items are labelled between 1 and 40. Originally, the Sleep test consisted of 40 items; but over the course of several administrations items 17 and 34 were deleted. The original item labels have been retained because these match the score sheets which have been used in previous administrations.

Table 5-13: Item statistics for Sleep

Item	Mean	SD	Item-total correlation
SL item 1	.877	.329	.220
SL item 2	.269	.444	.318
SL item 3	.344	.476	.541
SL item 4	.193	.396	.584
SL item 5	.052	.222	.361
SL item 6	.519	.501	.427
SL item 7	.514	.501	.494
SL item 8	.170	.376	.520
SL item 9	.519	.501	.450
SL item 10	.359	.481	.369
SL item 11	.585	.494	.467
SL item 12	.406	.492	.523
SL item 13	.514	.501	.413
SL item 14	.142	.349	.338
SL item 15	.113	.318	.453
SL item 16	.538	.500	.297
SL item 18	.406	.492	.329
SL item 19	.340	.475	.490
SL item 20	.415	.494	.453
SL item 21	.500	.501	.280
SL item 22	.708	.456	.421
SL item 23	.807	.396	.274
SL item 24	.693	.462	.359
SL item 25	.830	.376	.284
SL item 26	.335	.473	.449
SL item 27	.236	.426	.375
SL item 28	.759	.428	.371
SL item 29	.354	.479	.333
SL item 30	.340	.475	.321
SL item 31	.642	.481	.170
SL item 32	.491	.501	.159
SL item 33	.745	.437	.146
SL item 35	.481	.501	.346
SL item 36	.420	.495	.504
SL item 37	.788	.410	.313
SL item 38	.717	.452	.394
SL item 39	.099	.299	.372
SL item 40	.255	.437	.576

Table 5-14: Item statistics for The Oldest Old

Item	Mean	SD	Item-total correlation
OO item 1	.660	.475	.258
OO item 2	.462	.500	.467
OO item 3	.241	.428	.539
OO item 4	.387	.488	.592
OO item 5	.505	.501	.457
OO item 6	.434	.497	.493
OO item 7	.689	.464	.476
OO item 8	.406	.492	.545
OO item 9	.778	.416	.251
OO item 10	.656	.476	.175
OO item 11	.057	.232	.474
OO item 12	.142	.349	.072
OO item 13	.024	.152	.312
OO item 14	.175	.380	.324
OO item 15	.038	.191	.287
OO item 16	.245	.431	.581
OO item 17	.778	.416	.299
OO item 18	.689	.464	.386
OO item 19	.689	.464	.386
OO item 20	.208	.407	.519
OO item 21	.028	.166	.347
OO item 22	.113	.318	.428
OO item 23	.434	.497	.351
OO item 24	.316	.466	.408
OO item 25	.288	.454	.367
OO item 26	.231	.423	.595
OO item 27	.028	.166	.383
OO item 28	.226	.420	.475
OO item 29	.057	.232	.365
OO item 30	.109	.312	.516
OO item 31	.094	.293	.470

5.4.2   Language Experience Questionnaire analysis

Aside from the elicitation of biographical data which is presented in 5.4.1, the chief purpose of the LEQ was to provide a measure of familiarity by which it would be possible to categorise participants as either familiar or unfamiliar with a given accent. To this end, the familiarity self-rating (in section 2 of the LEQ) was designed to provide suitable evidence of experience with the target accents: Australian English, Japanese and Chinese. However, because the self-report has known limitations as a method, before the data was utilised, a series of analyses were conducted with the ratings from section 2 to assess their validity as measures of familiarity with accent.

The self-report question asked participants to indicate their familiarity with Australian English, Japanese and Chinese accents of English on a scale of 1 (not familiar) to 5 (very familiar). Descriptive statistics (Table 5-15) showed that the full scale was utilised for each of the accents, and the group as a whole were more familiar with an Australian English accent than either a Japanese accent or a Chinese accent:

Table 5-15: Mean familiarity self-ratings by accent

Accent	N	Minimum	Maximum	Mean	SD
Australian English	213	1.00	5.00	3.49	1.01
Japanese	211	1.00	5.00	2.98	1.42
Chinese	212	1.00	5.00	2.92	1.49

These descriptive statistics provide some evidence to support the validity of the self-ratings on the grounds that the participants would be expected to be most familiar with the Australian English accent, having all lived in Australia for some period of time.

To further investigate the validity of the ratings for familiarity with Australian English the relationship between the self-reports and "length of residence in Australia" was investigated using Spearman's *rho*. The results of this analysis showed a weak, positive correlation between the two variables [*rho* = .199, n = 211, p = .004]. However, given that "length of residence" was highly skewed (see 5.3.1), it is not surprising that the relationship between the variables did not emerge as strong. Also, it would be mistaken to assume that because a person has lived in Australia for a certain amount of time, this would necessarily equate to contact with native speakers in the host community.

The ratings for familiarity with Japanese accent and familiarity with Chinese accent were analysed under the hypothesis that participants who shared those L1 backgrounds would be most familiar with their own accent (see Flowerdew, 1994). For familiarity with the Japanese accent, the frequency table and accompanying chart below illustrate that this hypothesis appears to be supported, with greater numbers of Japanese L1 participants responding at the upper end of the scale:

Table 5-16: Self-ratings of familiarity with Japanese accent by Japanese L1 status

Familiarity with Japanese accent	Other L1	Japanese L1
1	39	1
2	48	3
3	31	4
4	26	17
5	7	35

Figure 5-1: Familiarity with Japanese accent by Japanese L1 status

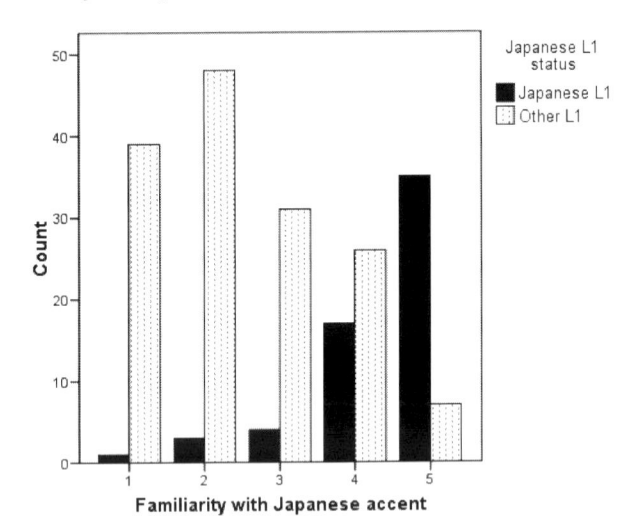

An independent t-test showed that there was a significant difference in self-rated familiarity scores between the Japanese L1 ($M = 4.37$, $SD = 0.94$) and other L1 groups [$M = 2.43$, $SD = 1.18$; $t(135.49) = 12.53$, $p < .001$].

Similarly, the great majority of responses by the Mandarin Chinese L1 group to "familiarity with Chinese accent" were at "familiar" or "very familiar", as illustrated in the table and chart below:

Table 5-17: Self-ratings of familiarity with Chinese accent by Mandarin Chinese L1 status

Familiarity with Chinese accent	Other L1	Mandarin Chinese L1
1	48	1
2	47	1
3	32	4
4	9	21
5	6	43

Figure 5-2: Familiarity with Chinese accent by Mandarin Chinese L1 status

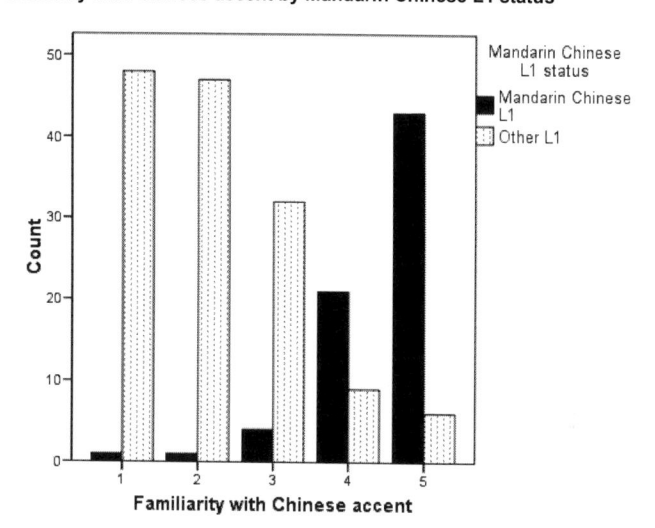

An independent samples t-test was conducted to compare the familiarity ratings of these two groups. This analysis showed a significant difference in the ratings of the Mandarin Chinese L1 group (M = 4.49, SD = 0.79) and the ratings of the other L1 group [M = 2.14, SD = 1.09; t (180.40) =17.80, p < .001]. Because the familiarity self-ratings were significantly different between these sets of groups that were expected to be different, these findings provide evidence to validate the self-reported ratings of familiarity with Japanese and Chinese accents.

Finally, the relationship between each set of familiarity ratings and responses to the remaining sections of the LEQ was explored. Sections three to seven of the LEQ asked participants to indicate whether their degree of regular experience with the target accents (among other accents) was "no contact", "some contact" or "regular contact". The domains of interest were contact "with teachers", "with other students", "at home", "at work" and "in the community". Although the participants were asked to respond for a number of accents, Australian, Japanese and Chinese were the primary foci of this study.

"Contact with teachers" was investigated separately first, because the response format of this section was "yes/no" rather than scaled like the other sections. In section (3a), 193 of the 213 original participants reported that their current teachers had Australian English accents. While this does not necessarily validate the results of the self-report measure, it does provide direct evidence that the majority of participants were, to some extent, familiar with Australian English. In section (3b), 31 participants reported that they had had contact with Japanese accented teachers in the past, and of these, 30 were from a Japanese L1 background. Similarly, 49 participants reported contact with a Chinese accented teacher, and 40 of these respondents were from a Mandarin Chinese L1 background. It was surprising that only around half of Japanese and Mandarin Chinese participants reported contact with a shared-L1 accented teacher, however this may be attributable to three reasons: (i) because students had primarily studied English with native-speaker teachers in their home country, (ii) because they believed their previous shared-L1 teachers spoke with native-speaker accents, or (iii) because the speaking in their English classes with shared-L1 teachers had been conducted in their L1. Nevertheless, given that almost all of the previous contact with Japanese and Chinese accented teachers was reported by Japanese and Mandarin Chinese L1 participants, this section of the questionnaire was considered redundant in light of the previous analysis of self-report ratings by the same L1 groups.

Next, correlation analyses were carried out between the self-rated familiarity scores and averaged "contact scores" derived from responses to the remaining sections of the questionnaire (4-7). To create a "contact score" for each accent in each domain, the responses were coded as "no contact" = 0, "some contact" = 1, and "regular contact" = 2. The scores across each of these domains for each accent were then averaged to arrive at an overall "contact score" for each of the three accents. The descriptive statistics for the whole group are presented in Table 5-18 below:

Table 5-18: Summary of contact scores by accent

Accent	N	Minimum	Maximum	Mean	SD
Australian English	211	0.00	2.00	0.97	0.53
Japanese	211	0.00	2.00	0.77	0.58
Chinese	211	0.00	2.00	1.05	0.63

The relationship between self-rated familiarity scores and contact scores was investigated using Spearman's *rho*. Firstly, for familiarity with an Australian accent, there was a weak, positive correlation between the two variables [rho = .182, p = .008], which suggests that the self-ratings were not accurate representations of reported contact with Australian English accented speakers in the real world. However, the correlations between these two variables were significant and stronger for familiarity with Japanese accent [$rho = .460$, $p < .001$] and familiarity with Chinese accent [$rho = .573$, $p < .001$]. These figures suggest a medium to large relationship (see Cohen, 1988) between the self-ratings of familiarity with Japanese and Chinese accents, and a separate measure of contact with speakers of those same accents in a range of real-world domains.

It was clear from the results of the procedures above that the familiarity self-ratings could be considered valid measures of familiarity with the Japanese and Chinese accents, but not for familiarity with Australian accent. The complication with rating familiarity with an Australian accent may have arisen from the fact that all participants were, to a certain extent, familiar with Australian English because they had all been living in Australia for different periods of time. It would have been easier to judge familiarity on the scale when considering accents such as Japanese and Chinese which would either have been familiar from a shared-L1 perspective, or through regular, sustained contact and communication with friends, housemates or other students.

For the purposes of this study it was not important to be able to establish degrees of familiarity with Australian English, but rather to find evidence (in addition to participants' current residence in Australia) that participants would be familiar with spoken Australian English. This evidence was seen in the high number of responses for contact with an Australian accented teacher, and supplemented by the reasonably high overall contact score for Australian English.

It was, however, important to be able to distinguish between degrees of familiarity with Japanese and Chinese accents, because the aim of the familiarity questionnaire was to be able to separate participants into two distinct groups based on their familiarity scores. A decision was made to use the self-ratings of familiarity, and to divide the cohort into "low familiarity" and "high familiarity" groups based on their scores. The "low familiarity" group would include participants who had responded 1, 2 or 3 on the scale, and the "high familiarity" group would include those who had responded 4 or 5 on the scale. This cut point was initially based on the observation that the majority of Japanese L1 and Mandarin Chinese L1 listeners had rated familiarity with their own accent at 4 or 5. The decision was further supported by examining the means of the two groups in each of the familiarity conditions which are presented in Tables 5-19 and 5-20. It can be seen that in each case, the mean for the low familiarity group is between 1 and 2, which is the lowest interval of the scale, and for the high familiarity group, the means are between 4 and 5 which is the highest interval of the scale.

Table 5-19: Descriptive statistics for familiarity with Japanese accent by familiarity group

Japanese accent (JA) familiarity group	N	Mean	SD
High familiarity	85	4.49	0.50
Low familiarity	126	1.96	0.77

Table 5-20: Descriptive statistics for familiarity with Chinese accent by familiarity group

Chinese accent (CA) familiarity group	N	Mean	SD
High familiarity	79	4.62	0.49
Low familiarity	133	1.90	0.80

Differences between these groups were confirmed through Mann-Whitney U tests. On the familiarity with Japanese accent measure, there was a significant difference in the average ranks of the high familiarity group (169.00) and the low familiarity group [63.50; $z = 12.78$, $p < .001$]. Similarly, on the familiarity with Chinese accent measure, there was a significant difference in the mean rank of the high familiarity group (173.00) and the low familiarity group [67.00; $z = 12.44$, $p < .001$].

Finally, it should be noted that there is a good deal of overlap between the shared-L1 group and the "high familiarity" group for both Japanese accent and Chinese accent, however this simply reflects that sharing a speaker's accent is a very good predictor of high familiarity with that accent in general.

5.4.3 Between-groups performance

In order to make some initial comparisons between groups in their overall performance with particular speakers, the total scores on each of the three DA-UTESL versions were converted to z-scores, a procedure by which test scores are transformed to a standardised measure with a mean of 0 and a standard deviation of 1. The standardization of test scores enabled an analysis of the relative performance of different listener groups on each test delivered by an accented speaker. These preliminary findings, presented below, are treated with caution because "speaker" is confounded with "test" in such a design: there was variability between each of the tests, most notably in their topic, but also in their range and representation of item types. However the results of these analyses do point towards some trends in listener group performance on tests with the different speakers, which are then examined on a more micro scale in the DIF analyses to follow.

Separate analyses were conducted to specifically compare the performances of shared-L1 listeners versus all other L1 listeners, and high familiarity versus low familiarity groups on the Japanese and Mandarin Chinese accent tests. In each case, performance with an accented speaker was compared with the "benchmark" performance on the Food Technology test with the Australian accented speaker.

Overall performance on Sleep – Kaori (Japanese-accented speaker)

In the first analysis, a mixed between-within subjects (2 x 2) ANOVA was run with "Japanese L1 status" as the between-groups factor and test/speaker as the within-groups factor. There were two levels to the "Japanese L1 status" factor: Japanese L1 and Other L1 (which included all non-Japanese L1 participants). There were also two levels in the test/speaker factor: FT – Henry and SL – Kaori. The means and standard deviation for each Japanese L1 status group with each test/speaker are presented below.

Table 5-21: Mean performance on Food Technology and Sleep by Japanese L1 status (z score conversion)

Test/Speaker	Japanese L1 status	N	Mean	SD
Food Technology (z score) Henry: Australian English accent	Japanese L1	60	0.10	0.96
	Other L1	152	-0.04	1.01
Sleep (z score) Kaori: Japanese accent	Japanese L1	60	0.12	1.01
	Other L1	152	-0.05	0.99

Figure 5-3: Performance on Food Technology and Sleep by Japanese L1 status

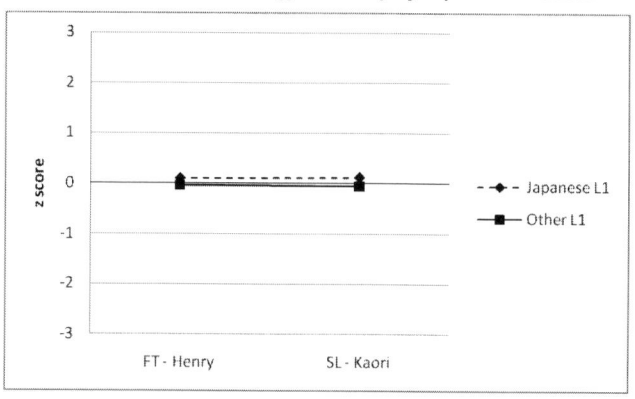

There was no statistically significant effect for test/speaker [Wilks' Lambda = 1.00, $F(1, 210) = 0.03$, $p = .87$] although this was expected because the z score conversion had already equalized the means of the tests. However there was also no significant interaction between Japanese L1 status group and test/speaker [Wilks' Lambda = 1.00, $F(1, 210) = 0.133$, $p = 0.72$]. This lack of interaction is shown clearly in Figure 5-3; although the Japanese L1 group was of a slightly higher listening ability than the Other L1 group, there was no clear test/speaker effect.

The same 2 x 2 analysis was conducted with "Familiarity" as the between-groups factor and test/speaker as the within-groups factor. The two levels of the "Familiarity" factor were "low familiarity" and "high familiarity". Again, there were two levels in the test/speaker factor: FT – Henry and SL – Kaori. The means and standard deviation for each familiarity group with each test/speaker are presented in Table 5-22.

Table 5-22: Mean performance on Food Technology and Sleep by JA familiarity group (z score conversion)

Test/Speaker	JA familiarity group	N	Mean	SD
Food Technology (z score) Henry: Australian English accent	High familiarity	85	0.02	1.02
	Low familiarity	125	-0.02	1.00
Sleep (z score) Kaori: Japanese accent	High familiarity	85	0.02	1.08
	Low familiarity	125	-0.01	0.95

There was no significant interaction between familiarity group and test/speaker [Wilks' Lambda = 1.00, $F(1, 210) = 0.133$, $p = 0.72$]. Figure 5-4 shows clearly that the relative performance of these familiarity groups was very even across both tests.

Taken together, these results would suggest that any initial trend for a shared-accent advantage or a familiarity advantage on the Sleep test is extremely minimal, and is not observable at the score level.

Figure 5-4: Performance on Food Technology and Sleep by JA familiarity group

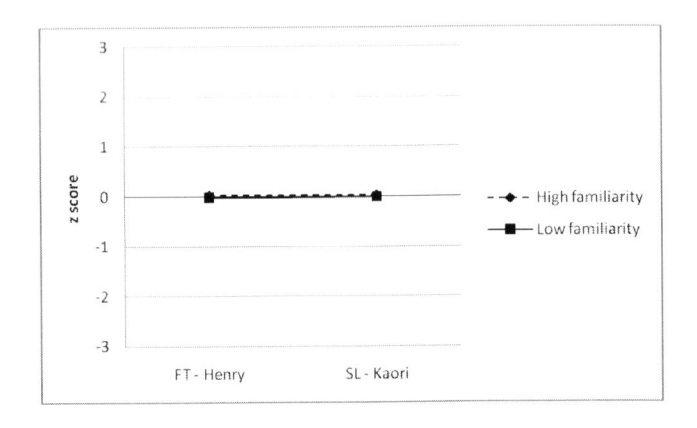

Overall performance on The Oldest Old – Jun (Mandarin Chinese accented speaker)

The same analytical procedures were conducted with a different set of factors to compare listener performance across the Food technology test and the Oldest Old test. A 2 x 2 ANOVA was run with "Chinese L1 status" as the between-groups factor and "test-speaker" as the within-groups factor. The two levels of the "Chinese L1 status" factor were Mandarin Chinese L1 and Other L1 (which included all non-Mandarin Chinese L1 participants). The two levels of the "test-speaker" factor were z scores for "FT – Henry" and "SL – Kaori". The descriptive statistics for this analysis are presented in Table 5-23 below.

Table 5-23: Mean performance on Food Technology and The Oldest Old by Mandarin Chinese L1 status (z score conversion)

Test - Speaker	Mandarin Chinese L1 status	N	Mean	SD
Food Technology (z score) Henry: Australian English accent	Mandarin Chinese L1	70	-0.02	1.17
	Other L1	142	-0.01	0.91
Oldest Old (z score) Jun: Mandarin Chinese accent	Mandarin Chinese L1	70	0.30	1.17
	Other L1	142	-0.15	0.88

It is clear from the means presented in Table 5-23 that the Mandarin Chinese L1 group scored relatively higher on the Oldest Old test compared with the Food Technology test, and the Other L1 group relatively lower. The ANOVA results confirmed that there was a significant interaction between Mandarin Chinese L1 status group and test-speaker [Wilks' Lambda .859, $F(1, 210) = 34.548$, $p < .001$] and the effect size was large [multivariate partial eta squared = .141]. This is most clearly illustrated in Figure 5-5.

Figure 5-5: Performance on Food Technology and the Oldest Old by Mandarin Chinese L1 status

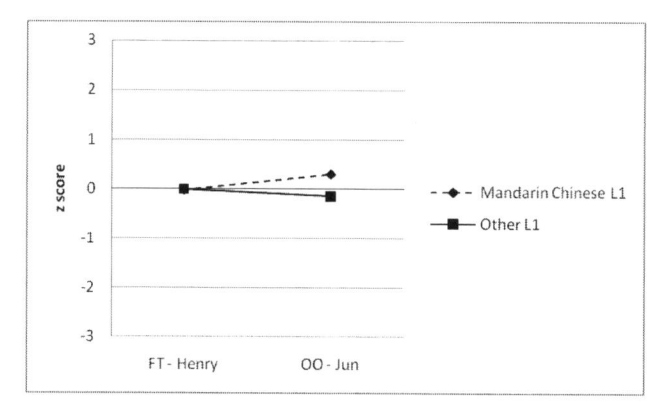

The final analysis compared the performances of Chinese accent familiarity groups across both tests in a 2 x 2 ANOVA. The two levels of the "Chinese accent familiarity" factor were "low familiarity" and "high familiarity" as determined by the language experience questionnaire, with FT – Henry and OO – Jun the two levels in the within-subjects factor. The means and standard deviation for each familiarity group with each test/speaker are presented below.

Table 5-24: Mean performance on Food Technology and The Oldest Old by CA familiarity group

Test - Speaker	CA familiarity group	N	Mean	SD
Food Technology (z score) Henry: Australian English accent	High familiarity	79	0.00	1.08
	Low familiarity	132	0.00	0.96
Oldest Old (z score) Jun: Mandarin Chinese accent	High familiarity	79	0.22	1.11
	Low familiarity	132	-0.14	0.91

In a similar way to the shared-L1 listeners in the previous analysis, the "high familiarity" listeners showed a marked increase in average standardized score on the Oldest Old test, and the "low familiarity" listeners a proportional decrease. The results of the ANOVA showed that there was indeed a significant interaction between familiarity group and test-speaker [Wilks' Lambda = .915, $F(1, 209) = 19.305$, $p < .001$], however the effect size [multivariate partial eta squared = .085] was moderate. The interaction effect is clearly illustrated in Figure 5-6.

Figure 5-6: Performance on Food Technology and the Oldest Old by CA familiarity group

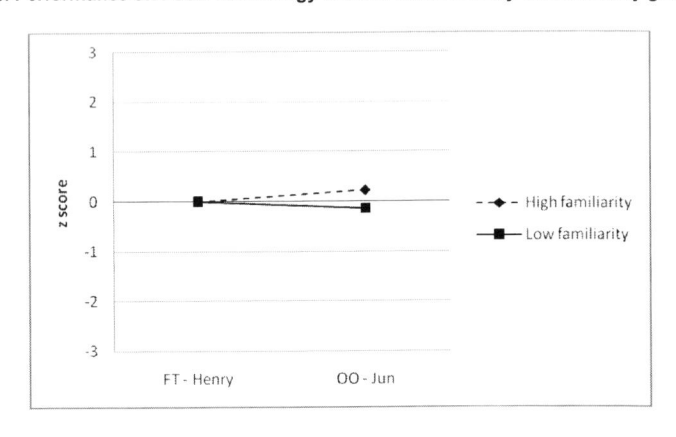

Thus, in contrast with the shared-L1 analysis and the familiarity analysis of the Sleep test, the analyses of relevant groups on the Oldest Old test suggested that

there was some advantageous relationship between Mandarin Chinese L1 background, or high familiarity with a Chinese accent, and performance on the Oldest Old test delivered by a Mandarin Chinese L1 speaker. As stated earlier, the confounding of test and speaker does not allow for specific conclusions to be drawn from these preliminary analyses regarding an accent advantage in either case. However, these results do suggest the potential for such a finding, and indicate that more detailed, rigorous exploration is warranted. Such an approach is now described in the next sections which outline the procedures and findings of the differential item functioning analyses.

5.5 DIF detection procedures

5.5.1 Overview of analytical procedures

In the same manner as the preliminary analyses above, four separate analyses were undertaken to detect DIF in the data: a "shared-L1 analysis" and a "familiarity analysis" within the Sleep test (Kaori – Japanese accent), and a "shared-L1 analysis" and a "familiarity analysis" within the Oldest Old test (Jun – Mandarin Chinese accent). In each shared-L1 analysis, the focal group was defined as shared-L1 listeners, and the reference group consisted of all other L1 listeners. In each familiarity analysis, the focal group was comprised of all "high familiarity" listeners, and all "low familiarity" listeners made up the reference group. Furthermore, within each of these four separate analyses, two methods of DIF detection were used: the standardization procedure and the Mantel-Haenszel procedure. An illustration of this design is shown in Figure 5-7.

Figure 5-7: An overview of DIF detection procedures

		Sleep test: Kaori (Japanese accent)	Oldest Old test: Jun (Mandarin Chinese accent)
Shared L1 analyses	Focal group	Japanese L1 background (N = 60)	Mandarin Chinese L1 background (N = 70)
	Reference group	Other L1 background (N = 152)	Other L1 background (N = 142)

Familiarity analyses	Focal group	High familiarity with Japanese accent (N = 85)	High familiarity with Chinese accent (N = 79)
	Reference group	Reference group: Low familiarity with Japanese accent (N = 125)	Low familiarity with Chinese accent (N = 132)

5.5.2 Matching groups

The matching criterion

The standardization method and the Mantel-Haenszel procedure both require groups of test-takers to be matched at ability level. This has been most commonly achieved in previous DIF studies by matching test-takers on their total test score, or on their score for the particular test component under focus, and is known as "internal matching". However the logic of internal matching is inherently circular; if DIF is pervasive throughout a test then DIF items may not be detected if ability is matched using total score on the same test. One way to avoid this problem is to "purify" the matching criterion by taking out items which initially show DIF, recalculating total scores, and matching groups based on this condensed version. Yet the purification approach can lead to the problem faced by Elder (1997) that when a substantial amount of DIF exists within a test, a purified form will necessarily consist of substantially fewer items. This remaining set of items may not represent a reliable measure of the construct, or it may result in further DIF findings within the refined criterion.

The alternative solution, and one less common in the literature, is to match groups according to an external criterion measure. This was seen as a useful alternative in the current study, especially because a shared-accent or familiarity advantage, as hypothesized, had the potential to be pervasive rather than located in a small number of items, making such an investigation prone to the problems inherent in internal matching. However there are potential disadvantages in the choice of an external criterion as well. Part of the reason that their use is rare is that in operational testing contexts the only available measure of candidates' ability is usually the test under investigation. Also, when external criteria do exist, they may not be valid measures of the same construct that is the focus of the test under investigation. However, Ferne and Rupp (2007) state:

> One can overcome such problems if one is willing to conduct a research study in which two parallel forms of a test are given to examinees from the reference and focal groups so that the scores from one form, or a purified version of it, are used as the external matching criterion on the second form.
>
> (p.129)

This method was adopted in the current study, with the Food Technology test version (Henry - Australian English accent) used as the external criterion. No purification procedure was carried out on the Food Technology test as the rationale behind its use was that it represented the "status quo" approach of the UTESL to speaker accent: standard native-speaker English. If DIF were then to be found on tests delivered by Jun or Kaori, this would be in relation to candidates' performance on this orthodox, unmodified UTESL which represents an existing, reliable measure of the construct of interest: EAP listening proficiency.

The matching process

In the calculation of DIF statistics, according to Clauser and Mazor (1998), "valid comparison of performance across groups requires that examinees be matched as accurately as possible" (p.37). To achieve an accurate match (using total test score as a matching variable, whether internal or external), DIF practitioners generally advise that the matching criterion should include as many score levels as the data allows (e.g. Angoff, 1993). This is most often practiced in the matching of candidates at every available score level, known as "thin matching". The "thin matching" approach has been validated in simulation studies which have shown that matching on the greatest number of available score levels produces the most accurate detection of DIF. Thin matching, however, is not always possible in practice, and is problematic when sample sizes are small. Thin matching with small samples may lead to lack of stability in p value estimates at each score level (in the case of the standardization procedure), or the loss of useful data (in the case of the Mantel-Haenszel statistic)[18]. Thus, in order to avoid these problems, a "thick matching" system was employed following Donoghue and Allen (1993) in which total score levels on the matching criterion are pooled.

Two principles guided this process. The first aim was to ensure that there was a minimum of five members in each group at each of the score levels to ensure a greater stability of results, and the higher likelihood that data would not be discarded in the Mantel-Haenszel analysis. To achieve this aim, score levels were kept as equal as possible, but varied in size to meet this requirement, especially at the extreme ends of the scale. This was, in effect, a form of minimum frequency matching (see Donoghue & Allen, 1993). Secondly, given that "thick matching" means score levels span more than one possible score unit, the other aim was to establish that means for focal and reference groups differed significantly across ability levels, but not between reference and focal groups within matched ability levels (as any pre-existing significant difference between groups of matched ability would confound the results of a DIF analysis). This was achieved through the statistical procedures, the results of which are described below.

Score levels were initially determined by examining total score on the Food Technology test through the "Table of Frequencies" function in SPSS with the relevant groups as "subgroups". Consequently, four tables were created which showed the frequencies of responses at each possible total score level of Food Technology for "Japanese L1 background" versus "Other L1 background"; "High familiarity with JA" versus "Low familiarity with JA"; "Mandarin Chinese L1 background" versus "Other L1 background"; and "High familiarity

---

18 The Mantel-Haenszel statistic assigns a zero weight to any level of a 2 x 2 table which contains cells of zero frequency (see Donughue & Allen, 1993).

with CA" versus "Low familiarity with CA". These tables were then inspected with the aim of identifying the maximum number of thick matched score levels with at least five members in each contrasting group. This process resulted in a set of six score levels which fit the data in all but one of the four situations. Because of the relatively lower sample size of the "Japanese L1 background" listener group, five score levels were created to be used for that particular analysis. The score levels and their N sizes are shown in Tables 5-25, 5-26, 5-27 and 5-28.

Table 5-25: Score levels and sample sizes by Japanese L1 status

	1 - 10	11 - 16	17 - 21	22 - 27	28 - 37	Total
Focal group (Japanese L1)	6	22	17	7	8	60
Reference group (Other L1)	30	53	32	24	13	152
Total	36	75	49	31	21	212

Table 5-26: Score levels and sample sizes by JA familiarity group

	1 - 9	10 - 14	15 - 19	20 - 24	25 - 29	30 - 37	Total
Focal group (High familiarity)	8	27	22	11	11	6	85
Reference group (Low familiarity)	17	29	38	20	13	8	125
Total	25	56	60	31	24	14	210

Table 5-27: Score levels and sample sizes by Mandarin Chinese L1 status

	1 - 9	10 - 14	15 - 19	20 - 24	25 - 29	30 - 37	Total
Focal group (Mandarin Chinese L1)	15	17	12	12	6	8	70
Reference group (Other L1)	10	39	50	19	18	6	142
Total	25	56	62	31	24	14	212

Table 5-28: Score levels and sample sizes by CA familiarity group

	1 - 9	10 - 14	15 - 19	20 - 24	25 - 29	30 - 37	Total
Focal group (high familiarity)	13	18	21	12	7	8	79
Reference group (low familiarity)	12	38	40	19	17	6	132
Total	25	56	61	31	24	14	211

In order to satisfy the second requirement – that groups within these thickly-matched score levels did not differ from each other at each stratified score level – a series of two-way ANOVAs were conducted with Food Technology total score as the dependent variable, and group membership and score level as independent variables. Results showed that for each of the four group contrasts there was no significant interaction between group membership and score level at $p < .05$. This lends validity to the argument that groups were indeed of matched ability at each step of the stratified score levels. These findings are presented visually in the charts shown in Figure 5-8.

Figure 5-8: Focal and reference groups on matching criterion by score level

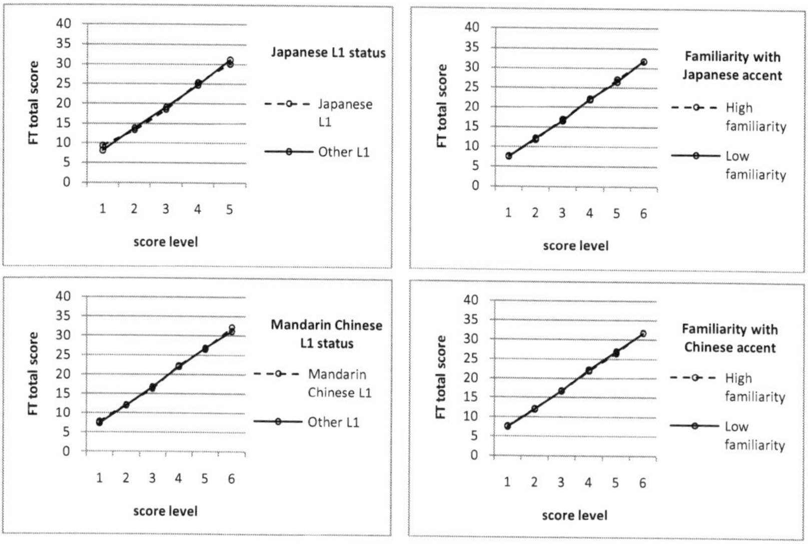

5.5.3 Calculating DIF

Calculating standardized p difference

The essence of the standardization procedure is the weighting procedure. Dorans (1989) and Dorans and Holland (1993) provide a range of options for selecting an appropriate weight, but suggest that the most common weight used is that of number of focal group members at score level (see also Roever, 2007). This in effect gives group differences more weight "at those score levels most frequently attained by the focal group under study" (Dorans & Holland, 1993, p.49). The formula for calculating the standardized p-difference with focal group N size at each score level is given by Dorans (1989) as:

$$D_{STD} = \sum_{s=1}^{S} N_{fs} (P_{fs} - P_{bs}) / \sum_{s=1}^{S} N_{fs}$$

Where:
- s = score level (otherwise known as ability level)
- P_f = observed performance of focal group on item
- P_b = observed performance of "base group" on item (otherwise known as reference group)

Thus the standardized p difference for an item is calculated by multiplying the difference between group means at each ability level by the number of focal group members, summing these values across ability levels, and then dividing the summed figure by the total number of focal group members.

For each analysis, these calculations were performed on each item using SPSS and Microsoft Excel. First, a table was created through the "custom tables" function of SPSS using data from a large spreadsheet which contained all cases and variables involved in the study. Each item was entered as a row with ability levels nested. Group membership (focal or reference) was entered as a categorical variable into the column function, and within each, nested adjacent columns for frequency counts and means at each ability level (as shown in Figure 5-9).

Figure 5-9: Custom table generated for calculation of standardised p difference

		focal group		reference group	
Item	Ability level	N	Mean	N	Mean
1	1				
	2				
	etc …				

The resulting table was copied from SPSS output into Microsoft Excel for two reasons. Firstly to format the table to be pasted back into SPSS (pasting the table from SPSS output directly into back into an SPSS data file caused formatting problems), and secondly so that charts could be easily produced from the data. Once the data in Excel had been reformatted, it was then entered into a new SPSS file with six variables: item number, ability level, focal group N, focal group mean, reference group N and reference group mean.

The first step in calculating the standardized p-difference was achieved by computing a seventh variable: "weighted mean difference". This was ("focal group mean" – "reference group mean") x "focal group N". A weighted mean difference was thus provided for each ability level within each item. The second step involved creating another custom table. "Item number" was entered as row and "weighted mean difference" as a column, with the summary statistic specified as "sum". The resulting table showed a summed, weighted mean difference for each item on the test. The final step, conducted with a calculator, was to divide each summed figure by the total focal group N size to calculate the standardized p-difference (see Appendix D for results for all items).

The resulting figure – the standardized p-difference – ranges from -1 to +1, with each interval of .1 indicating a ten percent advantage for one group over the other on a given item. In the context of test development, Dorans and Holland (1993) suggest that values of .1 or above and -.1 or below "should be examined very carefully", while Roever (2007) considers such values evidence of "large DIF" (p.179). Although the standardization approach is not normally accompanied by a significance test, it does have the advantage of enabling the researcher to map the performance of the reference and focal groups visually, and this is drawn upon in the interpretation of results below.

Calculating Mantel-Haenszel DIF statistics

For each of the four analyses, the Mantel-Haenszel statistic was calculated for each item through the Crosstabs function of SPSS. Following Roever (2007) this involved inputting the group membership variable (e.g., Japanese L1 status; Familiarity with Chinese accent) as a row, the item as a column, and the score level as a layer. SPSS then computed the Mantel-Haenszel odds ratios, logarithmic transformation of the odds ratio, and the significance level for the item. This procedure was followed for each item under investigation in each of the four analyses.

In many studies utilising the Mantel-Haenszel procedure, logarithmic transformations are converted to the delta metric, which is a scale that has a mean of 13 and a standard deviation of 4. This is accomplished by multiplying the natural logarithm of the odds ratio by -2.35. The resulting value is known as the Mantel-Haenszel delta difference or MH D-DIF. Conversion to the delta metric allows for easier comparisons between items where, intuitively, items with greater values show stronger DIF in either a negative or positive direction. All results were converted to MH D-DIF for ease of presentation, although the original statistics yielded from the analysis are presented in Appendix D.

Dorans (1989) suggested that a MH D-DIF of larger than 1 may be "a reasonable flagging criterion value" (p.228). However these flagging rules were expanded by Dorans and Holland (1993) who suggested that items where MH D-DIF was lower than one, or where the finding was not statistically significant, should be consider "negligible DIF", which they classify as Type A. Where MH D-DIF is significant and over the value of 1, Dorans and Holland classify the item as "moderate DIF" or Type B. Type C items – showing "large DIF" – are those which have an MH D-DIF of above 1.5, and where this value is significantly different from a value of 1. Because of the small sample size in this study, the results below will report all findings where the criteria for Type B DIF are met. Thus the findings include items with at least moderate DIF, and potentially some with large DIF.

5.6 DIF in Sleep (Kaori – Japanese accent)

5.6.1 Shared-L1 analysis results

The shared-L1 analysis compared the performance of listeners from Japanese L1 backgrounds (focal group) with listeners from all other L1 backgrounds (reference group). Of the 38 items in the Sleep test, the standardization procedure detected ten items (26%) as having a standardized p-difference of over .1, and the Mantel-Haenszel procedure detected seven items (18%) which were significant at $p < .05$, and where MH D-DIF was higher than 1. DIF items were found to advantage both the focal group and the reference group, but with a slight tendency towards the Japanese L1 background listeners as shown in Table 5-29.

Table 5-29: Number of DIF items detected in Sleep by method (shared-L1 analysis)

DIF detection method	Focal group advantaged	Reference group advantaged	Total
Standardization	6	4	10
Mantel-Haenszel	4	3	7

There was considerable overlap in these findings; all seven items flagged by the MH were also flagged by the standardization method. In addition, the standardization method flagged three items that that MH did not (29, 30 and 31). There were no disagreements between the methods in whether DIF favoured focal or reference groups. Table 5-30 shows the details and DIF indices of flagged items.

Table 5-30: Overview of flagged items in Sleep and DIF indices (shared-L1 analysis)

Item	Item type	STD P-DIF	MH D-DIF	p	Advantaged group
2	sentence completion	.163	2.026	.017*	focal
6	gap fill	-.209	-2.357	.005*	reference
10	gap fill	.198	2.096	.006*	focal
12	gap fill	.146	1.626	.041*	focal
19	listing	-.131	-1.786	.050*	reference
26	sentence completion	-.149	-2.117	.028*	reference
27	sentence completion	.149	-2.108	.018*	focal
29	multiple choice	-.101	(-1.314)	.124	reference
30	short answer question	.130	(1.426)	.070	focal
31	matching	.137	(1.537)	.061	focal

The findings of this analysis show that DIF items were somewhat balanced in whether they favoured the reference group or the focal group, though with a slightly higher number of DIF items favouring the shared-L1 listeners. This is not uncommon in testing practice, and McNamara and Roever (2006) note that "DIF favouring the reference group is often balanced out by DIF favouring the focal group" (p.85). This rough balance seems to fit with the findings of the preliminary analysis, which showed no discernible difference between Japanese L1 listeners and Other L1 listeners on the Sleep test. This is not to say that a shared-L1 effect may not have been present on those items favouring the focal group (see Section 5.8 below), but that this effect seems to have been equalised, to a certain extent, by items which favoured the reference group.

5.6.2 Familiarity analysis results

The familiarity analysis of the Sleep test compared the performance of listeners who reported that they were highly familiar with a Japanese accent (focal group) with listeners who had low familiarity (reference group). Fewer DIF items were flagged compared with the previous analysis. The standardization procedure detected six items (16%) with a standardized p-difference of over .1, and MH detected five items (13%) which were significant at $p < .05$, and where MH D-DIF was higher than 1. In a similar way to the previous analysis, DIF items were found to advantage both the focal group and the reference group, but with a more even spread between the two (see Table 5-31).

Table 5-31: Number of items detected in Sleep by method (familiarity analysis)

DIF detection method	Focal group advantaged	Reference group advantaged	Total
Standardization	3	3	6
Mantel-Haenszel	3	2	5

There was less overlap in these findings across both measures. Four items (2, 4, 6 and 19) were flagged by both procedures. MH flagged one item that the standardization procedure did not, and the standardization method identified two items uniquely. Table 5-32 shows the details and DIF indices of flagged items.

Table 5-32: Overview of flagged items in Sleep and DIF indices (familiarity analysis)

Item	Item type	STD P-DIF	MH D-DIF	p	Advantaged group
2	sentence completion	.145	1.896	.018*	focal
4	listing	.103	2.580	.018*	focal
5	listing	(.066)	4.113	.027*	focal
6	gap fill	-.199	-2.258	.003*	reference
19	listing	-.121	-1.755	.040*	reference
24	information transfer	-.103	(-1.260)	.104	reference
27	sentence completion	.105	(1.661)	.057	focal

There was some overlap between these results and the results of the shared-L1 analysis. Considering that a good proportion of Japanese L1 background listeners were "high familiarity" listeners and "Other L1 listeners" were "low familiarity" listeners, it is not surprising that several of the items in the table above (2, 6, 19, 27) were also identified in the shared-L1 analysis. These findings also reflect the rough balance between items favouring the focal group and those favouring the reference group that was seen in the previous analysis. Again, this reflects the findings of the preliminary analysis which focused on familiarity groups.

5.7 DIF in The Oldest Old (Jun – Mandarin Chinese accent)

5.7.1 Shared-L1 analysis

The shared-L1 analysis of the Oldest Old test compared the performance of listeners from a Mandarin Chinese L1 backgrounds (focal group) with listeners from all other L1 backgrounds (reference group). This analysis produced markedly different results for that conducted on the Sleep test. Of the 31 items on the Oldest Old, the standardization procedure identified ten items (32%) as having a standardized p-difference of over .1, and the Mantel-Haenszel procedure detected eight items (26%) which were significant at $p < .05$, and where MH D-DIF was higher than 1. Of particular interest, DIF items were found to advantage the focal group over the reference group in all but one case (see Table 5-33).

Table 5-33: Number of DIF items detected in The Oldest Old by method (shared-L1 analysis)

DIF detection method	Focal group advantaged	Reference group advantaged	Total
Standardization	9	1	10
Mantel-Haenszel	8	0	8

Again, there was a strong agreement between the methods. All of the eight items flagged by the MH were also flagged by the standardization method. In addition, the standardization method flagged two items that that MH did not (7 and 24). Table 5-34 shows the details and DIF indices of flagged items. In contrast to the shared-L1 analysis on the Sleep test, these findings show that DIF favoured the focal group on all by one of the items. This suggests that Mandarin Chinese L1 listeners were clearly advantaged on the Oldest Old test. The finding reflects the results of the preliminary analysis which showed that shared-L1 listeners performed better than Other L1 listeners in relative terms on the Oldest Old compared with their performance on the Food Technology test. However, although these findings suggest a consistent advantage for Mandarin Chinese L1 listeners, they do not provide direct evidence that this advantage is related to speaker accent. This evidence will be discussed in Section 5.8 below.

Table 5-34: Overview of flagged items in The Oldest Old and DIF indices (shared-L1 analysis)

Item	Item type	STD P-DIF	MH D-DIF	p	Advantaged group
1	short answer question	.235	2.693	.002*	focal
2	short answer question	.166	2.148	.014*	focal
3	short answer question	.219	4.385	.000*	focal
7	listing	.109	(1.488)	.106	focal
8	listing	.166	2.517	.004*	focal
17	information transfer	.155	2.583	.015*	focal
22	table completion	.104	2.688	.034*	focal
23	table completion	.296	3.071	.000*	focal
24	table completion	-.106	(-1.788)	.058	reference
25	gap fill	.193	2.458	.002*	focal

5.7.2 Familiarity analysis

The familiarity analysis of the Oldest Old test compared the performance of listeners who reported that they were highly familiar with a Chinese accent (focal group) with listeners who had low familiarity (reference group). Slightly fewer DIF items were flagged compared with the shared-L1 analysis. The standardization procedure detected seven items (23%) with a standardized p-difference of over .1, and MH detected the same number as being significant at $p < .05$, and where MH D-DIF was higher than 1. In a similar way to the previous analysis, DIF items were found to advantage the focal group in all but one case (see Table 5-35).

Table 5-35: Number of DIF items detected in The Oldest Old by method (familiarity analysis)

DIF detection method	Focal group advantaged	Reference group advantaged	Total
Standardization	6	1	7
Mantel-Haenszel	6	1	7

There was perfect overlap in these findings across both measures. All of the items flagged by the standardization method were also flagged by Mantel-Haenszel. Table 5-36 shows the details and DIF indices of flagged items.

Table 5-36: Overview of flagged items in The Oldest Old and DIF indices (familiarity analysis)

Item	Item type	STD P-DIF	MH D-DIF	p	Advantaged group
1	short answer question	.153	1.596	.032*	focal
3	short answer question	.183	3.511	.001*	focal
8	listing	.135	1.906	.019*	focal
17	information transfer	.132	2.030	.027*	focal
23	table completion	.263	2.773	.000*	focal
24	table completion	-.154	-2.336	.010*	reference
25	gap fill	.124	1.659	.028*	focal

All of the items flagged in this analysis had also been flagged in the results of the shared-L1 analysis. This may be explained partly by the make-up of the group. Like the Japanese familiarity analysis, a high proportion of listeners who were "highly familiar" with a Chinese accent were also Mandarin Chinese L1 background listeners (81%). However it also lends support to the notion that observed DIF may be accent-related, because the same findings were noted for these two groups of interest.

5.8 Evidence of accent-related DIF

It was not within the scope of this study to explain all of the DIF flagged by the statistical procedures. Rather, the aim of the DIF analysis was to provide preliminary statistical evidence of differential performance by shared-L1 and highly familiar listeners on items in the tests under investigation. A second stage was required to establish whether differential performance on flagged items was in fact substantively related to a shared-L1 or familiarity advantage with a speaker's accent. In order to achieve this second aim, a reduced set of items which exhibited significant DIF were chosen so that a detailed *post hoc* analysis could be conducted to uncover evidence of a shared-L1 or familiarity advantage related to accent and intelligibility. These "exemplar items" were chosen systematically. Firstly, the items which had been found to advantage the reference group were not subjected to further scrutiny. This is not to say that these items were not of interest in their own right, but that in attempting to explain DIF favouring reference groups the analysis would stray from the research questions. Secondly, as space does not permit all items favouring the focus group to be examined in detail, it was decided that items where DIF was, theoretically, most likely to be accent-related would be chosen. Given that, if an accent effect exists, then it would most likely emerge in items which were flagged by the shared-L1 analysis *and* the familiarity analysis, the following system was followed:

> An item was chosen for detailed analysis if:
> - the item favoured the focal group
>
> AND
> - the item was flagged by both procedures in the shared-L1 analysis
>
> AND
> - the item was flagged in the familiarity analysis (by at least one procedure)

The following items were analysed more closely following the DIF detection process to attempt to locate evidence of an accent-related basis for differential group performance:

Sleep: items 2 and 27
Oldest Old: items 1, 3, 8, 17, 23 and 25[19]

Throughout the analyses below, the following terms will be used: "more familiar listeners" will refer to shared-L1 *and* high familiarity listeners consid-

---
[19] For reference, plots of each of these items by L1 group and by familiarity group are presented in Appendix E.

ered together. "less familiar listeners" will refer to Other L1 *and* low familiarity listeners considered together.

5.8.1 Analysis of exemplar items in Sleep

Item 2

Sleep item 2 showed fairly large DIF in favour of both shared-L1 (STD P-DIF = .163) and highly familiar listeners (STD P-DIF = .145). The item requires that the listener extract the specific information from the text that "sleep revives us", or to provide a conceptually equivalent answer. It is not a straight-forward listening task, however, because it also requires that the listener infer that this information is the "main reason" for sleep – something that is not explicitly stated in the text. These task demands are reflected in the overall difficulty value which was .269. The details of this item are shown in Figure 5-10.

Figure 5-10: Details of Sleep item 2

Task (sentence completion): The main reason for sleep is to .... **Key information from the lecture transcript:** Daily activities leave our bodies low in energy, making us tired and eventually exhausted: sleep revives us. **Desired response:** revive/regenerate us **OR** recover from tiredness

Because this item focuses on listening for a specific phrase in the text, it was useful to first consider Kaori's production of the key phrase in the lecture. A narrow phonetic analysis of Kaori's production of the particular lexeme "revives" in the lecture revealed several "non-standard" features[20]:

revives   us
[ɪˈvaɪvɪs   ʌs]

---

20 Narrow phonetic transcriptions were performed with Praat – a speech analysis software program available at www.fon.hum.uva.nl/praat. All transcriptions were checked by a trained phonetician.

Kaori had dropped the initial position /r/ in "revives" and also added an epenthetic [ɪ] in her pronunciation of the final consonant cluster /vz/. According to Thompson (2001), the insertion of short vowels into consonant clusters is a common feature of Japanese pronunciation of English. However there is no reason to suspect that the elision of /r/ is a characteristic pronunciation.

Nevertheless, it appears that Kaori's non-standard pronunciation may have resulted in differential intelligibility of Jun between more familiar and less familiar listeners. The tables below show that in each analysis, more familiar listeners, by proportion, provided a correct response including the specific term "revive" more often than less familiar listeners:

Table 5-37: Correct response with "revive" by Japanese L1 status

Japanese L1 status	Correct response with "revive"
Japanese L1 (N=60)	9 (15.00%)
Other L1 (N=152)	3 (1.97%)

Table 5-38: Correct response with "revive" by JA familiarity group

Familiarity with JA	Correct response with "revive"
High familiarity (N=85)	8 (9.41%)
Low familiarity (N=125)	3 (2.40%)

The notion that less familiar listeners may have struggled with Kaori's pronunciation is complemented by a second observation. A closer look at the responses from each group suggested that less familiar listeners had made a greater proportion of a particular type of error; many had provided an incorrect response based around the terms "rest" or "relax". The proportions of this error by group in each analysis are given in Tables 5-39 and 5-40 below.

Table 5-39: Sleep item 2 response type by Japanese L1 status

Japanese L1 status	Blank response	Response with "rest" or "relax"	Other incorrect response	Correct response
Japanese L1 (N=60)	17 (28.33%)	2 (3.33%)	17 (28.33%)	24 (40.00%)
Other L1 (N=152)	50 (32.89%)	20 (13.16%)	49 (32.24%)	33 (21.71%)

Table 5-40: Sleep item 2 response type by JA familiarity group

Familiarity with Japanese accent	Blank response	Response with "rest" or "relax"	Other incorrect response	Correct response
High familiarity (N=85)	30 (35.29%)	6 (7.06%)	19 (22.35%)	30 (35.29%)
Low familiarity (N=125)	37 (29.60%)	16 (12.80%)	45 (36.00%)	27 (21.60%)

Although it can only be speculative, this finding suggests that many listeners who were unable to decode the term "revives us", or were not able to select a suitable cognate based on a higher level understanding of the text, may have guessed. One might expect a high number of guesses on this particular item because it deals with a real-world phenomenon – sleep – about which test-takers have considerable personal knowledge. The terms "rest" and "relax" are not mentioned in the lecture by this point, and seem to be "common sense" answers to the question, supplied by listeners who did not "catch" the information. That less familiar listeners guessed more often than more familiar listeners provides a plausible explanation for group differences based on the available evidence. However, these observations do not provide a strong, definitive link that these guesses were related to difficulties with Kaori's pronunciation.

Item 27

DIF on item 27 was more clearly detected for shared-L1 listeners (STD P-DIF = .149); in fact, the Mantel-Haenszel statistic was not significant in the familiarity analysis (although STD P-DIF was .105). In similarity with item 2, item 27 was also somewhat difficult overall (p value = .236). As a sentence completion task, it required the listener to note-down the particular term "non-REM" (or a suitable alternative). The details of the task are shown in Figure 5-11.

Figure 5-11: Details of Sleep item 27

Task (sentence completion):

The first four stages of sleep are also known as ....

Key information in lecture:

The first four stages of sleep are now usually called non-REM sleep.

Desired response:

non-REM (sleep)

A common erroneous response on item 27 was a blank response. Tables 5-41 and 5-42 show that a higher proportion of less familiar listeners provided a blank response, although the differences in proportions of this error were clearer in the shared-L1 analysis. Overwhelmingly, though, the notation of "REM" without "non" was shown to be the major source of error in the response data for all groups. In the shared-L1 analysis, this error was made by a greater proportion of Other L1 listeners. In the familiarity analysis these proportions were much more even:

Table 5-41: Sleep item 27 response type by Japanese L1 status

Japanese L1 status	Blank response	"REM" only	Other incorrect response	Correct response
Japanese L1 (N=60)	10 (16.66%)	21 (35.00%)	7 (11.67%)	22 (36.67%)
Other L1 (N=152)	40 (26.32%)	65 (42.76%)	19 (12.50%)	28 (18.42%)

Table 5-42: Sleep item 27 response type by JA familiarity group

Familiarity with Japanese accent	Blank response	"REM" only	Other incorrect response	Correct response
High familiarity (N=85)	17 (20.00%)	33 (38.82%)	9 (10.59%)	26 (30.59%)
Low familiarity (N=125)	32 (25.60%)	53 (42.40%)	16 (12.80%)	24 (19.20%)

In effect, a correct response on item 27 was entirely reliant on recognising and transcribing the particular words "non" and "REM" in the stream of speech. However Kaori's production of this key information did not demonstrate any particular features which could be considered non-standard:

non   R   E   M
[nɒn   ɑɹ   i   em]

It is possible, then, that the statistical DIF finding relates to a more general processing "cost" of listening to Kaori's speech among shared-L1 and unfamiliar listeners, in the manner described by Munro and Derwing (1995b). This notion of a processing cost would fit the observation of a greater number of blank responses in the data of less familiar listeners. It would also indicate that the omission of "non" in responses did not indicate a struggle with Kaori's pronunciation of this particular phrase, but suggests that many of the less familiar listeners were not attending to every word uttered because of a greater difficulty in dealing with Kaori's accent more generally. On hearing the term "REM sleep", which is salient throughout the lecture, struggling listeners noted this down, or missed the information altogether. However the notion of a greater general processing cost for less familiar listeners is not supported in consistent DIF findings throughout the test, as might be expected if the explanation presented above held true.

A counter explanation would hold that less familiar listeners generally attended to the input in a bottom-up manner (as might be expected in a task of this kind), and were in fact overcompensating for Kaori's pronunciation in the manner described by Bond (1999; 2005). It is important to note that a cue word in the sentence stem written on the answer paper is "known". It is possible that listeners did indeed attend to Kaori's production of "non", but taking into account their knowledge of her pronunciation thus far on the test, parsed her utterance as "known". Although not syntactically coherent, a logical answer once such a misunderstanding had taken place would be "REM". By contrast, the shared-L1 and familiar listeners may have made fewer adjustments to Kaori's accent throughout the test, and would have parsed "non" as Kaori had intended. This theory gains support from the responses of two of the less familiar listeners who each provided the response "known REM sleep".

These potential explanations, taken together with the results of the response analysis, suggest that the DIF finding for this item was quite likely to have been related to different processes between groups in dealing with Kaori's pronunciation. The next section will turn to examine the exemplar items taken from the Oldest Old.

5.8.2 Analysis of exemplar items in the Oldest Old

Item 1

Item one on the Oldest Old showed reasonably strong DIF on both analyses, with a standardized p difference of .235 on the shared-L1 analysis and .153 on the familiarity analysis. It was not a particularly difficult item for listeners overall, with a p value of .660. The details for this item are shown in Figure 5-12.

Figure 5-12: Details of the Oldest Old item 1

Task (short answer question):

What is the lecturer's definition of "the oldest old?"

....

Key information in lecture:

By this I mean people who are aged over 95

Desired response:

(people) over/> 95

The task required that a listener extract and note down a particular phrase: "over 95". It is important to note, initially, that a correct response to this item is almost entirely reliant on bottom-up processing skills. Candidates may deduce from the question prompt, and the general context that has been set in the pre-reading, that they need to provide an answer related to age. However, to orient themselves in the lecture, listeners need to first understand the phrase signalling a definition – "by this I mean" – and then, more importantly, to be able to accurately perceive the number term "over 95".

Turning firstly to Jun's production of key information in the recorded input, a narrow phonetic transcription reveals two interesting characteristics:

        aged   over   ninety-five
       ['eɪdʒəd   'əʊvəɹ   'naɪntifaɪ]

Firstly, the stress in the word "ninety-five" was placed on the first syllable, and the final syllable – the word "five" – is weak. Secondly, in this weak syllable, Jun dropped the final position consonant [v] in "*five*". Final position consonant dropping is a documented characteristic of Chinese pronunciation of English (Chang, 2001), and has been related to transfer owing to the small number of words with final position consonants in Chinese.

An analysis of test-taker responses (Tables 5-43 and 5-44) suggested that Jun's non-standard pronunciation may have resulted in lower intelligibility for less familiar listeners:

Table 5-43: The Oldest Old item 1 response type by Mandarin Chinese L1 status

Mandarin Chinese L1 status	Blank response	Incorrect number only	Other incorrect response	Correct response
Mandarin L1 (N=70)	3 (4.29%)	5 (7.14%)	5 (7.14%)	57 (81.42%)
Other L1 (N=142)	17 (11.97%)	25 (17.61%)	17 (11.97%)	83 (58.45%)

Table 5-44: The Oldest Old item 1 response type by CA familiarity group

Familiarity with Chinese accent	Blank response	Incorrect number only	Other incorrect response	Correct response
High familiarity (N=79)	4 (5.06%)	9 (11.39%)	6 (7.59%)	60 (75.95%)
Low familiarity (N=132)	16 (12.12%)	18 (13.64%)	18 (13.64%)	80 (60.61%)

Two noteworthy points arise from these tables. The first is that in each analysis very few of the more familiar listeners provided no response. Conversely, a greater proportion of unfamiliar listeners had trouble even attempting a response. This is the beginning of the Oldest Old test, and the key information for item one is heard after less than one minute of exposure to Jun's voice. These figures for "blank response" may represent a period during which a number of less familiar listeners found it difficult to adjust to the new accent, to the degree that they did not attempt an answer. It is worth noting, however, that this phenomenon was mostly confined to the lower ability listeners. 15 of the 17

Other L1 listeners, and 14 of the 16 low familiarity listeners who provided a blank response were at ability level three or below.

Secondly, it is clear from the shared-L1 response table that the most common error for Other L1 listeners was to note down an incorrect number. This, however, was not as clear for the familiarity analysis, where the spread of error types was more even. Focusing on the shared-L1 analysis, the frequencies of particular incorrect numbers are provided in Table 5-45 for each analysis:

Table 5-45: Range of incorrect number responses by Mandarin Chinese L1 status

Incorrect number	Mandarin Chinese L1 (N = 70)	Other L1 (N = 142)
"50"	-	2
"54"	-	1
"65"	-	1
"75"	-	2
"80"	-	2
"85"	3	7
"90"	1	2
"99"	-	3
"100"	1	3

At least one of these incorrect responses – "100" – is quite unlike the target utterance, and may be explained as deriving from information heard later in the script relating to centenarians (see below). However in the remainder of these cases, two explanations may explain the higher proportion of "wrong numbers" in the responses of the reference group. Firstly, it is feasible that these wrong numbers represent actual misperceptions of the input. For those listeners who were unfamiliar with these patterns of pronunciation, the number "ninety-five" may have been misheard as a different number, some of which are close phonemic matches to Jun's actual production (e.g., 90, 99).

A second explanation is that these incorrect numbers provide evidence of guesses based on "world knowledge" where listeners' bottom-up processing had failed. This would fit the observation that many of the incorrect numbers noted down ("75", "80", "85") were not phonemically similar to Jun's utterance. A scenario of this kind would be explained by the "interactive-compensatory" mechanism proposed by Stanovich (1980) and explored in the context of L2 listening comprehension by Field (2004). In the "interactive-compensatory" view, top-down strategies – in this case the activation of knowledge about the world – are drawn upon to compensate for deficiencies at the perceptual level. For item one, listeners who failed to "catch" the specific age but knew that a "number" response was required may have provided any of the numbers in this range based on their own notions of what the "oldest old" might mean.

In either case, the clear finding that less familiar listeners were less able to provide the correct number uttered by Jun, together with the non-standard characteristics of Jun's production of this key information, provide evidence that at least some of the DIF found on item 1 may be explained as related to differential intelligibility of Jun between listener groups.

Item 3

Item 3 on the Oldest Old test showed fairly large DIF in favour of both shared-L1 (STD P-DIF = .219) and highly familiar listeners (STD P-DIF = .183). It was also a difficult item for all test-takers; the p value in the overall item statistics was .241. The details of this item are shown in Figure 5-13.

Figure 5-13: Details of the Oldest Old item 3

Task (short-answer question):

What is the *specific term* used in the lecture for "people aged 100 or more"?
....

Key information in lecture:

Demographers, who are experts who study populations statistics, predict that by the year 2050 there'll be 20 to 40 million people in the world who'll be a hundred years old or more. We call these people centenarians ...

Desired response:

Centenarians

The general difficulty of this item may be attributed to several factors. Firstly, the task requires that test-takers provide a "specific term" given by Jun, which in effect makes this item a transcription task. Secondly, the term that is to be transcribed – "centenarians" – is not a common word, and may be assumed to be an unfamiliar term for many test-takers. Chapter 3 showed that transcription tasks are as much a measure of speaker intelligibility as they are listening ability (which is why they may be used as a measure of intelligibility). For this reason, it is useful to first consider Jun's production of the key information:

we	call	these	people	centenarians
[wɪ	kɔː	dɪs	ˈpipəʊ	sentɪˈnerɪns]

Jun's production contained several "non-standard" features in the words preceding "centenarians" including dropped final position [l] on "call" and "people". The word "centenarians" itself was produced with fully articulated consonants and a standard stress pattern, but with the elision of what would usually be a schwa between [ɪ] and [n], making the word one syllable too short. This might be more accurately described as a mispronunciation than a characteristic feature of Chinese pronunciation[21].

An analysis of responses (Tables 5-46 and 5-47) showed that the most common answer among all test-takers was a blank response, although this was represented much more in the test papers of less familiar listeners.

Table 5-46: The Oldest Old item 3 response type by Mandarin Chinese L1 status

Mandarin Chinese L1 status	Blank response	Attempt or mishearing	Other incorrect response	Correct response
Mandarin L1 (N=70)	16 (22.86%)	11 (15.71%)	14 (20.00%)	29 (41.43%)
Other L1 (N=142)	53 (37.32%)	29 (20.42%)	38 (26.76%)	22 (15.49%)

Table 5-47: The Oldest Old item 3 response type by CA familiarity group

Familiarity with Chinese accent	Blank response	Attempt or mishearing	Other incorrect response	Correct response
High familiarity (N=79)	21 (26.58%)	12 (15.19%)	17 (21.52%)	29 (36.71%)
Low familiarity (N=132)	48 (36.36%)	28 (21.21%)	35 (26.52%)	21 (15.91%)

We might infer from these tables that the difficult terminology of "centenarians", together with the Jun's non-standard pronunciation, resulted in a communication breakdown for many listeners; particularly those from Other L1 or low familiarity groups.

Unfamiliar listeners also provided a proportionally greater number of attempts at the word "centenarian" (e.g. "sendinatory", "senti narrow") that could not be marked as correct under the strictures of the marking guidelines. From observing these responses alone, it is difficult to know whether such responses are exact orthographic representations of perceptual errors, or poor orthographic representations of correctly perceived phonetic information. In some cases, these attempts formed distinct, other words (e.g., centenaries, sentinale) in which case they may signify either mishearings, or may be the result of listeners drawing on top-down processing to arrive at a known word based on the phonetic information available.

It is clear that, as a measure of listening comprehension, item three was a poor task. It did not measure understanding so much as an accurate transcription

---

21 In the recording studio Jun had struggled with the pronunciation of this word, having never encountered it before herself.

of a relatively uncommon word. However, item three proved more problematic for the analysis after it became apparent that the term "centenarians" appeared in a question stem later in the same test. This left the possibility that test-takers who initially transcribed the lexical item incorrectly, or who had initially left a blank response, may have turned back to fill in the answer in the latter stages of the test when they encountered the written term. As such, although there appeared to be evidence of proportionally greater numbers of more familiar listeners transcribing this word accurately, this cannot be taken as clear evidence of differential intelligibility.

Item 8

Item 8 showed DIF in favour of both shared-L1 (STD P-DIF = .166) and highly familiar listeners (STD P-DIF = .135). Its overall difficulty was in the mid-range (.406). The details of this item are shown in Figure 5-14.

Figure 5-14: Details of the Oldest Old item 8

Task (listing):

Name *two* effects of Alzheimer's disease on people's behaviour. (second effect)

ii) ....

Key information in lecture:

The effect on the person is that there is a deterioration of memory, deterioration of intellect and of judgement. A person suffering from Alzheimer's gradually loses the ability to care for himself or herself and loses the ability to use language and to recognise familiar faces and places.

Desired response:

(Any of the following not given in item 7) loss of: intellect/judgment/ability to care for themselves/language/recognition of people/recognition of places

---

An analysis of test responses revealed no evidence of misperceptions of key information among listener groups. Rather, as Tables 5-48 and 5-49 below illustrate, the clear basis of the focal-group favouring DIF statistic in each analysis appears to be the proportionally greater number of blank responses provided by less familiar listeners.

Table 5-48: The Oldest Old item 8 response type by Mandarin Chinese L1 status

Mandarin Chinese L1 status	Blank response	Other incorrect response	Correct response
Mandarin L1 (N=70)	24 (34.29%)	10 (14.29%)	36 (51.43%)
Other L1 (N=142)	64 (45.07%)	28 (19.72%)	50 (35.21%)

Table 5-49: The Oldest Old item 8 response type by CA familiarity group

Familiarity with Chinese accent	Blank response	Other incorrect response	Correct response
High familiarity (N=79)	26 (32.91%)	14 (17.72%)	39 (49.37%)
Low familiarity (N=132)	62 (46.97%)	24 (18.18%)	46 (34.85%)

Again, we might interpret this finding as evidence of increased processing costs for Other L1 and low familiarity listeners. However, without accompanying evidence of intelligibility-related difficulty in the form of misperceptions among the responses of less familiar listeners, it is difficult to definitively ascribe an intelligibility-related reason to the DIF found on this item.

Item 17

Item 17 on the Oldest Old test showed fairly strong DIF in favour of both shared-L1 (STD P-DIF = .155) and highly familiar listeners (STD P-DIF = .132). It is interesting to note that the overall item analysis showed it to be the easiest item on the test (equal with item 9) with a p value of .778. The details of this item are shown in Figure 5-15.

Figure 5-15: Details of the Oldest Old item 17

Task (information transfer):

Listen to the description of the bar graph and fill in the two missing age groups:

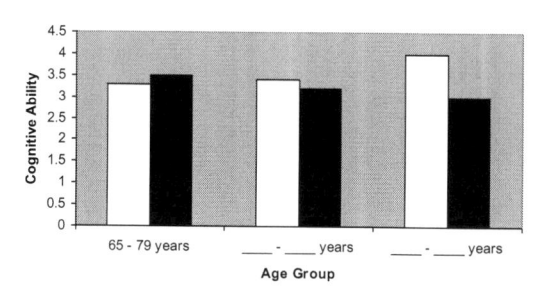

[Bar graph: Cognitive Ability (y-axis, 0 to 4.5) vs Age Group (x-axis) with three pairs of bars labeled "65 - 79 years", "___ - ___ years", "___ - ___ years"]

Key information in lecture:

These are, beginning from the left, the 65 to 79 age group, then in the middle, the 80 to 89 age group, and finally, on the right, the 90 to 99 age group.

Desired response:

80 – 89 **AND** 90 – 99

Item 17 was similar to item 1 in that a correct answer depended on the accurate perception and transcription of a set of numbers. For this reason, an analysis of Jun's production of this key information is particularly important in understanding candidate responses. The phonetic transcriptions of key information below shows that although Jun used a weakened schwa in the "to" of "90 to 99", she articulates a full [u:] in the "to" of "80 to 89":

eighty	to	eighty-nine		ninety	to	ninety-nine
['eɪti:	tu:	'eɪtɪnaɪ?]		['naɪnti:	tə	naɪntɪ'naɪ]

The Chinese accent characteristic of stressing syllables which would typically be reduced in native varieties of English has been noted by Chang (2001, p.312) who points out that Chinese speakers tend to "give the weak syllables a full rather than reduced pronunciation". Chang attributes this characteristic of Chinese pronunciation of English to L1 transfer: "reduced syllables are far less frequent in Chinese than in English. Moreover, these syllables in Chinese are usually pronounced more prominently than in English, and undergo fewer phonetic changes" (2001, p.312).

Evidence from the analysis of candidate responses suggested that Jun's pronunciation of this information may have impacted on how the numbers were perceived. A large number of candidates who scored zero had written down a response which included "82" rather than "80". Further, Tables 5-50 and 5-51 below demonstrate that the frequency and proportion of this particular incorrect response was higher for less familiar listeners in each analysis:

Table 5-50: The Oldest Old item 17 response type by Mandarin Chinese L1 status

Mandarin Chinese L1 status	Blank or incomplete response	Response including "82"	Other incorrect numbers	Correct response
Mandarin L1 (N=70)	1 (1.43%)	3 (4.29%)	5 (7.14%)	61 (87.12%)
Other L1 (N=142)	9 (6.34%)	19 (13.38%)	10 (7.04%)	104 (73.24%)

Table 5-51: The Oldest Old item 17 response type by CA familiarity group

Familiarity with Chinese accent	Blank or incomplete response	Response including "82"	Other incorrect numbers	Correct response
High familiarity (N=79)	1 (1.27%)	5 (6.33%)	5 (6.33%)	68 (86.08%)
Low familiarity (N=132)	9 (6.82%)	17 (12.88%)	10 (7.58%)	96 (72.73%)

The finding that many of the reference group members were more likely to note down "82-89" may be attributable to their expectations of a weakened production of "to" in a context where a range of numbers was being described ("x" to "y"). It is worth noting that the high degree of misperceptions seems to run counter to Jenkins' (2000) placing of weak stress into the non-core features of ELF phonology, and her doubt of "the argument that it is necessary to weaken an unimportant item in order to highlight an important one, provided that the latter is adequately stressed" (p.146). Given the nature of the input – "80" followed by "to" – it is not surprising that Jun's fully articulated [tuː] may have led to misperceptions of the type observed above. Of most interest, however, is that the more familiar listeners made this misperception on far fewer instances proportionally. This finding suggests that in this particular instance Jun was more intelligible for shared-L1 or highly familiar listeners through their increased knowledge of the stress patterns of Chinese English pronunciation.

Tables 5-50 and 5-51 indicate that unfamiliar listeners also had more trouble in noting down a complete response to item 17. This phenomenon was mostly located at the lower ability levels, and was possibly due to the general cognitive demands involved in accurately perceiving the set of numbers which were uttered, and noting them down in real-time. That listeners did not "catch" particular numbers is evidenced by the nature of some of the unfamiliar listener responses:

Example 1: (Participant 12, L1: Indonesian, ability level: 2)

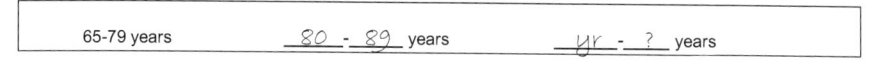

| 65-79 years | __80__ - __89__ years | __yr__ - __?__ years |

Example 2: (Participant 102, L1: Arabic, ability level: 1)

| 65-79 years | __80__ - ____ years | __90__ - __99__ years |

In the first example, Participant 12 is clearly aware that she needs to provide a response in the form of an age in years, but clearly "misses" the information necessary to fill in the second part of the answer signaled by her question mark in the final space. Similarly Participant 102 seems to have "missed" the particular number "89" – even though the co-textual information provided in her own response makes clear what the missing answer must be. This may indicate that less familiar listeners at low proficiency levels were so taxed at the perceptual level, they were not able to utilize top-down knowledge to assist in interpreting an answer.

There is sufficient evidence in the relationship between the production of the key information and the responses of candidates presented above to suggest that the score level DIF found in item 17 was attributable to differential intelligibility of Jun between the groups.

Item 23

According to the standardization method, item 23 on the Oldest Old test showed the strongest DIF in both analyses, with a STD P-DIF of .296 in the shared-L1 analysis, and of .263 in the familiarity analysis. Overall figures put the item in the midrange of difficulty, with a p value of .434. The details of the item are shown in Figure 5-16.

Figure 5-16: Details of the Oldest Old item 23

Task (table completion)
Complete the following table: [*relevant row of table shown below*]
Factors affecting the health of the oldest old
	Biological Factors	(ii).................................... Factors	
Key information in the lecture:
They can be classified in two groups: in one: biological factors and the second: environmental factors.
Desired response:
Environmental

Like all of the items discussed so far, item 23 requires that the listener extract a specific piece of information, and thus it primarily taps bottom-up listening skills. Indeed, item 23 hinges on the correct recognition of a single word – environmental – within the stream of speech. It is therefore useful to first consider Jun's production of this key information, a phonetic transcription of which is provided below given below:

environmental   factors
[ˈɪmərəməntʊ   faektəɹs]

Jun's delivery of "environmental" is noteworthy for several reasons. The first has to do with the placement of nuclear stress. While a standard pronunciation would place stress on the fourth syllable of the word environ<u>men</u>tal, Jun placed stress on the first syllable. Moreover, Jun's production was also a misplacement of nuclear stress. According to Jenkins (2000), "the nucleus is the most prominent syllable in any group of words … it is the one the speaker has chosen to highlight (by means of extra length and loudness, and a change in pitch level) as carrying the most salient part of his or her message" (p.42). Jenkins argues further that the correct placement of nuclear stress is crucial for EIL intelligibility in situations where information is "contrasted", as it is in the key information of item 23: "biological factors" versus "environmental factors". Jenkins (2000) found that nuclear stress errors formed a substantial source of unintelligibility in her ILT data, and has labelled them "the most serious word stress deviations of all" (p.42). Also noteworthy are the segmental characteristics of the utterance. Jun substituted the consonant [m] for the consonant cluster [nv], and she also dropped the final position [l].

An analysis of responses showed evidence of a relationship between Jun's pronunciation and two particular types of error among less familiar listeners. It is clear from Tables 5-52 and 5-53 that listener groups in each analysis were fairly even in their proportion of blank responses or "other" incorrect responses. However, less familiar listeners provided greater proportions of unacceptable attempts at the word "environment" and other words similar to "environment".

Table 5-52: The Oldest Old item 23 response type by Mandarin Chinese L1 status

Mandarin Chinese L1 status	Blank response	Attempt at "environ-mental"	Similar actual word	Other incorrect response	Correct response
Mandarin L1 (N=70)	16 (22.86%)	1 (1.43%)	2 (2.86%)	9 (12.86%)	42 (60.00%)
Other L1 (N=142)	38 (26.76%)	25 (17.61%)	11 (7.75%)	18 (12.68%)	50 (35.21%)

Table 5-53: The Oldest Old item 23 response type by CA familiarity group

Familiarity with Chinese accent	Blank response	Attempt at "environ-mental"	Similar actual word	Other incorrect response	Correct response
High familiarity (N=79)	15 (18.99%)	5 (6.33%)	3 (3.80%)	10 (12.66%)	46 (58.23%)
Low familiarity (N=132)	39 (29.55%)	21 (15.91%)	10 (7.58%)	17 (12.88%)	45 (34.09%)

Attempts at "environmental" were identified as responses which were phonemically similar to Jun's utterance, or which appeared to be partially completed "transcriptions" of what was heard. Similar actual words were those responses that formed a separate lexeme altogether, though one which appeared to correspond to the phonetic information derived from Jun's production. Table 5-54 gives a list of all attempts at environmental and similar actual words provided by Other L1 listeners. In the list of attempts made by unfamiliar listeners, there is only one response which includes a "v", thus it seems that the absence of this phoneme misled listeners to some extent, and provides evidence that listeners were attending very carefully to the phonetic information in the input. The placement of the nuclear stress on the first syllable may have added further complexity for listeners who were struggling to recognise the word.

Table 5-54: Approximations of "environmental" by Other L1 listeners

Attempt at "environmental"	Similar actual word
Emmotical	elementary
Enro mental	Erementary22
illmental	External
im	Immersion
immanterl	intelligence
immarteal	interactive
imornant	irrelevant
imoronal	Irrelevant
in	Mental
in	Mental
In	Mentally
In -	
in ... ment	
incoment	
indorolated	
inmen	
Inmenetal	
Inroman	
Inroman-	
inroment	
Inromental	
invoriment	
Iremended	
Iremental	
Iromental	

The question remains that with "incorrect" placement of nuclear stress and non-standard segmental features how were the Mandarin Chinese L1 and highly familiar listeners able to respond accurately? Two explanations may fit. Firstly, the table in the answer booklet provides a visual "scaffold" upon which listeners may have utilised top-down knowledge to either predict the answer "environmental" or to "fill in" the answer if bottom-up processing failed. More familiar listeners may have been better able to utilise top-down knowledge because they were not as "taxed" at the perceptual level more generally.

A second explanation, which is in fact closely related to the first, is that the higher number of "attempts" made by less familiar listeners is related to an interaction between their generally lower knowledge of Jun's phonology, the difficulty of the input material, and the difficulty of the surrounding vocabulary.

---

22 Although this word is not spelled correctly, it seems to be a clear attempt at the word "elementary" rather than an attempt at "environmental".

If we are to reconceptualise Jun's production in this instance as a "mispronunciation" rather than as a pronunciation characteristic of a Chinese English variety, then we might understand the group differences. More familiar listeners who heard the mispronounced word may have realised that this was a mispronunciation, and quickly drawn on other contextual cues to make sense of what they heard. Less familiar listeners, on the other hand, may not have detected this as a mispronunciation, and given the difficulty and novelty of surrounding vocabulary in the text (e.g., "cognitive abilities", "longevity genes", "adaptive capacity"), together with their lack of experience with Jun's phonology, assumed that this was also an unfamiliar lexical item rather than a mispronunciation of a known word. In short, when more familiar listeners heard a mispronunciation, they noticed quickly (based on its deviation from their phonological expectations) and activated top-down processing. When unfamiliar listeners heard the same mispronunciation in a novel lexical environment, they assumed it was a novel word, rather than a mispronunciation of a common word, and attempted to transcribe phonetically what they heard.

There is clear evidence in the range of responses that the DIF on this item can be attributed to differential intelligibility of Jun between groups.

Item 25

Item 25 of the Oldest Old test was reasonably difficult with a p value of .288. It also showed strong DIF in the shared L1 analysis (STD P-DIF = .193) and moderately strong DIF in the familiarity analysis (STD P-DIF = .124). The details for this item are shown in Figure 5-17.

Figure 5-17: Details of the Oldest Old item 25

Task (gap-fill):
Complete this statement:
The oldest old have _____ of E-4.
Key information in lecture:
It's been found that the oldest old may have an unusually low number of a gene variant called E-4.
Desired response:
(an unusually) low number/amount

Like almost all of the other items submitted to this detailed analysis, item 25 tests listening for a specific detail: what the oldest old "have" in relation to "E-4". However, given the very close match between the spoken input and the written prompt, item 25 is essentially an utterance recognition task. Listeners who hear "the oldest old may have" simply need to write down the next phrase they hear. A layer of difficulty is added in that listeners must select which information is necessary to fill the gap. This may require perceiving and parsing what is heard, before deciding to note down the key information "low number", and discard "gene variant", which is simply an elaboration of "E-4". However many listeners may not reach the parsing stage, and may simply note down words perceived immediately following the cue "have".

Building on this argument that item 25 is primarily testing utterance recognition, in order to understand candidate performance it is first necessary to analyse Jun's production of the key information:

low	number	of	a	gene	variant
[leʊ	'lʌmbər	ɒv	ə	dʒin	vaɪrənt]

It is immediately noticeable that Jun's production of the initial consonant /n/ in number has been articulated as [l]. Chang (2001) notes that, from an L1 transfer perspective, Mandarin Chinese does not contain [n] sounds, and that [l] and [n] may often cause perceptual confusion for learners. From a production perspective an interesting parallel for this characteristic of Jun's pronunciation is found in Hung's (2000) study of the phonology of Hong Kong English. Hung noted that in syllable onset positions speakers of Hong Kong English often interchange [l] and [n], and this was particularly marked in the word "number" where 20 percent of his speakers pronounced initial "n" as [l]. While it is clear that these findings for Hong Kong English cannot be generalised to account for Jun's pronunciation, Hung's attempt to understand this phenomenon is worth noting when he suggests that the particular frequency of an onset position [l] in "number" might be because "the word number has been borrowed into Cantonese as [lʌmba]" (p.355). No evidence of the borrowing of "number" in Mandarin was noted.

It was clear from the response analysis (Tables 5-55 and 5-56) that greater proportions of blank responses and responses which included "low" plus an error (or simply "low" on its own) were the main contributors to the DIF finding.

Table 5-55: The Oldest Old item 25 response type by Mandarin Chinese L1 status

Mandarin Chinese L1 status	Blank response	"Low" + error	Error + "number"	Other incorrect response	Correct response
Mandarin L1 (N=70)	17 (24.29%)	6 (8.57%)	4 (5.71%)	13 (18.57%)	30 (42.86%)
Other L1 (N=142)	54 (38.03%)	21 (14.79%)	2 (1.41%)	34 (23.94%)	31 (21.83%)

Table 5-56: The Oldest Old item 25 response type by CA familiarity group

Familiarity with Chinese accent	Blank response	"Low" + error	Error + "number"	Other incorrect response	Correct response
High familiarity (N=79)	21 (26.58%)	5 (6.33%)	4 (5.06%)	18 (22.78%)	31 (39.24%)
Low familiarity (N=132)	50 (37.88%)	22 (16.66%)	1 (0.76%)	29 (21.97%)	30 (22.73%)

It is, again, difficult to assert conclusively that the greater proportion of blank responses among unfamiliar listeners was related to differential intelligibility. However given that Jun's production of "number" was non-standard, and that the accurate production of consonants has been shown to be a crucial factor in intelligibility (Jenkins, 2000), particularly in syllable initial positions (Zielinski, 2006) it can be assumed that this may have caused intelligibility difficulties for listeners generally, and perhaps more so for those less familiar with the phonological features of Jun's Chinese accent. Any difficulty at the perceptual level would have been compounded by attempting to understand the remainder of the phrase ("gene variants"), and this may have led to a general breakdown in communication.

Further, and more solid, evidence of differential intelligibility – particularly relating to Jun's pronunciation of "number" – is found in the responses of those listeners who noted down the word "low", but not "number". The tables above show that this was a more common erroneous response among less familiar listeners. A closer inspection of responses which fall within this category shows that several unfamiliar listeners noted down the word "low" on its own, or alternatively latched onto the word "genes" in lieu of "number". In other cases the responses show evidence of "number" being misperceived as "lamber" (x 2), "lanber", "longer", "lumber" and "temper". By contrast, fewer of the less familiar listeners noted down "number" without "low", signaling that "number" was the problematic word in this item.

In a similar way to the misperception of "environmental" in the previously discussed item, this DIF finding may also relate to the nature of the surrounding text. Less familiar listeners may have been constrained in drawing on top-down knowledge to "correct" deficiencies at a perceptual level – as would be hypothesised in the interactive-compensatory mechanism – because of the technical vocabulary which was prevalent at that point of the lecture (e.g., "gene variants"). The nature of the surrounding text may have led less familiar listeners to assume that Jun's production was not a variant pronunciation of a relatively common word, but was in fact an unfamiliar lexical item. In such circumstances, listeners would have been likely to attempt to transcribe what they heard phonetically.

5.9 Discussion

5.9.1 Summary of main findings

The results of the DIF analysis and subsequent response analysis presented above show that shared-L1 and familiarity effects were not the same across two tests featuring highly intelligible speakers with L2 accents. Preliminary analyses of mean scores on the Sleep test (featuring Kaori) compared with the benchmark Food Technology test (featuring Henry) showed no significant interaction effects for either the Japanese L1 status or familiarity with Japanese accent groups with each test. However, there were significant interaction effects between test and both Mandarin Chinese L1 background and familiarity with Chinese accent groups when performance on The Oldest Old test (featuring Jun) and Food Technology were compared. These results suggested a general advantage at the test score level for more familiar listeners and a relative disadvantage for less familiar listeners on the test spoken by Jun. On these analyses, however, the variable of "speaker" was confounded with test version, and so differential performance could not be solely attributed to a shared-L1 or familiarity effect.

Nevertheless, the findings of the preliminary analyses were reflected at the item level through DIF analysis using two different methods. On the Sleep test, DIF was detected in 10 items using the standardization procedure and 7 items using Mantel-Haenszel in the shared-L1 analysis, and in 6 items using the standardization procedure and 5 items using Mantel-Haenszel in the familiarity analysis. However, in both cases DIF was fairly evenly balanced for focal and reference groups. On selected items where DIF was found to favour more familiar listeners, there was some evidence in the response analysis of two exemplar items that this statistical finding was the result of increased accent-related difficulty for the reference groups, however the findings were not unequivocal.

By contrast, DIF clearly favoured the focal groups in each analysis of the Oldest Old. In the shared-L1 analysis, of 10 items which were shown to exhibit DIF by the standardization or Mantel-Haenszel method, 9 advantaged the focal group. Similarly, in the familiarity analysis, of 7 items which showed DIF using the two procedures, 6 were found to advantage the focal group. Further, the response analysis showed clear evidence that the DIF finding on at least four of these items (1, 17, 23, 25) could be connected to differential intelligibility of Jun between matched-ability listeners from different listener groups.

The evidence of differential performance between listener groups on the Oldest Old test, *prima facie*, supports the idea that listeners may be advantaged over other listeners on a listening test featuring a speaker from the same L1 background, or with whose accent they are highly familiar. However, DIF was shown not to be pervasive on this test. By contrast, the results for analyses on the Sleep test provide evidence that an L2 speaker may be used on listening assessment without the threat of serious bias at the score level. These findings, then, reflect many of the preceding studies which have found contradictory evidence for a shared-L1 or familiarity effect (Munro et al., 2006; Major et al., 2002). To paraphrase Major et al.'s (2002) summation of their own findings: do listeners perform better on a listening test when the speaker shares their first language background or when they are highly familiar with a speaker's accent? The answer to this question was not a clear yes or no but, rather, sometimes.

5.9.2 Hypothetical conditions for accent-related DIF

Unlike the Major et al. (2002) study, however, the current study was afforded the opportunity to examine group differences at the item level. In this analysis, several similarities emerged across items where DIF was shown to be related to speaker accent. Thus, from the results of this detailed analysis, a set of conditions which facilitate differential performance by shared-L1 or highly familiar listeners may be hypothesised, which help to explain why a shared-L1 or familiarity effect was not the same across both tests, and was not pervasive across all items in the Oldest Old. This set of hypothesised conditions also leads to a clearer theoretical understanding of how accent-related DIF may manifest on tests of listening comprehension more generally.

A comparison of findings from the post hoc analysis of the Oldest Old test suggests a number of similar factors across items which showed accent-related DIF. These can broadly be classified under the topics of task characteristics, speaker pronunciation, and linguistic demands of the text. These factors all appear to serve as moderating variables in the influence of the listener background factors which have been investigated. Each is discussed briefly below.

Task characteristics

All of the items which showed substantive accent-related DIF on the Oldest Old test targeted listening for specific details. These tasks included short answer questions, gap-fills and information transfer. In two cases a correct response hinged on the accurate perception of numbers. In the case of item 23, a correct response required that the listener recognise a single a word – "environmental" – in Jun's speech. For item 25, it was argued above that a correct response was also a matter of utterance recognition. In completing these tasks, listeners would have been likely to primarily draw on bottom-up skills (see Vandergrift, 2007). The implication is that accent-related DIF items appear to have been measures of intelligibility as much as they were measures of listening ability. Thus, on these items differences between listener groups were arguably occurring at the level of speech perception, as the relative roles of listener- and speaker-factors which determine intelligibility were brought to the fore.

Speaker pronunciation

Although items which tap bottom-up processing skills heighten the importance of speaker intelligibility, not all of the items on the Oldest Old test (or for that matter the Sleep test) which focused on listening for specific details showed DIF. The response analysis showed that Jun's particular pronunciation of key information required for such tasks was also a contributing factor to the conditions under which differential intelligibility may manifest. Jun was shown to deliver key information on DIF items with non-standard features of pronunciation, some of which violated aspects of the Jenkins' (2000) lingua franca core. These included consonant substitutions (item 25), non-standard nuclear stress (item 23), final position consonant dropping (items 1 and 23), consonant substitution (item 25), and consonant deletion (item 23). Difficulties were also observed when weak forms were not used (item 17).

It is not surprising, then, that listeners may have had intelligibility problems with these pronunciations. What is interesting, though, is that shared-L1 and high familiarity listeners *did not* experience the same level of intelligibility difficulty – pointing towards a greater degree of mutual intelligibility between Jun and more familiar listeners for those particular utterances. In many cases, Jun's non-standard pronunciation was linked to previously documented characteristics of Chinese English phonology, which suggests that the greater degree of mutual intelligibility between shared-L1 and familiar listeners may provide evidence of an emerging L2 variety. This observation is echoed in Bent and Bradlow (2003) who draw implications from their own findings thus: "the demonstration of the interlanguage speech intelligibility benefit suggests a mechanism that may underlie the establishment of new pronunciation norms across a community of non-native talkers" (p.1609). Thus a DIF finding appears to be conditional on pronunciation which deviates from features deemed essential for common EIL intelligibility – such as those described in the LFC – but which represents features of pronunciation particular to an L2 variety shared by (or familiar to) listeners.

Linguistic demands of the text

The final factor concerns the linguistic demands of the text. This factor may be important in constraining less familiar listeners from activating top-down knowledge when they are struggling with an unfamiliar accent at the perceptual level. Technical or difficult vocabulary in surrounding text may potentially lead less familiar listeners to assume that a variant pronunciation is a new word rather than a non-standard realisation of a known word, or a mispronunciation – as was the case with Jun's production of "environmental" in item 23. Less familiar listeners may then be more likely to attempt to transcribe what they have heard phonetically, resulting in an incorrect answer.

A hypothetical model of conditions for accent-related DIF

These hypotheses are summarised in Figure 5-18, presented below, which offers a hypothetical model of conditions for accent-related DIF based on the observed DIF in the Oldest Old test. Three "moderating factors" give rise to particular scenarios in which shared-L1 or familiarity effects will be more pronounced, and potentially lead to score level differences. When these conditions are minimised, and where speakers of L2 varieties have a high level of general intelligibility, shared-L1 and familiarity effects may be constrained – as they were for the many of items on the Oldest Old, and for the Sleep test.

Figure 5-18: A hypothetical model of conditions for accent-related DIF

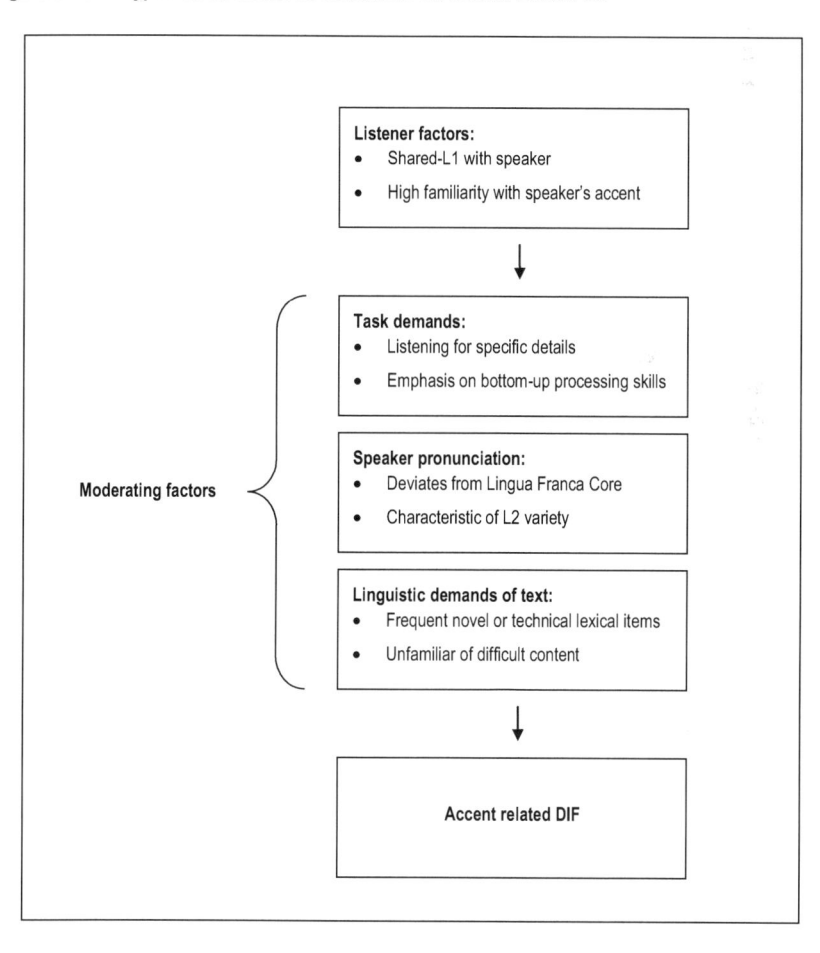

```
                    ┌─────────────────────────────────────┐
                    │ Listener factors:                   │
                    │  • Shared-L1 with speaker           │
                    │  • High familiarity with speaker's  │
                    │    accent                           │
                    └─────────────────────────────────────┘
                                      ↓
                    ┌─────────────────────────────────────┐
                    │ Task demands:                       │
                    │  • Listening for specific details   │
                    │  • Emphasis on bottom-up            │
                    │    processing skills                │
                    └─────────────────────────────────────┘
                    ┌─────────────────────────────────────┐
 Moderating factors │ Speaker pronunciation:              │
                    │  • Deviates from Lingua Franca Core │
                    │  • Characteristic of L2 variety     │
                    └─────────────────────────────────────┘
                    ┌─────────────────────────────────────┐
                    │ Linguistic demands of text:         │
                    │  • Frequent novel or technical      │
                    │    lexical items                    │
                    │  • Unfamiliar of difficult content  │
                    └─────────────────────────────────────┘
                                      ↓
                    ┌─────────────────────────────────────┐
                    │        Accent related DIF           │
                    └─────────────────────────────────────┘
```

5.9.3 Limitations of the study

This study was necessarily limited, firstly, by its small sample size. Although samples of over 200 are often considered large in the field of second language research or applied linguistics more generally, this N size precluded several of the more sophisticated approaches to DIF which are regularly taken in the fields of language testing or educational assessment more broadly. Even in the non-parametric approaches taken in the current study, the rate of DIF detection has been found to increase as sample size increases, meaning that the larger number of participants in a study, the less chance there will be of making a Type II error (false negative) (see Fidalgo, Ferreres & Muñiz, 2004). If this is the case, then it is possible that with a larger sample size, DIF may have been detected in more items on either of the tests under examination. However, a statistical DIF finding does not necessarily indicate substantive DIF, and as the analysis above has shown, several of the items which were identified as showing strong DIF were seemingly not related to an accent effect. More findings of statistical DIF would not necessarily have led to the finding of more accent-related DIF. Future studies, though, should aim for larger sample sizes if possible.

A second limitation concerns the constraints of the DIF methods used in the study. In order to distinguish between high and low familiarity listeners for the creation of focal and reference groups, the self-report scale was dichotomised. This is problematic in the first instance because dichotomisation necessarily results in a loss of information. However it also reveals a deficiency in the methods used in that the potential for a curvilinear relationship between accent familiarity and differential item functioning could not be captured.

A third limitation relates to the language experience questionnaire. Although care was taken in the design and trialling of this instrument, it ultimately depended on a participant's answer to a single key self-report measure. There is, perhaps, no straightforward way to measure the construct of "familiarity with an accent". Ideally, pre-test interviews would establish with greater validity how much exposure an individual had had with a given accent, but it would not be possible to conduct such interviews with large groups of test-takers. This study suggested, however, that one of the best predictors of familiarity with a particular L2 variety is whether a listener shares this variety – a finding similar to that proposed by Flowerdew (1994). As non-native varieties emerge, this will perhaps more likely be the case. For this study, the validity of the results for the familiarity group are supported by their similarity with the results for the shared-L1 listeners.

A final limitation of this study is that the response analysis was necessarily "etic"; that is, it relied on the researcher's speculation regarding attempts at words, processing costs and general difficulties experienced with speaker accent. In a more ideal situation, the research design might have included a number of participants taking part in a stimulated recall, where the veracity of the researcher's assumptions about attempts at words, and the reason why answers were left blank, might have been verified. Nevertheless, this limitation provides the impetus for the third study in this book – where test-taker performance with matched L1 and mismatched L1 speakers is explored utilizing verbal report methodology. The third study will approach the issues raised in this chapter from an "emic" perspective, albeit with a different group of test-takers, in an effort to further explain the nature of accent-related difficulty, and build upon the findings presented above.

Chapter 6: Attitudes towards speakers

This chapter presents the findings of study two, in which participants' attitudes towards the three speakers – Henry (Australian English accent), Kaori (Japanese accent) and Jun (Mandarin Chinese accent) – were measured using the verbal-guise technique. The chapter is divided into nine sections. In section 6.1, a set of research questions deigned to address the second "questionable assumption" is presented. Section 6.2 provides an overview of the speaker evaluation methods for measuring language attitudes with a focus on verbal guise procedure. Section 6.3 then presents the methods used in the data collection stage. Section 6.4 presents the results for all traits on the verbal guise scale, and Section 6.5 describes the process of data reduction using principal axis factor analysis. Section 6.6 presents the specific results for a "lecturer competence" factor, beginning with an overview of results for all listeners, and then a between-subjects analysis of L1 groups. The same pattern is followed in section 6.7 for a "social attractiveness" factor. Section 6.8 then explores the relationship between attitudes and subsequent test performance with each speaker. Section 6.9 provides a discussion of results and their connections with previous research.

6.1 Research questions

Study two was designed to provide evidence either to support or to refute the following assumption articulated in Chapter 3:

Assumption 3: Test-takers will not, overall, hold negative attitudes towards highly-intelligible speakers with L2 accents used on an EAP listening test.

Assumption 4: Test-taker attitudes towards diverse accented speakers will not affect their performance on a listening test featuring that speaker.

This assumption was broken down into a set of specific research questions:

Research Question 1:
a) What attitudes do test-takers hold towards diverse accented speakers used on an EAP listening test?
b) Do attitudes towards speakers vary according to listeners' L1 background?

Research Question 2:
   a) Is there a relationship between attitudes towards a particular speaker, and subsequent performance on a test featuring that speaker?

6.2 Methodological considerations

6.2.1 An overview of the speaker evaluation approach

Attitudes toward accent, as Chapter 2 illustrated, have been extensively researched from the fields of social psychology, communication studies and sociolinguistics. Within these related traditions, Cargile and Bradac (2001) note three broad investigative approaches: content analysis, direct methods and speaker-evaluations. Content analyses concern the "public treatment accorded to language varieties", and have been conducted through analyses of the media and language policy (Cargile & Bradac, 2001, p.349). Direct approaches encompass questionnaires, interviews and other similar methods in which participants are directly asked their opinions of particular varieties or speakers. An example of a direct method was Jenkins' (2007) study – reported in Chapter 2 – in which a map task was used to elicit attitudes towards particular native and non-native varieties. Indirect measures, on the other hand, gauge language attitudes through observation of listeners' reactions to speech samples, most often measured with rating scales. These are commonly referred to as speaker evaluation studies. Cargile and Bradac (2001) note that speaker evaluation studies have "dominated" the study of language attitudes – an observation shared by Giles and Billings (2004).

Speaker evaluation approaches are considered to have their origin in Lambert et al.'s (1960) study which saw the first use of the "matched-guise technique" (MGT). The matched-guise technique is an experimental approach in which listeners hear a single speaker assuming a range of "guises" such as different accents, dialects or languages, and then provide ratings of each guise on a set of subjective scales. These are usually semantic-differential scales (see Osgood, Suci & Tannenbaum, 1957) which cover a range of personality traits such as "intelligent-unintelligent" or "likeable-unlikable". Attitudes towards language varieties are inferred from these ratings, because it is assumed that hearing certain guises "triggers certain social characterizations that will lead to a set of group-related trait-inferences" (Giles & Billings, 2004, p.189). The inferences are further bolstered by the fact that aspects of voice quality are controlled in a matched-guise experiment because a single speaker is assuming each guise.

The development of the matched guise technique has been recognised as a tremendously significant contribution to language attitudes research in terms of the template it provides for language attitudes research, and also the considerable amount of research it has spawned (see Giles & Billings, 2004). However, it is not without its limitations. Garrett, Coupland and Williams (2003) raise a number of problems associated with the MGT which principally concern the nature of the stimulus. One serious concern is that by controlling other speech variables in the use of a single talker taking on multiple guises, the stimuli may become less genuine. Garrett et al. argue this point thus:

> The advantage of minimizing the effects of some of the more idiosyncratic variations in speech (for example, prosodic and paralinguistic features such as rate and voice quality) may mean that some of the other characteristics which normally co-vary with accent varieties (such as intonational characteristics, or even discourse patterning – so-called "discourse accent") are also eliminated. This raises issues of the authenticity of these voices/varieties.
>
> (2003, p.59)

In an effort to overcome this criticism of artificiality, an increasingly common variation on the methodological paradigm set down by the matched guise procedure has been the "verbal-guise technique" (VGT). The verbal-guise procedure is essentially the same in all respects to the MGT except that the speech samples are delivered by several speakers, rather than one individual speaker taking on different guises. This method has been used successfully in studies which have investigated attitudes towards various native and non-native speaker accents, where it was not feasible to have one single talker assume all guises (e.g., Al-Kahtany, 1995; Bresnahan et al., 2002; Chiba et al., 1995; Dailey et al., 2005; Gallois & Callan, 1989; McKenzie, 2008).

Although the verbal-guise technique allows for more authentic speech samples, it is less robust in its ability to generalise from speaker evaluations to attitudes about those varieties represented. The MGT, by comparison, controls all other speech-related variables, leaving phonology the sole independent variable. In recognition of this, several studies which have utilised the verbal guise technique have made a concerted effort to select speakers who are roughly similar in voice quality (see for example Ladegaard, 1998; McKenzie, 2008). Yet to some extent, the ability to generalise beyond speakers is an issue for all speaker evaluation research. Garrett et al. (2003) cite Edwards' (1982) argument that the MGT "does not measure language attitudes so much as attitudes to representative speakers of languages and language varieties" (p.53). Ultimately, the choice of procedure will depend on a trade-off between speaker authenticity (or feasibility) and the desire to generalise findings to broader attitudes about language with more confidence.

6.2.2 The use of the speaker evaluation approach in the current study

In the current study, a speaker evaluation approach was taken which followed, to the greatest extent possible, the verbal-guise technique. Because of the contextualised nature of the investigation, however, there was not scope for selecting speakers with comparable voice quality. The three speakers – Henry, Kaori and Jun – had already been chosen to take part in the study through the speaker selection procedure outlined in Chapter 4. This selection was necessarily based on their comparable levels of intelligibility. Therefore a range of speech factors other than accent which might have affected evaluations remained uncontrolled; chief among which was speaker gender. Nevertheless, the primary aim of this study was not to draw conclusions with regard to Australian, Japanese and Mandarin Chinese English accents in an abstract sense, but to gauge listeners' attitudes towards the three particular speakers in this study. This is not to say that the findings for these three "cases" (two of whom are speakers with L2 accent varieties) may not be compared with prior research on attitudes towards native and non-native varieties. Indeed it is the findings of this previous literature which have provided the impetus for this study. Rather, this study recognises the range of extraneous variables that may influence evaluations, and these will be acknowledged in the interpretation of results.

The verbal-guise method held a number of other benefits for the purposes of the study in other ways. Firstly, it was deemed to be appropriate for use with large sample sizes, with the data collection procedure relatively efficient and easy to administer. Also, as an indirect measure, it did not overtly "flag" the issue of speaker accent through its use. This was important given that data for studies one and two were collected in the same session (see 5.3.3) with the attitudes towards speakers collected first. Thirdly, as a speaker evaluation approach, the VGT yields data which are suitable for statistical analysis. This was necessary in order to investigate a relationship between an individual's attitude towards a given speaker, and their performance on a test featuring that speaker.

Finally, it was decided that the study – like many other VGT studies – would use semantic-differential scales. Originally developed in the 1950s by Osgood, the principles underlying these scales were documented at length in Osgood et al.'s (1957) *The Measurement of Meaning*. In most cases, the semantic differential consists of a seven-point rating scale (although some studies have used five- and six-point or nine-point scales) where "bipolar" adjectives frame each end. One feature that has been less exploited in speaker-evaluation research, which tends to focus on the ranking of speakers, is that the semantic-differential approach claims to show both the direction and intensity of attitudes towards a given object (or in this case, speaker). On a seven point scale, the point of "4" is considered neutral with each end representing either a very positive or negative attitude, and with grades of intensity in the steps between the neutral point and the extreme (Osgood et al., 1957). This is an important feature for this study, which is primarily interested in whether attitudes towards the selected speakers are generally positive or negative for a cohort of test-takers. The methods involved in setting up the verbal-guise procedure are described below, with a focus on the trialling of a speaker evaluation task.

6.3 Methods

6.3.1 Participants

Listeners

The participants in this study were the same sample of test-takers described in chapter five, including one participant who did not complete the diverse accents-UTESL, making a total sample size of 213.

Speakers

The speakers in this study were the same three speakers introduced in chapter four: Henry (Australian English accent), Kaori (Japanese accent) and Jun (Mandarin Chinese accent). As stated above, this study does not seek to generalize the findings of attitudes towards each speaker to attitudes towards their respective language varieties as a whole. Rather, the aim of the study is to gauge attitudes towards these three particular speakers in the specific context of a language test.

6.3.2 Instruments

Two instruments were utilised in this study: the diverse accents UTESL battery, and a Speaker Evaluation Task (SET). The construction of the DA-UTESL battery has been described in detail in chapter three; the development of the Speaker Evaluation Task is outlined below.

The Speaker Evaluation Task

Selecting and recording stimuli

The first step in constructing the Speaker Evaluation Task was to select an appropriate common script, and to record each speaker. It was of prime importance that the speech sample was of an identical type and quality to that of the materials that each speaker had recorded for the DA-UTESL, so that the speech sample would be an authentic sample of each speaker's formal academic speech. Thus, the sample script was drawn from a fourth existing UTESL. This script is shown below:

Biotechnology refers to the use of living things to make or change products, such as the food we eat. Although the word is a recent one, biotechnology is not a new idea. For centuries, farmers have tried to improve crop plants and reduce the losses caused by threats to their survival – threats such as pests, weeds, soil quality and the weather. Through selective breeding, by combining the best varieties of plants, they created new and better plant varieties. But these traditional methods are time-consuming and imprecise, so more recently scientists have looked for more effective ways of improving crops.

The stimuli for the SET were recorded by speakers in the same recording session that they recorded their respective DA-UTESL scripts. Following the same procedure as the recording for the DA-UTESL, speakers were monitored to ensure that all of the words within the common script were uttered. However, speakers were not otherwise guided in their delivery of the material. A fourth speaker – with a standard Australian English accent – was also recorded for the purposes of a practice task.

Selecting and trialling items

The scales used in the Speaker Evaluation Task were adapted from Zahn and Hopper's (1985a) Speech Evaluation Instrument which is discussed above (see Appendix F for Zahn and Hopper's full set of items). The adaptation had two aims. Firstly, the instrument needed to be shortened. Zahn and Hopper (1985a) include 30 items in their scale, and it was thought that completing a semantic-differential scale of this size between speech excerpts would add unreasonable length to the data collection procedure. The SEI is considered an "omnibus measure" (Zahn & Hopper, 1985a, p.113), and its use in reduced form has precedent in the research of Cargile (2002), Gundersen and Perrill (1989) and Zahn and Hopper themselves (1985b). Secondly, the items included on the shortened scale needed to fit the context of the investigation: gauging attitudes towards lecturers in a formal academic speech situation. With these aims in mind, it was also considered important that the scale retain items representing each of the three-factors of Zahn and Hopper's (1985a) original instrument: superiority/competence, attractiveness and dynamism.

To narrow Zahn and Hopper's original set of items the list of thirty items were inspected with a second researcher with experience in the construction of such scales. Based on collective judgment, half of the thirty items were discarded because (a) they were not directly relevant to evaluations within the context of an academic lecture (e.g., upper class-lower class, rich-poor); (b) they might be assumed given the information supplied about the speaker's role as an academic lecturer (e.g., literate-illiterate, white-collar-blue collar); (c) they were very similar to other items (e.g., several items covered similar notions of attractiveness-unattractiveness); or (d) they were judged to be potentially difficult for second-language learners of lower proficiency levels to interpret (e.g., complete-incomplete, sweet-sour).

The remaining items were set on a seven-point semantic-differential scale, with two items added: correct-incorrect, good pronunciation-bad pronunciation. Items were presented in a randomised order, and they were also randomly presented according to whether a positive adjective appeared on the left or right-hand side of the scale (following Burns, 1997). An initial "short-form" of seventeen items was trialled with a group of 20 students in a postgraduate applied linguistics course. Feedback from the trial indicated that the scale was easy to use, but ideally should be shorter than 17 items given the length of time participants needed to complete each item between excerpts. Upon inspection of initial results with a second researcher, further items were discarded because they appeared to be confusing for some participants (including the added item "correct-incorrect"), or, again, because they were seen to be overlapping with several other items. Feedback from the trial also raised the issue of creating clearly understandable negative forms, thus "disfluent" was changed to "not fluent". Finally, an "affective response" item was added which asked how "happy" the listener would be if the speaker was their lecturer. The final eleven items are shown in Figure 6-1 below (for the actual materials used in the study, see Appendix G).

Figure 6-1: Speaker evaluation task scales

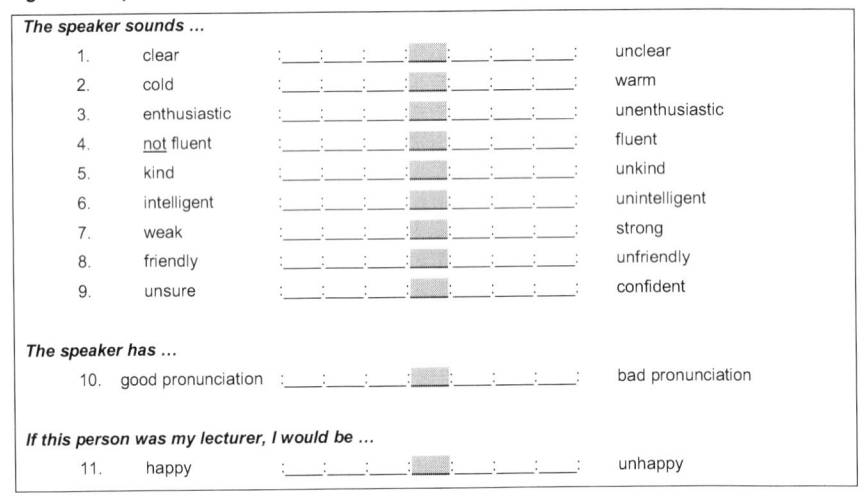

The speaker sounds ...

1.	clear	:___:___:___:___:___:___:	unclear
2.	cold	:___:___:___:___:___:___:	warm
3.	enthusiastic	:___:___:___:___:___:___:	unenthusiastic
4.	<u>not</u> fluent	:___:___:___:___:___:___:	fluent
5.	kind	:___:___:___:___:___:___:	unkind
6.	intelligent	:___:___:___:___:___:___:	unintelligent
7.	weak	:___:___:___:___:___:___:	strong
8.	friendly	:___:___:___:___:___:___:	unfriendly
9.	unsure	:___:___:___:___:___:___:	confident

The speaker has ...

10.	good pronunciation	:___:___:___:___:___:___:	bad pronunciation

If this person was my lecturer, I would be ...

11.	happy	:___:___:___:___:___:___:	unhappy

6.3.3 Data collection procedure

The Speaker Evaluation Task was administered in the same series of data collection trials described in Chapter 5. In each trial, the Speaker Evaluation Task was administered before any of the tests. Each trial was conducted in the same format:

Step 1

Consent was first gained from all participants in accordance with the University of Melbourne Human Research Ethics guidelines, which stipulates that participants receive a plain language statement and sign a consent form before they can take part in a project. This was the same plain language statement and consent form used in study one.

Step 2

Participants received the booklet containing the Speaker Evaluation Task along with the DA-UTESL battery and the Language Experience Questionnaire used in study one. The order of all data collection proceedings was explained.

Step 3

The researcher introduced the Speaker Evaluation Task. Participants were asked to read through the instructions to the task printed in the booklet, and the method of response on the semantic-differential scales was explained. Participants were also asked to read the adjectives in the practice task, and check the meaning of any words that they were unsure of either with a partner or with the researcher.[23]

Step 4

The practice task was conducted. Participants heard the practice speaker, and were given time after hearing the stimulus to complete their responses on the scales. Participants were then given the opportunity to ask any further questions about the task.

Step 5

Participants completed the Speaker Evaluation Task for each of the three speakers, with a one minute gap between speakers to allow respondents to

---

23 After the initial trial, it became clear that all of the adjectives were very familiar to participants except "enthusiastic", which was raised by several students as an unknown word. In the subsequent trials, the researcher made a point of checking whether test-takers understood "enthusiastic".

complete all items. Following the SET, participants continued with the tests and questionnaire discussed in the preceding chapter.

6.4 Results for all traits

Initial calculations are shown below of the mean evaluations of each speaker by all listeners on each item of the speaker evaluation task:

Table 6-1: Mean evaluations on all items by speaker

		Henry		Kaori		Jun	
		Mean	SD	Mean	SD	Mean	SD
1.	clarity	**6.33**	1.05	5.02	1.51	5.97	1.32
2.	warmth	3.64	1.81	4.56	1.54	**5.00**	1.50
3.	enthusiasm	4.01	1.65	3.63	1.50	**4.91**	1.45
4.	fluency	**6.07**	1.28	4.50	1.60	5.51	1.51
5.	kindness	4.08	1.62	4.94	1.43	**5.29**	1.27
6.	intelligence	**5.53**	1.38	4.50	1.27	5.22	1.33
7.	strength	**5.44**	1.37	3.65	1.29	4.95	1.40
8.	friendliness	3.85	1.71	4.79	1.54	**5.13**	1.37
9.	confidence	**5.69**	1.38	4.27	1.41	5.20	1.54
10.	pronunciation	**6.39**	.87	4.34	1.55	5.73	1.41
11.	affective response	**5.08**	1.65	4.13	1.59	**5.29**	1.49

Significance tests (with alpha set at .05, and Bonferroni adjustments for multiple comparisons) showed statistically significant differences between each speaker on all traits except the affective response item where there was no significant difference between Henry and Jun.

From these initial descriptive statistics it can be seen that Henry, the Australian English speaker, was evaluated most positively on "clarity", "fluency", "intelligence", "strength", "confidence" and "pronunciation". Jun, the Mandarin Chinese L1 speaker, was rated highest on "warmth", "enthusiasm", "kindness" and "friendliness", and was equivalent with Henry on the affective response item. Kaori, the Japanese L1 speaker, was not rated highest on any of the items, but was evaluated more highly than Henry, the native speaker, on "warmth", "kindness" and "friendliness".

Two points are noteworthy in these initial results. Firstly, the direction of attitudes for Jun and Kaori was almost always positive; that is, above the neutral threshold of 4. All of Jun's mean evaluations, and all but two of Kaori's, are above this figure. Attitudes towards Henry were also strongly positive on all traits except for "warmth" and "friendliness" on which he was evaluated, on average, in a negative direction on the scale. Secondly, Henry received his three most favourable average evaluations on three language-related traits: "clarity", "fluency" and "pronunciation". Two of these – "clarity" and "pronunciation" – also have the lowest standard deviations among all of the ratings, indicating a higher degree of homogeneity among the measured attitudes of listeners. Importantly, though, on these key language-related items – "clarity", "fluency" and "pronunciation" – listeners, on average, held positive attitudes towards Kaori's speech, and very positive attitudes towards Jun's.

6.5 Data reduction

From these descriptive statistics, it is immediately obvious that more than one dimension of evaluation existed within the data. Indeed, the hypothesized factor structure of the speech evaluation instrument would hold that three factors should emerge from the scales: a status/competence factor including "clarity", "fluency", "intelligence" and potentially "pronunciation"; a social attractiveness factor including "warmth", "kindness" and "friendliness"; and a dynamism factor including "enthusiasm", "strength" and "confidence". The "affective response" variable may be expected to correlate with several, if not all, dimensions of the scale.

To explore the possible dimensions of the scale, all data was collated in an SPSS file and subjected to an exploratory factor analysis using the principal axis technique. The choice of principal axis factoring from the broad family of factor analytical approaches followed Zahn and Hopper (1985). Following Pallant (2002), the data – which consisted of 213 ratings of each speaker on 11 traits (7029 data points in total) – were assessed for suitability. The data met the standard requirements for sample size, and the correlation matrix showed that a good number of the correlations had an r of greater than 0.3. Bartlett's test of sphericity was significant at <0.001, and the Kaiser-Meyer-Oklin value was 0.85, well exceeding the recommended value of 0.6. Based on these initial findings, it seemed feasible to conduct the factor analysis.

The principal axis analysis of the 11 items revealed two factors with eigenvalues exceeding 1, the first explaining 39.20% of the variance, and the second 21.13%:

Table 6-2: Total variance explained

Factor	Initial Eigenvalues			Extraction Sums of Squared Loadings		
	Total	% of Variance	Cumulative %	Total	% of Variance	Cumulative %
1	4.311	39.195	39.195	3.833	34.845	34.845
2	2.324	21.128	60.323	1.915	17.409	52.254
3	.767	6.976	67.299			
4	.652	5.931	73.230			
5	.612	5.561	78.791			
6	.560	5.092	83.883			
7	.445	4.044	87.927			
8	.411	3.740	91.667			
9	.387	3.515	95.181			
10	.291	2.642	97.824			
11	.239	2.176	100.000			

Extraction Method: Principal Axis Factoring.

The screeplot illustrated a very clear break between the second and third component (see below), suggesting that the scale did, in fact, comprise only two factors.

Figure 6-2: Screeplot

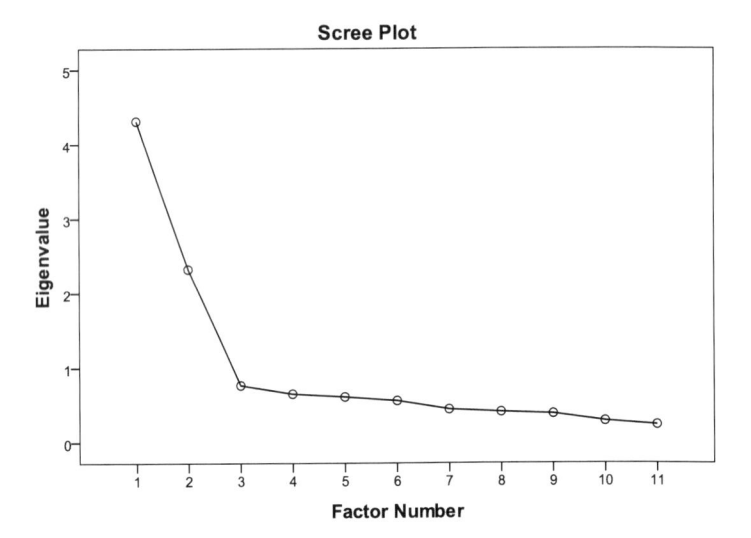

A varimax rotation was performed on the full set of data with two factors selected for extraction. The varimax rotation showed the emergence of a simple two-factor structure, though with the affective response item cross-loading on both factors (see Table 6-3).

Table 6-3: Rotated factor matrix

	Factor 1	Factor 2
pronunciation	.829	
clarity	.711	
confidence	.694	
strength	.687	
fluency	.686	
affective response	.615	.415
intelligence	.597	
kindness		.845
friendliness		.796
warmth		.696
enthusiasm		.473

Extraction Method: Principal Axis Factoring.
Rotation Method: Varimax with Kaiser Normalization.
Rotation converged in 3 iterations.

Because of the affective response item appeared to be cross-loading, a second analysis was run with the affective response item removed. Again, two factors emerged with eigenvalues exceeding 1 which explained just over 60% of the variance in the data:

Table 6-4: Total variance explained (affective response item removed)

Factor	Initial Eigenvalues Total	% of Variance	Cumulative %	Extraction Sums of Squared Loadings Total	% of Variance	Cumulative %
1	3.781	37.807	37.807	3.293	32.930	32.930
2	2.312	23.117	60.924	1.898	18.983	51.913
3	.734	7.335	68.259			
4	.651	6.510	74.769			
5	.610	6.104	80.873			
6	.536	5.356	86.229			
7	.425	4.252	90.481			
8	.390	3.896	94.377			
9	.291	2.913	97.290			
10	.271	2.710	100.000			

Extraction Method: Principal Axis Factoring.

The varimax rotation again produced a simple two-factor structure, each with a number of strong loadings, and this time with no items cross-loading:

Table 6-5: Rotated factor matrix (affective response item removed)

	Factor 1	Factor 2
pronunciation	.810	
clarity	.706	
fluency	.696	
confidence	.696	
strength	.688	
intelligence	.608	
kindness		.844
friendliness		.789
warmth		.698
enthusiasm		.480

Extraction Method: Principal Axis Factoring.
Rotation Method: Varimax with Kaiser Normalization.
Rotation converged in 3 iterations.

While a two-factor solution did not necessarily reflect the original properties of the speech evaluation instrument developed by Zahn and Hopper (1985), there was certainly precedent for such a solution in . Factor 1 was labelled "lecturer competence", and factor 2 was labelled "social attractiveness". Alpha coefficients showing the internal consistency of each subscale across the data set are given in Table 6-6.

Table 6-6: Cronbach's α reliability coefficients for the items comprising each factor

Factor name	Cronbach's α
lecturer competence	0.85
social attractiveness	0.79

6.6 Results for lecturer competence

6.6.1 All listeners

Descriptive statistics (Table 6-7) of the overall mean evaluations on the lecturer competence dimension suggested that listener attitudes followed a pattern familiar in the literature. Henry – the native speaker – was evaluated most highly, followed by Jun (Mandarin Chinese accent) and then Kaori (Japanese accent). The range of responses showed more homogeneous lecturer competence scores for Henry compared with Kaori and Jun, who received some scores within the extreme low scale points 1 and 2:

Table 6-7: Descriptive statistics of lecturer competence by speaker

Speaker	N	Mean	SD	Min.	Max.	Range
Henry (Australian English accent)	213	5.91	0.84	3.50	7.00	3.50
Kaori (Japanese accent)	213	4.38	0.97	1.67	6.67	5.00
Jun (Mandarin Chinese accent)	213	5.43	1.05	1.67	7.00	5.33

A one-way repeated measures ANOVA was conducted in order to compare the mean lecturer competence scores between all three speakers. The results showed a significant main effect for speaker [Wilks' Lambda = .35, $F(2, 211) = 196.17$, $p < .001$], and the effect size was very large [multivariate partial eta squared = .650]. Pairwise comparisons using Least Significant Difference demonstrated that the mean scores for all speakers were significantly different from each other (see Table 6-8).

Table 6-8: Pairwise comparisons of speakers on lecturer competence

Compared speakers		Mean difference	Standard error	Sig.
Henry	Kaori	1.53	0.08	.000
	Jun	0.48	0.09	.000
Kaori	Henry	-1.53	0.08	.000
	Jun	-1.05	0.09	.000
Jun	Henry	-0.48	0.09	.000
	Kaori	1.05	0.09	.000

Based on estimated marginal means
* The mean difference is significant at the .05 level.
a Adjustment for multiple comparisons: Least Significant Difference (equivalent to no adjustments).

These findings imply that listeners clearly distinguished between speakers on the dimension of lecturer competence, with Henry rated most highly, followed by Jun and then Kaori.

While listeners distinguished between speakers in rank, the findings also demonstrate that all three speakers were, on average, viewed positively on the dimension of lecturer competence. Each speaker had a mean evaluation score of over 4, suggesting a positive direction on the semantic differential scales. However it should be noted that Kaori's mean evaluation on the lecturer competence factor was nearing 4, while Henry and Kaori were rated well over 5. Mean evaluations of each speaker on lecturer competence are illustrated in Figure 6-3.

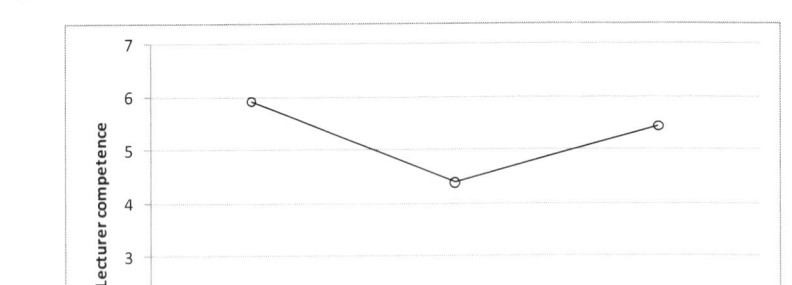

Figure 6-3: Mean lecturer competence scores by speaker

6.6.2 L1 groups

As the literature suggests that familiarity with accent or sharing a speaker's accent may influence attitudes towards that speaker, the effect of listener L1 background was also explored. Listeners were divided into four L1 groups: "other-East Asian L1", "Mandarin Chinese L1", "Japanese L1" and "Other Mixed L1". The rationale behind splitting other L1 listeners into two separate groups was based on two reasons. Firstly, listeners from the East Asian region may have been expected to be more familiar with the accents of Jun and Kaori than listeners from the Middle East, Europe or South America given that English is increasingly used as a lingua franca within the Asia Pacific region (see Kirkpatrick, 2007b). Secondly, Chapter 4 demonstrated that although listeners were not particularly accurate in identifying the accents of the three speakers, they typically categorised them as an East Asian variety. As such, it might be hypothesized that listeners from non-Asian L1 backgrounds may respond to the accents in different ways to those listeners from other East Asian L1 backgrounds. The demographic of each group is given in Table 6-9.

Table 6-9: Overview of the four L1 groups

Other East-Asian L1 N = 53	Mandarin Chinese L1 N = 70	Japanese L1 N = 60	Other mixed L1 N = 30
Korean (N = 35) Indonesian (N = 10) Thai (N = 4) Vietnamese (N = 4)	Mandarin Chinese (N = 70)	Japanese (N = 60)	Spanish (N = 13) Arabic (N = 9) French (N = 3) Turkish (N = 2) Portuguese (N = 1) Hindi (N = 1) West Ambae (N = 1)

A mixed between-within subjects (3 x 4) ANOVA was run with "lecturer competence" as the dependent variable, "speaker" as the within-subjects factor, and "L1 group" as the between-subjects factor. The speaker factor had three levels: Henry, Kaori and Jun. The L1 group factor had four levels: Other East-Asian L1, Mandarin Chinese L1, Japanese L1 and Other Mixed L1. The averaged mean scores for each speaker within each L1 group are shown in Table 6-10.

Table 6-10: Mean lecturer competence scores by speaker and L1 group

Speaker	L1 group	N	Mean	SD
Henry: Australian English accent	Other East-Asian L1	53	5.93	0.79
	Mandarin Chinese L1	70	5.98	0.81
	Japanese L1	60	5.67	0.83
	Other Mixed L1	30	6.18	0.92
Kaori: Japanese accent	Other East-Asian L1	53	4.48	1.07
	Mandarin Chinese L1	70	4.45	0.94
	Japanese L1	60	4.31	0.94
	Other Mixed L1	30	4.17	0.91
Jun: Mandarin Chinese accent	Other East-Asian L1	53	5.61	0.95
	Mandarin Chinese L1	70	5.47	1.06
	Japanese L1	60	5.34	1.14
	Other Mixed L1	30	5.21	1.02

Results of the ANOVA again showed a significant main effect for speaker [Wilks' Lambda = .353, $F(2, 208) = 190.845$, $p < .001$] with a large effect size of .647 (multivariate partial eta squared). There was, however, no significant effect for L1 group [$F(3, 208) = 5.729$, $p = .179$]. Further, the interaction effect between speaker and L1 group was not statistically significant [$F(6, 416) = 1.414$, $p = .208$]. These results suggest that listeners from different L1 backgrounds were remarkably uniform on average in their evaluations of speakers on the lecturer competence dimension. The findings also show that each speaker was evaluated, on average, in a positive direction by listeners from these four L1 background groups. Henry was viewed most positively on this factor, followed by Jun. Kaori, on the other hand, was slightly above the mid-value 4 in the average evaluations of each L1 group. These findings are illustrated in Figure 6-4.

Figure 6-4: Mean lecturer competence score by speaker and L1 group

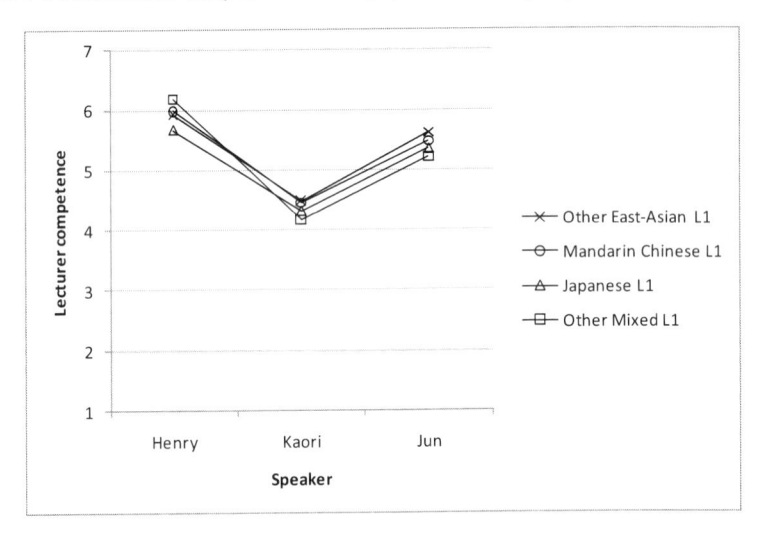

While there was no significant interaction between L1 group and speaker, there was a trend in the data – visible in the graph above – in which the Other Mixed L1 group provided the most positive evaluations of Henry, and the least positive evaluations of Kaori and Jun. By contrast, the Other East-Asian L1, Mandarin Chinese L1 and Japanese L1 groups remained relatively stable in their attitudes towards Henry, Kaori and Jun. This pattern is noticeable in Table 6-11 (below) which summarises the position of each L1 group in relation to others in attitudinal responses towards each speaker.

Table 6-11: Attitudes towards each speaker by L1 group

Attitude	Henry	Kaori	Jun
Most positive	Other Mixed L1	Other East-Asian L1	Other East-Asian L1
⇩	Mandarin Chinese L1	Mandarin Chinese L1	Mandarin Chinese L1
	Other East-Asian L1	Japanese L1	Japanese L1
Least positive	Japanese L1	Other Mixed L1	Other Mixed L1

The highlighting of this trend is useful in considering the findings presented in the next section.

6.7 Results for social attractiveness

6.7.1 All listeners

The overall mean evaluations of speakers on the social attractiveness dimension showed a markedly different pattern of attitudes compared with lecturer competence. Descriptive statistics (Table 6-12) indicated that the pattern was almost reversed: on average Henry was evaluated lowest, whereas Jun (Mandarin Chinese accent) and Kaori (Japanese accent) were rated highest and second highest respectively. The minimum and maximum ratings showed a wide spread, indicating that attitudes towards speakers on the social attractiveness dimension were more diverse across the cohort compared with evaluations of the same speakers on lecturer competence. While Kaori and Jun are rated reasonably positively on average, Henry is evaluated slightly negatively with an average score slightly lower than the neutral point of 4.

Table 6-12: Descriptive statistics of social attractiveness scores by speaker

Speaker	N	Mean	SD	Min.	Max.	Range
Henry (Australian English accent)	212	3.90	1.39	1.00	7.00	6.00
Kaori (Japanese accent)	212	4.48	1.11	1.50	7.00	5.50
Jun (Mandarin Chinese accent)	209	5.09	1.01	2.25	7.00	4.57

Again, a one-way repeated measures ANOVA was conducted in order to compare social attractiveness scores between all three speakers. The results showed a significant main effect for speaker [Wilks' Lambda = .652, $F(2, 206)$ = 54.878, $p < .001$], and the effect size was large [multivariate partial eta squared = .348]. As with lecturer competence, pairwise comparisons using Least Significant Difference (Table 6-13) demonstrated that the mean scores for all speakers on social attractiveness were significantly different from each other.

Table 6-13: Pairwise comparisons of speakers on social attractiveness

Compared speakers		Mean difference	Standard error	Sig.
Henry	Kaori	-0.59	0.12	.000
	Jun	-1.19	0.12	.000
Kaori	Henry	0.59	0.12	.000
	Jun	-0.60	0.10	.001
Jun	Henry	1.19	0.12	.000
	Kaori	0.60	0.10	.000

Based on estimated marginal means
* The mean difference is significant at the .05 level.
a Adjustment for multiple comparisons: Least Significant Difference (equivalent to no adjustments).

The graph below illustrates these findings with clear distinctions between Henry, Kaori and Jun.

Figure 6-5: Mean social attractiveness scores by speaker

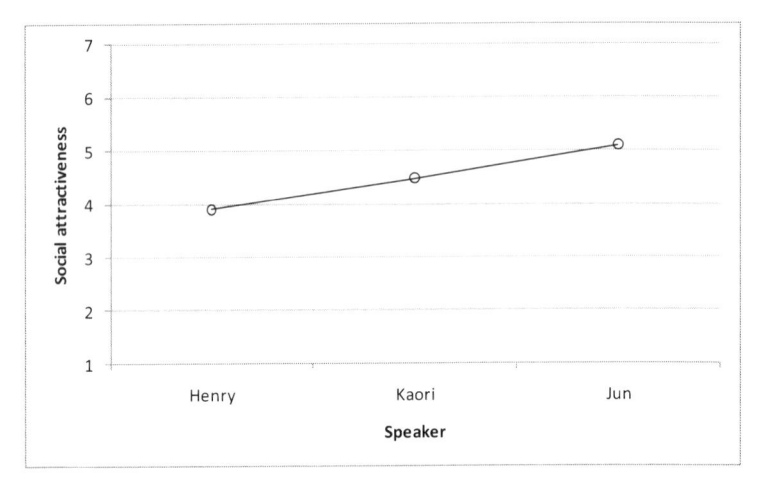

6.7.2 L1 groups

As with the previous section, an L1 group effect on mean evaluations was also investigated. Descriptive statistics showed that while Henry and Kaori were evaluated on social attractiveness in a positive direction by each L1 group, attitudes towards Henry on this factor were slightly negative among Mandarin Chinese L1 and Japanese L1 listeners.

Table 6-14: Mean social attractiveness scores by speaker and L1 group

Speaker	L1 group	N	Mean	SD
Henry: Australian English accent	Other East-Asian L1	53	4.09	1.24
	Mandarin Chinese L1	68	3.82	1.35
	Japanese L1	58	3.37	1.35
	Other Mixed L1	29	4.77	1.43
Kaori: Japanese accent	Other East-Asian L1	53	4.25	1.14
	Mandarin Chinese L1	68	4.92	1.13
	Japanese L1	58	4.39	1.06
	Other Mixed L1	29	4.08	0.89
Jun: Mandarin Chinese accent	Other East-Asian L1	53	5.06	1.06
	Mandarin Chinese L1	68	5.26	0.96
	Japanese L1	58	4.98	1.07
	Other Mixed L1	29	4.96	0.96

A mixed between-within subjects (3 x 4) ANOVA was run with "social attractiveness" as the dependent variable, "speaker" as the within-subjects factor, and "L1 group" as the between-subjects factor. As with the previous L1 group analysis, the speaker factor had three levels: Henry, Kaori and Jun, and the L1 group factor had four levels: Other East-Asian L1, Mandarin Chinese L1, Japanese L1 and Other Mixed L1. Results of the ANOVA showed significant effects for speaker and L1 group at $p < .01$. However, there was also a statistically significant interaction effect between speaker and L1 group [Wilks' Lambda = .863, $F(6, 406) = 5.19$, $p < .001$]. A graphical representation of the mean evaluations by speaker and L1 group (see Figure 6-6) showed that this interaction effect was most likely caused by the Other Mixed L1 group's ranking of Henry over Kaori, and almost equivalent to Jun. However, the Other East-Asia L1 group also appeared to be evaluating Henry slightly more positively in relation to Kaori than the Japanese L1 and Mandarin Chinese L1 listeners.

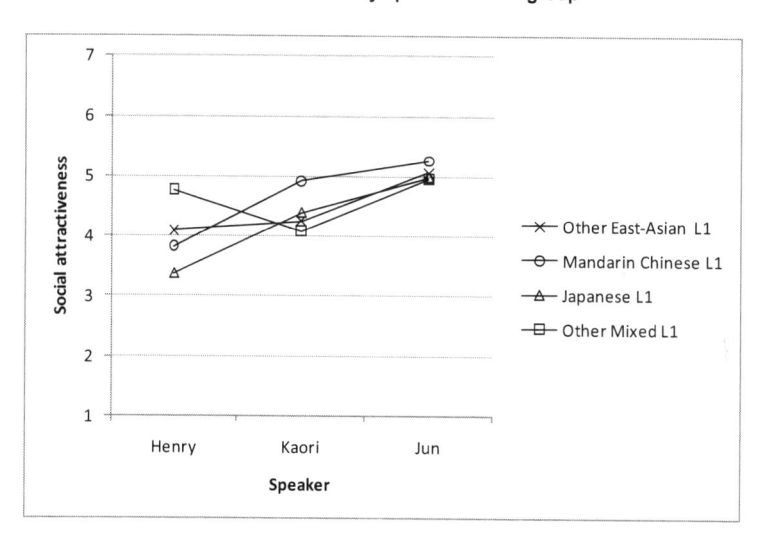

Figure 6-6: Mean social attractiveness score by speaker and L1 group

The cause of the interaction effect was investigated in a follow-up analysis in which the ANOVA was run a second time with the Other Mixed L1 group removed. The results still showed a significant interaction effect between speaker and L1 group [Wilks' Lambda = .938, $F(4, 350) = 2.86$, $p = .024$], suggesting that the Other East-Asia L1 group was also contributing to the initial effect in the Four L1 groups analysis.

To understand this interaction effect further, separate within-subjects ANOVAs were run for each L1 group. Because multiple comparisons were being performed, a Bonferroni adjustment was made in the post-hoc comparisons for each analysis. All of the listener groups seemed to show different evaluative patterns in their data (see Table 6-15). The Other East-Asian L1 group rated Jun significantly higher than Henry and Kaori, whom they evaluated at roughly the same level. The Mandarin Chinese L1 group evaluated Kaori and Jun highly – with no significant difference between them – but had significantly less positive attitudes towards Henry. The Japanese L1 listener group evaluated each speaker differently, with Jun ranked highest, followed by Kaori and Henry. Finally, although the Other Mixed L1 group's average evaluation of Henry was quite high – attitudes towards Henry were not significantly different from attitudes towards Kaori or Jun. However, this group's evaluation of Kaori was significantly lower than their evaluation of Jun.

Table 6-15: Multiple pairwise comparisons by L1 group

L1 group	Talker pairs		Sig.
Other East-Asian L1	Henry	Kaori	1.000
	Henry	**Jun**	.000*
	Kaori	**Jun**	.000*
Mandarin Chinese L1	Henry	**Kaori**	.000*
	Henry	**Jun**	.000*
	Kaori	Jun	.127
Japanese L1	Henry	**Kaori**	.000*
	Henry	**Jun**	.000*
	Kaori	**Jun**	.019*
Other Mixed L1	Henry	Kaori	.094
	Henry	Jun	1.000
	Kaori	**Jun**	.006*

Bolded and underlined names indicate the speaker awarded the higher evaluation score.

These findings suggest that the patterns of evaluation of the three speakers were different among each listener group. However there were some similarities between the Mandarin Chinese L1 group and the Japanese L1 group: both rated Kaori and Jun significantly higher than they did Henry. Also, the Other East Asian L1 group and the Other Mixed L1 group were similar in that their ratings for Kaori and Henry were not significantly different. What seems clear is that the two shared-L1 groups appear to have been functioning somewhat differently to the other two groups in their evaluations of Kaori in relation to Henry.

6.8 Attitudes and test performance

In order to assess the relationship between attitudes towards each speaker on the two factors – lecturer competence and social attractiveness – and subsequent performance on a listening test featuring that same speaker, three multiple regressions were initially planned. However, in the case of each speaker there was no need to proceed beyond the initial inspection of Pearson correlations, because relationships between attitudes and test performance were demonstrated to be weak.

6.8.1 Performance with Henry (Australian English accent)

Initial Pearson correlations showed that there was a significant, positive correlation between each listener's individual attitude towards Henry on the lecturer competence factor and their total score on the Food Technology test, although the relationship was weak [$r = .19$, n = 212, $p = .005$]. There was also a very weak, negative correlation between attitudes towards Henry on the social attractiveness dimension and total score on Food Technology that did not reach significance [$r = -.11$, n = 212, $p = .105$]. The lack of a strong relationship between each attitudes measure and FT total score is shown in the two scatter-plots in Figures 6-7 and 6-8.

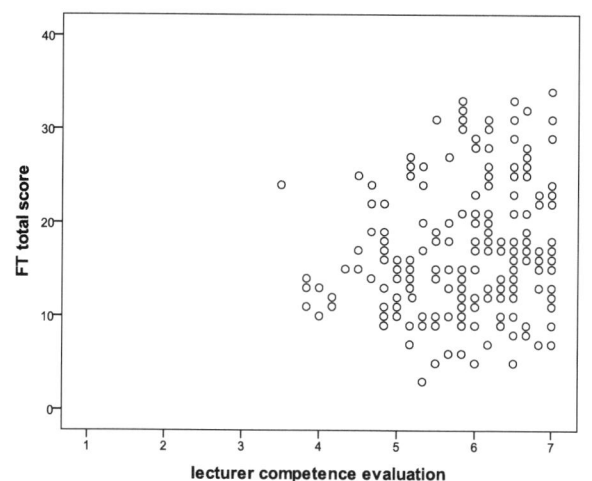

Figure 6-7: Relationship between lecturer competence evaluation and FT total score

Figure 6-8: Relationship between social attractiveness evaluation and FT total score

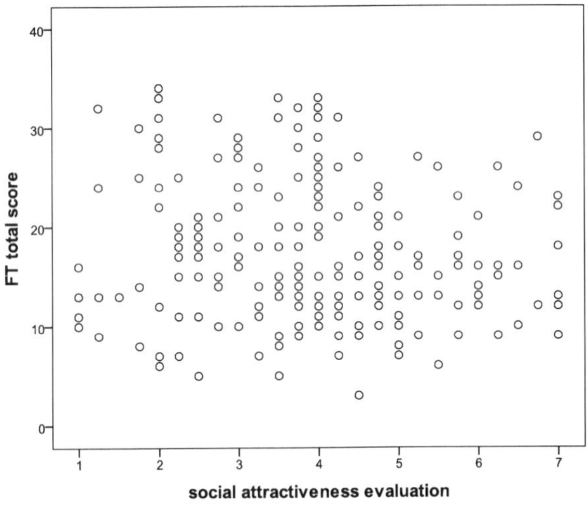

6.8.2 Performance with Kaori (Japanese accent)

For performance with Kaori, initial inspections of correlation coefficients revealed a slightly different pattern from that reported above. A very weak relationship was found between listeners' attitudes towards Kaori on the lecturer competence factor and their total score on the Sleep test, and this was not statistically significant [$r = .10$, $n = 212$, $p = .169$]. There was a significant, though still weak, positive correlation between evaluations of Kaori's social attractiveness and total score on Sleep [$r = .19$, $n = 211$, $p < .005$]. These relationships are illustrated in the scatterplots shown in Figures 6-9 and 6-10. The calculated coefficient of determination indicated that 3.72% of variance on the Sleep test could be explained by variance on attitudes towards Kaori on the social attractiveness dimension.

Figure 6-9: Relationship between lecturer competence evaluation and SL total score

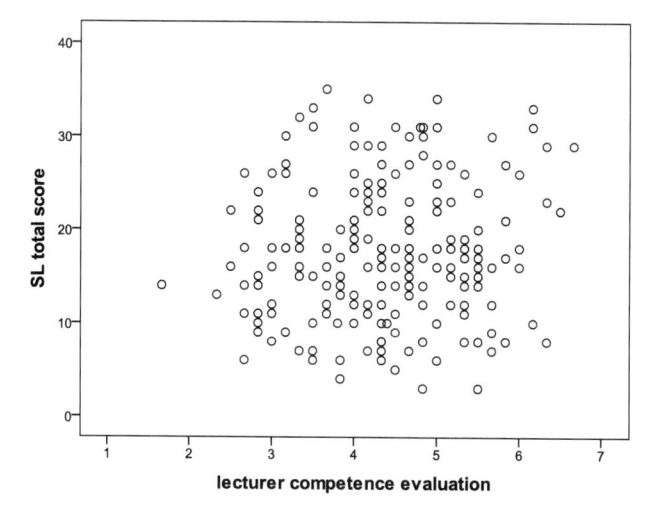

Figure 6-10: Relationship between social attractiveness evaluation and SL total score

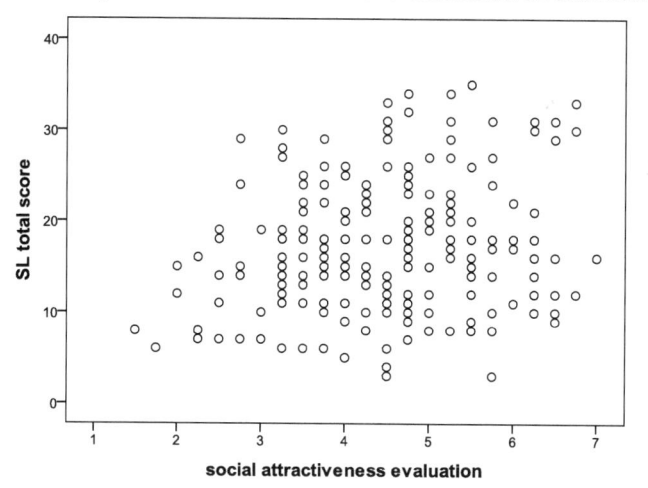

6.8.3 Performance with Jun (Mandarin Chinese accent)

Finally, the initial correlation coefficients for listening performance with Jun and the two speaker evaluation measures revealed a slightly different pattern again. There was a negligible negative correlation between lecturer competence and total score on the Oldest Old test which was not statistically significant [$r =$

-.06, $n = 212$, $p = .356$]. There was a stronger (though still very weak) positive correlation between evaluations of social attractiveness and total score which was significant [$r = .17$, $n = 208$, $p = .016$]. These relationships are illustrated in the scatterplots shown in Figures 6-11 and 6-12.

Figure 6-11: Relationship between lecturer competence evaluation and OO total score

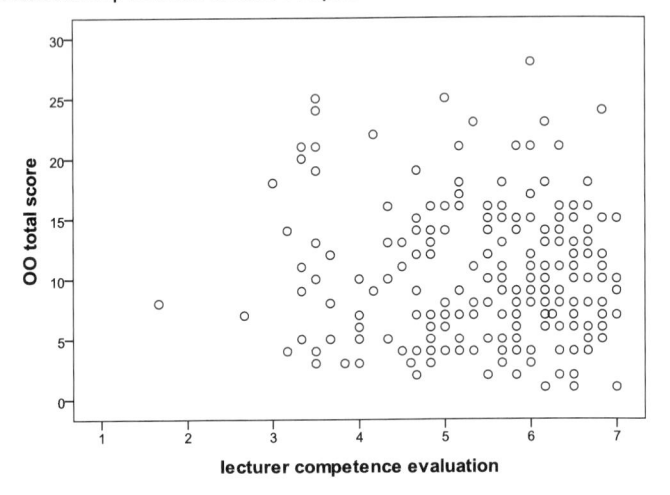

Figure 6-12: Relationship between social attractiveness evaluation and OO total score

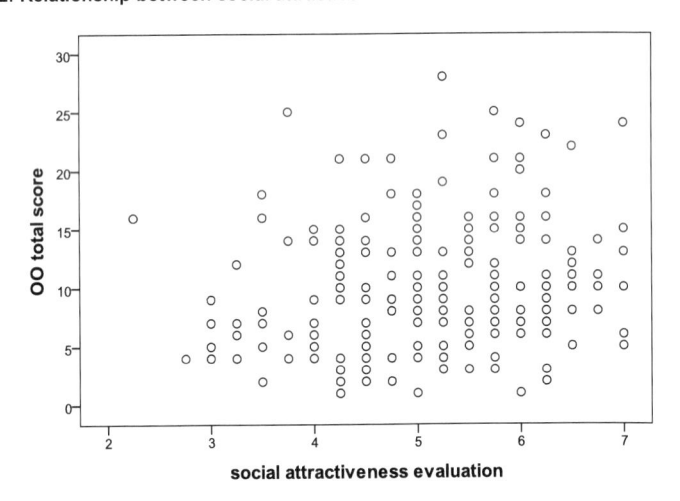

As with the significant finding for Henry, the relationship between evaluations of Jun's social attractiveness and subsequent test score on the Oldest Old was not considered strong enough to warrant further investigation, as it indicated a shared variance of only 2.25%.

6.9 Discussion

This section set out to address two related aims: to gauge the attitudes of test-takers towards the three speakers, and to establish whether attitudes were related to test performance. Each of these is addressed separately in the sections below.

6.9.1 Attitudes and acceptability

This study showed firstly that, on average, L2 listeners held generally positive attitudes towards the speech of Henry, Kaori and Jun on most traits as indicated by the directionality of their averaged ratings on the speaker evaluation task. At first glance, the generally positive attitudes directed towards Kaori and Jun seem at odds with the previous research on attitudes towards L2 accents by L2 listeners which was presented in the literature review. It may have been expected that the listeners would react more negatively to the presence of L2 speech in the same way as those listeners in Dalton-Puffer et al.'s (1997) study, for example. However, the findings do find support in speaker evaluation studies where native speaker raters have viewed an "intelligible foreign accent" positively than an accent characterised as "unintelligible" (e.g., Bresnahan et al., 2002). This may be attributed in part to the nature of the speaker evaluation task itself, which has been found to be subject to information processing effects (see Cargile & Bradac, 2001; Cargile, 2002). In this respect, Cargile (2002) argues that "speaker evaluations should be a reflection not only of evoked information (both individuating and attitudinally-derived), but also of the process that integrates this information into a response" (p.181). Listeners who are less challenged by a speaker's intelligibility may be more inclined to rate them favourably – particularly on those traits related to their linguistic performance.

Secondly, the study showed that evaluations could be reduced to a set of two factors: lecturer competence and social attractiveness. On the lecturer competence factor, it appeared that attitudes towards the three speakers were strongly speaker-determined: there was no interaction between speaker and listeners' L1 background in evaluations of lecturer competence, and listeners from these different groups were remarkably uniform, on average, in their judgments.

Overall, listeners evaluated Henry highest on this factor, followed by Jun and then Kaori. This fit with the common observation that speakers of standard accents tend to be rated more positively on competence or status dimensions than speakers of non-standard varieties (see Giles & Billings, 2004; Ryan, Hewstone & Giles, 1984). An alternative interpretation of this ranking pattern relates to the effect of speaker gender. Previous research has suggested that male speakers are often evaluated more favourably than female speakers on traits such as strength (see Cargile & Bradac, 2001). However this has not always translated to lower ratings for female speakers on competence-type traits. For example, Bayard, Weatherall, Gallois and Pittam (2001) found that an American female voice was rated most highly on power and status dimensions by listeners from New Zealand and America, compared with a range of male and female speakers of other inner-circle varieties.

Irrespective of the bases of speaker rankings, however, the analyses conducted on lecturer competence scores provide further evidence that Kaori and Jun were accepted, on the whole, as competent speakers in this particular context. Both speakers were evaluated, on average, in a positive direction to varying degrees, with a particularly positive appraisal of Jun. This is important to establish, because perceptions of speaker competence have been connected to the "believability" of speakers in the context of listening assessment. In a preliminary study (Harding, 2008), it was found that listeners who perceived speakers as "not competent" – particularly on judgments of their language skills – also lost belief in those speakers in their role as lecturers (see also Markham, 1988).

Analyses conducted on the social attractiveness factor also suggested that listeners, overall, evaluated Jun and Kaori within the positive range. It was also noteworthy that attitudes towards Henry were slightly negative overall. Again, the general pattern of ratings appeared to fit with currently accepted norms in the rating of non-standard accents:

> When [standard and non-standard] speakers are evaluated on traits related to kindness, solidarity, and overall attractiveness, speakers with a non-standard accent often compare much more favorably, sometimes even being rated as more attractive, especially by nonstandard speaking listeners.
>
> (Cargile & Bradac, 2001, p.350)

As with lecturer competence, there is also the possibility that the ranking of speakers indicated more positive reactions towards female voices on the social attractiveness factor. Research on the role of speaker gender in language attitudes has shown that women are often evaluated more highly on aesthetic traits (Mulac, 1998). However the fact that the Japanese L1 and Mandarin Chinese L1 listeners in particular evaluated Kaori and Jun significantly more favourably than they did Henry lends weight to the argument that these generally higher ratings indicate some level of solidarity with fellow speakers of an Asian variety. Although this interpretation does not account for the evaluations of the Other East-Asian L1 group, it does fit with emerging research on the growing acceptance of Japanese accents among Japanese learners (see McKenzie, 2008).

In sum, though, with reference to the first specific aims of the study, the findings of the analyses discussed above provide evidence to support questionable assumption 3, which stated that test-takers would not, overall, hold negative attitudes towards highly-intelligible L2 accented speakers used on an EAP listening test.

6.9.2 Attitudes and test performance

Turning to the second aim, the findings of the second part of the study demonstrated that attitudes towards a speaker were not a strong predictor of an individual's score on a version of the UTESL which was delivered by the same speaker. It may be inferred from this finding that negative attitudes towards a speaker were not related to poor performance on a test featuring that speaker, and inversely that positive attitudes did not engender high levels of comprehension. Thus, this study provides evidence to support questionable assumption 4 which stated that test-taker attitudes towards diverse accented speakers will not affect their performance on a listening test featuring that speaker.

The lack of any substantial results on this question may be explained in two ways. Firstly, apart from Lindemann (2002) and Rubin (1992), there have been very few studies which have addressed the direct impact of attitudes on comprehension. Despite this, the notion that attitudes towards speakers affect listening comprehension appears to have become commonly accepted. For example, the following statement was excerpted from the literature review of Major et al. (2005, p.44): "it is widely known that attitudes toward different varieties influence comprehension: Positive attitudes aid comprehension, while negative attitudes interfere with comprehension." In actuality, the relationship between attitudes to accent and actual comprehension (as opposed to perceived comprehensibility) has not been well established, and therefore should not be expected.

Secondly, although it is reasonable to believe that attitudes have some influence on comprehension in the context of face-to-face conversation (such as has been shown in Lindemann's [2002] work), the context of a simulated language test is an entirely other matter. It is likely that in the simulated trials conducted for this study any negative attitudinal response to a given speaker was tempered by the desire to attend to, and complete, a task. This would be even more pronounced in an authentic testing situation where the motivation to succeed may outweigh concerns about the nature of input. The exception would be when an attitudinal response is so strong that it leads to test anxiety among participants, which then constrains their performance (see Arnold, 2000).

The final point to be made on this issue is a critique of the basis of the questionable assumption itself. The question remains that if attitudes had been shown to affect performance, would this actually be a problem? As argued in Chapter 1, ability to cope with variation can be understood as a form of strategic competence, and is a feature of intercultural communicative competence (Alptekin, 2002). Consider the case of Kaori. It has been demonstrated in Chapter 4 that Kaori was highly intelligible to a range of listeners, and in Chapter 5 that more familiar listeners did not find her substantially more intelligible than less familiar listeners. If a listener held a negative attitude towards Kaori's speech, and this had some deleterious effect on that listener's performance, then the problem may be conceptualised as a lack of sociolinguistic competence or strategic competence on the part of the listener. If the operationalisation of these elements of communicative competence is desirable, then an argument may be advanced that any variance in the listener's test score related to attitudes towards Kaori should be considered construct-*relevant*. This idea will be extended in the final chapter of the book.

6.9.3 Limitations of the approach

The major limitations of the approach taken in this study were acknowledged in the discussion of methodological considerations. It is not defensible to generalise from these findings to make claims about the relative competence or social attractiveness of, say, Japanese-accented speakers based on the results for Kaori. However these findings do provide a useful set of case studies through which previous hypotheses concerning attitudes towards speakers with non-native accents have been tested. In this respect, the study provides evidence that the speech of highly-intelligible speakers with L2 accents does not necessarily evoke negative attitudes in a typical cohort of ESL participants.

On reflection, it is somewhat curious that Kaori was viewed less positively than Jun on both lecturer competence and social attractiveness measures by all listener groups when the test delivered by Jun – The Oldest Old – was shown to contain greater levels of accent-related DIF than the Sleep test. It would logically follow that if Jun's voice was shown to cause more accent-related difficulty for less familiar listeners, then it might have been expected that listeners would have evaluated her less positively than Kaori on the speaker evaluation task, at least on the linguistic traits. This disparity is made clearer when marginal comments given by two test-takers during The Oldest Old are taken into consideration:

Margin comments 1: (Participant 12, L1: Indonesian)

> **Position:** End of Section A
>   *"not clear Chinese pronunciation, maybe"*
> **Position:** End of Section B
>   *"very unclear!"*
> **Position:** Next to Section D
>   *"oh please too unclear and fast"*

Margin comments 2: (Participant 69, L1: Korean)

> **Position:** Next to Section A
>   *Chinese speaker ... don't use her ever, ever!*

These comments suggest that attitudes towards speakers which are activated in the specific context of a listening test may be different in nature from those elicited during a speaker evaluation task. It is possible that, in a testing situation, reactions to speakers may be only partly a function of attitudes towards a particular variety, but also partly related to the extent to which task demands have increased as the result of an unfamiliar accent. Thus the results of this study may only tell part of the story of listeners' attitudes towards speakers in a listening test. The issue of online attitudinal response towards speakers will be explored in more detail in the next chapter.

Chapter 7: Verbal reports

This chapter presents the findings of a study in which participants from Mandarin Chinese and Japanese L1 backgrounds provided introspective verbal reports while completing the Japanese-accent UTESL and the Mandarin Chinese-accent UTESL. The chapter is divided into eight sections. In section 7.1, a set of research questions deigned to triangulate and expand upon the findings of studies one and two is presented. Section 7.2 provides an overview of verbal report methods, and discusses the approach taken in the current study. Section 7.3 then describes the methods used in the study. Section 7.4 discusses the initial analysis of data, including a description of coding and an overview of the data. Section 7.5 presents a qualitative analysis of data which demonstrate the nature of accent-related difficulty for listeners. Section 7.6 presents a qualitative analysis of data which demonstrate the nature of attitudinal response to accent during a listening test. Section 7.7 presents an analysis and discussion of test-takers' post hoc comments. Finally, section 7.8 summarises the main findings of the study.

7.1 Research questions

This study was designed to triangulate the findings of the two preceding studies through qualitative methods. Thus, guided by the overarching concerns of differential performance and attitudes, and informed by the results of the studies presented in Chapters 5 and 6, a set of research questions was posed:

Research Question 1:
- a) To what extent do test-takers experience accent-related difficulty while completing the Sleep test and the Oldest Old test?
- b) To what extent is accent-related difficulty more pronounced for non-shared-L1 listeners in each case?
- c) What is the nature of accent-related difficulty experienced by test-takers?
- d) What strategies do test-takers use to deal with accent-related difficulty?

Research Question 2:
- a) To what extent do test-takers express attitudinal responses to Kaori and Jun while completing the Sleep test and the Oldest Old test?
- b) What is the nature of these attitudinal responses?
- c) To what extent do negative evaluations appear to affect listening performance?

Research Question 3:
In their *post hoc* comments:
  a) How do test-takers retrospectively identify Jun's and Kaori's accents?
  b) How do test-takers evaluate the general fairness and acceptability of using speakers with L2 accents in listening assessment?

Throughout this chapter, findings associated with these research questions will be compared and contrasted with findings from study one and study two in an overarching convergence approach.

7.2 Methodological considerations

7.2.1 An overview of verbal report methods

According to Gass and Mackey (2000) verbal reporting may be broadly defined as "gathering data by asking individuals to vocalise what is going through their minds as they are solving a problem or performing a task" (2000, p.13). As a type of introspective method, verbal reports have been used over the past century within the field of psychology, although always with some degree of controversy. Faerch & Kasper (1987) describe the turn away from introspective methods during the behaviourist era, and their gradual re-embrace as interest in cognitivism grew in the latter part of the twentieth century. However, it was not until Ericsson and Simon's (1984; 1993) landmark text *Protocol Analysis* that the verbal report method received a robust theoretical framework – rooted in the information processing paradigm. This growing acceptance of verbal reports as a legitimate methodology has also seen their emergence as a method of investigation in the field of second language acquisition (see Gass & Mackey, 2000).

Although they have been used more widely to investigate other language skills, verbal reports have been utilized in a small but diverse range of studies related to second-language listening. Some of the features of listening which have been investigated include: strategy use (e.g., Goh, 1998; O'Malley, Chamot & Kupper, 1989; Vandergrift, 2003), the nature of listening difficulty (e.g. Goh, 2000), and the utilisation of visual information in video texts (e.g., Gruba, 1999; Ockey, 2007; Wagner, 2008). Verbal reports are also increasingly being used in language testing research (see Green, 1998; Lumley & Brown, 2005). In her monograph on the particular application of the method in test contexts, Green (1998) suggests that verbal reports may be used to address validation questions such as "do two different versions of the same test measure the same skills?", and "does the content of a particular item effect performance?". Within the testing field, two prominent studies have drawn on verbal report methods to investigate the processes of test-takers on listening assessment tasks: Buck (1990)[24] and Wu (1998).

Within the literature, the label "verbal report" provides an umbrella term for a number of differing approaches, all with differing theoretical assumptions. The most exhaustive treatment of this method is provided by Ericsson and Simon (1993), who proceed from the notion that "cognitive processes could be described as sequences of heeded information and cognitive structures" (p.372), and that verbal reports correspond to this heeded information. Ericsson and Simon draw a clear distinction between "concurrent" verbal reports and "retrospective" verbal reports. Concurrent reports involve a participant "talking-" or "thinking-aloud" as they complete a task, whereas retrospective reports involve the participant recollecting their thought processes after completing a task. Concurrent are considered the purest type of verbal reports as they elicit information heeded which is stored in short-term memory. By contrast retrospective verbal are seen as less reliable, and Ericsson and Simon (1993) recommend that concurrent verbal reports are preferable to retrospective reports. Yet while it is argued that think-aloud methods have high "veridicality" – that is the verbal report is an accurate reflection of cognitive processes processes – an ongoing issue of validity concerns "reactivity" – the extent to which the method itself affects task performance.

Verbal reports are considered more broadly by Cohen (1987; 1996; 1998) with respect to their use in language research. Cohen (1996) states that the term, "encompasses a variety of measures intended to provide mentalistic data regarding cognitive processing" (p.13). In his own work, primarily investigating strategy use, Cohen classifies verbal reports into three types: self-report, self-observation and self-revelation. Definitions of each category are given below:

Self-report: "Learners' descriptions of what they do, characterized by generalized statements about learning behavior."
Self-observation: "The inspection of specific rather than generalized language behavior, either introspectively, i.e., within 20 seconds of the mental event, or retrospectively."
Self-revelation: "'Think-aloud'" stream-of-consciousness disclosure of thought processes while the information is being attended to."

(Cohen, 1996, p.13)

The chief distinction between the categories of self-observation and self-revelation are that the latter includes only those reports where a learner "thinks aloud" without analysis. By contrast, self-observation necessarily involves some level of analysis of a process, as well as a recollected description of the process.

---

24 See also Buck (1991).

As such, under Cohen's classification, Ericsson and Simon's think-aloud protocols map onto the self-revelation category – as unanalyzed disclosure. However, Cohen (1987) also suggests that in many cases it is very difficult to tell separate the act of "thinking aloud" and the act of "observing behaviour", and that many verbal reports – even those collected concurrently – may contain elements of both.

In many cases, the use of retrospective reports is unavoidable because of the nature of a task. This is the case with listening research, where it is not feasible to concurrently report on cognitive processes as spoken input is being heeded in real-time. All of the listening studies cited above have used retrospective reports of some kind. For example, in Goh's (1998) study of listening comprehension strategies and tactics among ESL learners, the researcher utilized what she labelled an "immediate verbalization" procedure during which she read a passage aloud to a single participant, paused after "each part"[25], and then asked the participant to report how he/she had understood the passage. Goh suggests that with this method, listeners were able to access their short-term memory, and that this provided richer data than a second method used in the study: listening-related diary entries.

One verbal report procedure which has been little used in listening studies is the stimulated recall method. Gass and Mackey have written extensively on stimulated recall as a type of retrospective self-observation (see 2000; 2007; Mackey & Gass, 2005). Like other forms of retrospective verbal reporting, stimulated recalls "are used to explore learners' thought processes or strategies by asking learners to reflect on their thoughts after they have carried out a task" (p.25). What distinguishes stimulated recall from other retrospective verbal report methods is the use of a stimulus or prompt to aid recall. The basis of the method assumes that,

> some tangible (perhaps visual or aural) reminder of an event will stimulate recall of the mental processes in operation during the event itself. In other words, the theoretical foundation for stimulated recall relies on an information-processing approach whereby the use of and access to memory structures is enhanced, if not guaranteed, by a prompt that aids in the recall of information.
> (Gass & Mackey, 2000)

Gass and Mackey (2000) distinguish between three types of stimulated recall: consecutive (immediately after finishing a task); delayed (up to 24 hours after a task) and non-recent (longer than one day). The method is more susceptible to veridicality problems than think-aloud or immediate retrospections, especially as

---

25 Goh (1998) does not indicate the length of each section between pauses, however the passages used were around 250 words in length, and these were divided into "short segments" (p.131).

the distance between the event and the recall increases. However, in their delayed form, they avoid the problem of reactivity.

7.2.2 The use of verbal reports in the current study

The broad aim of this study was to investigate whether test-takers experienced accent-related difficulty or provided attitudinal responses towards speakers while completing the DA-UTESL through verbal reports. The nature of the UTESL meant that certain methods of collecting verbal report data were not feasible. The UTESL is for the most part a note-taking test; almost all tasks require a written response, and test-takers are expected to answer items as they are listening. This constrained the choice of verbal report method to those which were retrospective. However it was necessary to develop a specific procedure for a retrospective verbal report which was workable within the UTESL format, and which elicited data to address the research questions. Because there has been little verbal report research conducted specifically on listening assessment, the two most relevant studies – Buck (1990) and Wu (1998) were initially surveyed to see if methods were transferable to the current context.

The Buck (1990) method

Buck conducted verbal report interviews with nine Japanese university students while they took an English language comprehension test. The VR method used in the Buck study may be described as retrospective self-observation according to Cohen's (1996) criteria. A text was broken into short sections, each with accompanying comprehension questions. The recording was paused after each section, and participants answered the questions. Buck then interviewed the participants using a series of standardised probe questions to prompt introspection. These types of questions included, for example, "how much of this do you feel that you understood in this section" and "why do you think you didn't understand very well?"

Through this procedure, Buck was able to glean information from his participants regarding their processes, strategy use and the nature of their listening difficulty. With specific reference to the aim of this study, Buck claimed that listeners were able to introspect in interesting ways about the "results of decoding", stating that "they usually (but not always) know when their understanding is incomplete and can often identify where it is deficient and what caused the problem ..." (p.169). Buck's method is (perhaps necessarily) susceptible to problems of reactivity given the detailed amounts of introspection that were elicited on very short excerpts of text. However, the method is a useful template in that is was workable in the context of a set of assessment tasks, and it elicited rich and useful information in relation to his research questions.

The Wu (1998) method

Although Wu adhered more closely to the methodology advised by Ericsson and Simon (1993), the data yielded in the study included both self-revelation and self-observation. The test used by Wu involved multiple choice listening tasks. Wu's participants completed the test (including tasks) in a "first pass". Then, in the second pass, test-takers were asked to provide retrospective reports. Wu also used probe questions to explore participants' initial responses; however it is unclear what these particular probe questions were from the paper.

Wu's initial aim seems to have been to collect Level 1 and Level 2 verbalisations. According to Ericsson and Simon (1993), Level 1 and 2 verbalisations are the unanalysed thoughts of the test-takers. Level 3 responses, however, concern specific information, such as "reasons and explanations" (Wu, 1998, p.25). Wu found, however, that Level 3 verbalisations inevitably arose in the data. Furthermore, Wu noted that that these types of responses yielded some of the most useful data, stating, "Level 3 verbalizations were especially informative about possible causes of the subjects' comprehension breakdowns". Wu likens this observation to that of Brown (1995, p.42) who has noted that, "we can learn rather little about the processes of comprehension when they flow comfortably . . . We have an opportunity of learning rather more where understanding is difficult to come by, where interpretation is only partially achieved, or where an attempt to communicate results in misunderstanding."

The current study

The current study drew on the basic structure of Buck (1990) in that it was most feasible for the test to be broken into sections, and for test-takers to report retrospectively on their responses to test tasks. It also drew on Buck (1990) and Wu (1990) in that it was deemed necessary to elicit Level 3 data – allowing for self-analysis – in order to explore the research questions in sufficient depth. Thus, the study was a retrospective self-observation under Cohen's classification. However the study also utilised the methods proposed by Gass and Mackey (2000) in that the test-taker's written response to an item was used as a stimulus to aid the memory process. In this sense, the method might also be classified as a type of immediate/consecutive recall.

To refine the general approach, two methods were pre-piloted with one second language listener. In the first method – trialled with the Oldest Old test – the recording was paused at the end of each of the existing four sections of the test. The listener was then asked to report on what they had been thinking while answering each of the items in that section, with recall stimulated by the direction to look back at their answer for each particular question. This method elicited some useful data, but was somewhat unwieldy for Section C of the test, which is quite long. Although this method lessened the problem of reactivity, it may have compromised the veridicality of recalled processes. However the trial participant reported that she felt it was not particularly challenging to recall her thoughts for each question.

The second method – trialled with the Sleep test – involved breaking each section of the test into even smaller "chunks" of roughly equal length. For example, Section A of the Sleep test was broken into four sub-sections, section B into three sub-sections and so on. The same stimulated recall procedure as before was followed with the participant instructed to recall what they were thinking while they were answering the question. Because the test-taker was required to report on fewer items during each pause in the recording, this technique proved to be more manageable than the previous method. The reports were performed closer in time to the listening "event", and each series of reports was not especially time-consuming. This second method was judged as easy to use by the trial participant, and appeared to elicit more detailed data for each item on recalled processes, strategies and comprehension difficulties. The trial participant also appeared keen to express general comments on the test – and occasionally the speaker – during these pauses. On observing this, it was felt that allowing scope for the expression of "general comments" throughout the procedure would provide more opportunity to elicit data on the research questions of interest in this study – particularly the expression of "online" attitudes towards speakers.

Based on this pre-pilot, an approach was decided on for use in the main study. This approach involved breaking each section into manageable subsections for the purposes of stimulated recall. A more detailed description of how each test was modified is provided in the methods section below. In addition, a uniform series of points at which general comments would be elicited was devised. These points were at the end of each of the four main sections, and during the first pause (after verbal reports had been completed). The rationale behind asking for general comments at the first pause was to elicit any first impressions test-takers may have developed in the first 1 – 2 minutes of the test. A flow chart of the approach is shown in Figure 7-1 below.

Figure 7-1: Verbal report procedure

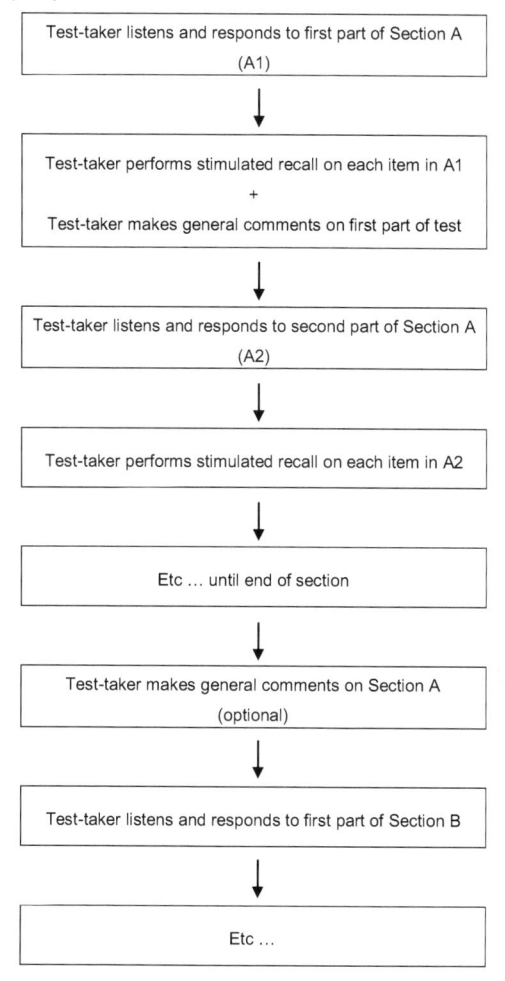

```
┌─────────────────────────────────────────────────────────┐
│ Test-taker listens and responds to first part of Section A │
│                        (A1)                              │
└─────────────────────────────────────────────────────────┘
                            ↓
┌─────────────────────────────────────────────────────────┐
│ Test-taker performs stimulated recall on each item in A1 │
│                         +                                │
│ Test-taker makes general comments on first part of test  │
└─────────────────────────────────────────────────────────┘
                            ↓
┌─────────────────────────────────────────────────────────┐
│ Test-taker listens and responds to second part of Section A │
│                        (A2)                              │
└─────────────────────────────────────────────────────────┘
                            ↓
┌─────────────────────────────────────────────────────────┐
│ Test-taker performs stimulated recall on each item in A2 │
└─────────────────────────────────────────────────────────┘
                            ↓
┌─────────────────────────────────────────────────────────┐
│                 Etc … until end of section               │
└─────────────────────────────────────────────────────────┘
                            ↓
┌─────────────────────────────────────────────────────────┐
│       Test-taker makes general comments on Section A     │
│                      (optional)                          │
└─────────────────────────────────────────────────────────┘
                            ↓
┌─────────────────────────────────────────────────────────┐
│ Test-taker listens and responds to first part of Section B │
└─────────────────────────────────────────────────────────┘
                            ↓
┌─────────────────────────────────────────────────────────┐
│                         Etc …                            │
└─────────────────────────────────────────────────────────┘
```

The final methodological issue to be determined was the nature of the probe questions. It was decided – following Buck (1990) – that probe questions would be standardized. Test-takers would first be oriented towards a particular item with the question "what answer did you have for question (…)?" in order to stimulate recall for a particular listening episode. Following this, the primary recall question would be "what were you thinking while you were answering that question?" In addition to these two core questions, a range of possible follow-up probe questions were devised to encourage test-takers to talk more freely about their listening experience, including "how did you arrive at that answer?" "How did you approach the question?" "What difficulty did you experience?" and "What do you recall hearing?" among others. These questions were trialled together with the verbal reports procedure with two Mandarin Chinese L1 speakers. During these trials, the range of questions were assessed by the researcher for how well they were understood by the listener, and they consistency with which they elicited a targeted issue. It was found that each trial participant elaborated quite well on the initial recall question "what were you thinking …?". However it was also found that various follow-up probes worked better than others. It was also noted that participants were quite adept in reflecting at length on the reasons for their own difficulty with a given task. The final set of standardised questions is presented below:

- **Orientation to stimulus**
    - What answer did you have for question (__)?
- **Core recall question**
    - What were you thinking when you answered question (__)?
- **Probes**
    - Did you have any difficulty answering question (__)?
    - (If so) what particular difficulty did you have?
    - Could you explain a bit more about x ?
    - Could you talk a bit more about x ?
    - How did you arrive at that answer?

A further question was devised for the general comments sections, which occurred in the first pause, and then at the end of each of the four major sections:

- Do you have any general comments at this point in the test?

7.3 Methods

7.3.1 Participants

Eight participants were selected for the study: four from a Japanese L1 background, and four from a Mandarin Chinese L1 background. Seven of the participants were females drawn from the same first-year tertiary course (Nursing) at a university in Australia. The eighth participant was a male who had also had experience in the health sector, and was engaged in tertiary study in the field of hospitality. These particular participants were selected for a number of reasons. Firstly, based on their common situations, it was estimated that their level of English proficiency would at least be above, and very probably still near, a threshold proficiency required to be able to enter a bachelor degree program (IELTS 6.0 or 6.5). Further, this threshold proficiency is also the equivalent level of most students who are required to take UTESL, so these participants – regardless of any individual variations in their proficiency – could be considered typical of the test-taking population. Also, given that the verbal reports and interviews were conducted in English, it was considered important to use students with suitably high levels of proficiency. It was also believed that in selecting participants from the same academic background, they would have similar levels of background knowledge on each the topics (which are in the general health field). Brief profiles[26] of each listener are given below:

Japanese L1 participants

Mana

Mana (22) was from Chiba prefecture. She had studied English throughout junior high school and high school exclusively with Japanese teachers. On arriving in Australia she studied English intensively for five months in an ELICOS (English Language Intensive Course for Overseas Students) program before taking an IELTS test and enrolling in a nursing diploma program. This one year diploma provided a direct pathway into the Bachelor of Nursing. Mana reported that she spent most of her time in Australia with people from Japanese, Chinese, Korean and Australian backgrounds. She also added that she spent time occasionally with South American, French, German and Italian people, indicating a good level of general experience with diverse accents.

Takahiro

Takahiro (36) was the only male in the group. He was from Kyoto, and had been living in Australia for four years at the time of data collection. In Japan he had studied Danish (which he reported that he speaks fluently), and had worked in various labouring and sales roles. After arriving in Australia, Takahiro studied English for a number of months, during which time he sat IELTS. He went on to complete a diploma course in remedial massage at a Technical and Further Education (TAFE) college, and at the time of the interview was enrolled in a commercial cookery course, also at a TAFE college. In terms of experience with different accents, Takahiro reported that he spent most of his time in Australia with people from Japanese and Indian backgrounds, and that he also has a very good friend who is Chilean.

---

26 This information was derived from responses to the modified language experience questionnaire, as well as in a follow-up interview after the data collection session (see 7.3.3).

Akiko

Akiko (29) was from the Kansai region of Japan where she had previously worked as an administrator at a construction company. In Japan she had been primarily exposed to American and Japanese accents in her English classes. Akiko had had considerable test taking experience; during her time in Japan she had sat for TOEIC, TOEFL and IELTS. Having gained a sufficient score, she entered a diploma course in Australia from which she had recently progressed into a Bachelor of Nursing. Akiko reported that the people she spent most time with in Australia were from Korean, Japanese, Taiwanese and Malaysian backgrounds.

Tomoko

Tomoko (22) was from Sapporo, Hokkaido. In Japan, Tomoko had experienced a wide range of inner-circle varieties among her English teachers – American, Australian, British, Canadian and New Zealand – as well as Japanese accents. While still in Japan, Tomoko had taken the TOEFL. At the time of data collection she had been living in Australia for three years. Upon first arriving, Tomoko had entered a three month ELICOS program, after which she entered a foundation course in nursing. From here she had progressed into the Bachelor of Nursing. Tomoko circle of friends in Australia consisted of a diverse group of nationalities, including people from Japan, Malaysia, Vietnam, Thailand, Korea and Taiwan.

Mandarin Chinese L1 participants

Wai

Wai (21) was from Shanghai, and had studied exclusively with Chinese English teachers before coming to Australia. At the time of data collection Wai had been living in Australia for three-and-a-half years. She had taken a different pathway into her current course of study from the cases presented so far, having arrived in Australia when she was only seventeen. Wai enrolled in an English language course for six months before entering an Australian high school for two years. She then progressed into a Bachelor of Nursing. Because of this experience, Wai did not have any prior experience with tests of academic English. Wai reported that most of her friends were Chinese, but her boyfriend was Australian.

Ying

Ying (23) was also from Shanghai. She had studied English in China with both Chinese and Canadian teachers, and on finishing high-school took an IELTS test on which she gained a score (above IELTS 5.5). This was sufficient for Ying to be accepted into the diploma of nursing course in Australia. From the diploma,

Ying progressed into the Bachelor of Nursing degree at the same university. At the time of data collection, Ying had been living in Australia for two-and-a-half years, and reported that she spent most of her time with other students from a Chinese background.

Li

Li (25), too, was from Shanghai, and had been living in Australia for 2 years. In China, Li had learned English from Chinese and British teachers. She took an IELTS exam in China and was accepted into the diploma of nursing at a university in Australia. Like Ying, Li followed a pathway from nursing diploma into the Bachelor of Nursing degree. Li reported that her friends and roommates in Australia were Chinese, but that she had considerable contact with teachers and classmates with an Australian English-speaking background. Li also worked part-time in an aged care facility, and so had contact with Australian English-speaking colleagues.

Xiao

Xiao (29) was from Henan Province in China where she had previously worked as a maths teacher in a primary school. In China Xiao learned English exclusively from Chinese teachers, and sat an IELTS exam. At the time of data collection she had been living in Australia for three years. She had gained an English qualification by completing the final year of an Australian high-school certificate (as a mature student), and had then enrolled in a Bachelor of Nursing. Like Li, Xiao worked part-time in nursing home. She reported that her interaction with different nationalities in Australia was "half-half", stating that she spends half of her time "with Australians and people from other countries" and half "with Chinese people."

7.3.2 Instruments

The instruments used in study two were the same as those used in study one: the DA-UTESL and the Language Experience Questionnaire. However modifications were made to both instruments given the different requirements of the second study.

Modifications to the DA-UTESL

Participants in the second study were presented with only two of the three tests in the original DA-UTESL: Sleep (Japanese accented speaker) and the Oldest Old (Mandarin Chinese accented speaker). The decision not to include the Food Technology test (Australian English accented speaker) was made because the focus of this part of the study was on listeners' experiences with their own, familiar accent, and with another, potentially unfamiliar. To include the Food Technology test would not have helped to address this aim, and would have extended the length of the verbal report sessions to an unreasonable level of three hours.

The recordings for Sleep and the Oldest Old were re-edited with a series of ten-second pauses, preceded by tones, inserted at regular intervals within each of the four sections. These tones served a dual purpose; they indicated to the listener that they should finish writing their answer and prepare to report, and also signalled to the researcher the point at which the CD should be paused. The ten-second pause in the recording was designed to provide the researcher with ample time to pause the CD. The decision of where to insert pauses within sections on each of the tests was guided by two principles: that no sub-section be longer than two-minutes in length; and that pauses come at a natural break in the discourse. Following this procedure, the Sleep test was divided into fourteen subsections, and the Oldest Old test was divided into twelve subsections.

Modifications to the Language Experience Questionnaire

The Language Experience Questionnaire was shortened for the case study investigation; only section one was used. The principle rationale behind abridging the questionnaire was to shorten the length of the data collection session (which was already two-hours long). Also, the small number of participants allowed scope for the researcher to ask a range of follow-up questions, in the period following the data collection session, on participants' experience with accents in language learning and social settings. Thus the same information elicited in the long-form questionnaire was attained through direct correspondence with participants.

7.3.3 Procedure

The verbal report interviews were conducted with each of the eight participants in one-on-one sessions between October and December 2007. Each interview was conducted in a quiet room which contained a CD player and a lap-top computer with a connected USB microphone (set up to record through Audacity). Each session followed the same format:

Step 1

Consent was first gained from all participants in accordance with the University of Melbourne Human Research Ethics guidelines, which stipulates that participants receive a plain language statement and sign a consent form before they can take part in a project.

Step 2

Participants were given a brief outline of the session, based on the following pre-amble:

> Over the next two hours, you are going to take two English language listening tests. Please try to complete each test to the best of your ability.
>
> You will hear all of the instructions for each test on the CD recording. Please follow all of these instructions carefully.
>
> At regular points during the test, I'm going to pause the CD and ask you some questions about your experience on the section of the test you just completed. The black dots next to the questions on the answer paper indicate where each section will be broken by a pause. You will hear a short beep, after which I will pause the CD, and you should finish what you are writing (if you are still writing).
>
> I will then ask you some questions about your listening experience during that sub-section. Please talk as much as you can. I will not converse with you, but I might ask some follow-up questions.
>
> As you talk during these breaks, I will be recording your voice. This recording is for research purposes, and no-one else will hear this recording except me.

During this introduction, participants were free to ask clarification questions. Participants did not complete any specific training task, because, as Gruba (1999) found, this may have led to confusion, and may have been counter-productive in trying to get participants to relax in order to introspect freely. Given that the verbal reports were stimulated, and that specific probe questions were used, it was felt that enough structure was provided in procedure itself that participants would not feel "lost" in any way. This was supported by the trials (previously mentioned) where the participants were able to introspect readily.

Step 3

The CD was played, and participants completed the test. During pauses, the test-taker was asked the standardised questions and probes (or closely matching alternatives) which were presented in 7.2.2.

Step 4

After both tests had been administered according to Step 3, participants were asked to the following discussion questions:

- Could you identify the accents of each of the speakers you heard?
- Do you have any comments on the use of accented speakers on a listening test?

Step 5
Following the post-hoc interview, participants were asked to complete the modified language experience questionnaire.

Step 6
Participants were given the opportunity to ask any questions about the research, and were given a short debrief on the aims of the research and the way in which their data was to be used. Participants were also invited to request their test scores tests at a later date once their papers had been marked. Participants also received payment for their participation.

7.4 Initial analysis

7.4.1 Coding
Participants' verbal reports on each test were transcribed and initially analysed for instances where listeners oriented towards the speaker in a general sense, and more specifically towards the speaker's pronunciation or accent. This process was aided by observational notes taken during the verbal report procedure, which flagged instances where listeners had made reference to the speaker's pronunciation or accent in any way. The instances which were identified in the data were considered "speaker, pronunciation or accent-related episodes" (SPAREs). Guided by the aims of the study, the SPAREs were further subdivided in the following manner:

I. Instances relating to accent-related difficulty
- Explicit mention of listening difficulty related to speaker's accent or pronunciation
- Explicit mention of listening ease related to speaker's accent or pronunciation

II. Instances relating to test-taker attitudes towards speaker
- Negative evaluative or affective response towards a speaker
- Positive evaluative or affective response towards a speaker

Further instances stood out in the data, however, where listeners had not made any explicit mention of speaker, pronunciation or accent, but where it appeared that an incorrect response on an item was the result of an intelligibility-related difficulty. These were also considered in the analysis, and classified as "apparent intelligibility-related difficulty" (AIRD).

7.4.2 An overview of the data

Figures 7-2 and 7-3 presented overleaf illustrate the frequency and patterns of different types of SPARE and AIRD on each test by across listener groups. In these tables, each item on the test represents a row, and "GC" refers to the uniform points at which "general comments" were sought from test-takers. SPAREs and AIRD are indicated with the following symbols:

✗	Explicit mention of listening difficulty related to speaker's accent or pronunciation
✓	Explicit mention of listening ease related to speaker's accent or pronunciation
−	Negative evaluative or affective response towards speaker
+	Positive evaluative or affective response towards speaker
■	Apparent intelligibility-related difficulty

Figure 7-2: SPAREs and AIRD on the Sleep test by listener

	Japanese L1 listeners				Mandarin Chinese L1 listeners			
	Mana	Takahiro	Akiko	Tomoko	Wai	Ying	Li	Xiao
SL1						+		
SL2					— ✗			
GC1							— ✗	
SL3					✗			
SL4								
SL5							✗	
SL6								
SL7								
SL8								
SL9								
SL10								
SL11								
SL12								
SL13								
SL14								
SL15								
SL17								
GC2					—			
SL18								
SL19								
SL20								
SL21								
SL22								
SL23								
SL24								
SL25		✓						
GC3								
SL26								
SL27								
SL28					✗			
SL29								
SL30								
SL31								
SL32								
SL33								
GC4								
SL35					■			
SL36	✗ —							
SL37								
SL38								
GC5							— ✗	

196

Figure 7-3: SPAREs and AIRD on the Oldest Old test by listener

	Japanese L1 listeners				Mandarin Chinese L1 listeners			
	Mana	Takahiro	Akiko	Tomoko	Wai	Ying	Li	Xiao
OO1		■						
OO2								
OO3								
GC1							✗ —	
OO4								
OO5								
GC2					—			
OO6								
OO7								
OO8								
OO9								
OO10								
OO11								
OO12	✗							
OO13								
OO14								
GC3								
OO15		■	✗					
OO16								
OO17						■		
OO18								
OO19								
OO20								
OO21								
OO22							■	
OO23		✗						
OO24								
OO25	■			■				
OO26		■	✗					
OO27								
GC4		✗						
OO28					— ✗			
OO29								
OO30								
OO31								
GC5					—			

The Sleep test (Kaori)

Regarding the Sleep test (featuring Kaori), the data suggest that the participants overall did not experience regular accented-related difficulty while listening to Kaori. Instances across all items were sparse, and for three of the eight listeners there were no reports of accent-related difficulty in the data. Nevertheless, of the instances that were observed, the patterns suggest that across this small sample accent-related difficulty with Kaori was more pronounced in the responses of the Mandarin Chinese L1 listeners. Among the Japanese L1 listeners, only Mana provided an instance of accent-related difficulty in her verbal report data, while Takahiro provided a report of listening ease related to Kaori's accent. On the other hand, there were six sites within the Mandarin Chinese L1 listeners' data where participants expressed explicit difficulty with Kaori's accent or pronunciation, and one site of apparent intelligibility-related difficulty. These sites of difficulty, however, were limited to the data of Wai and Li.

The pattern was somewhat similar for instances relating to test-taker attitudes towards Kaori. Examples in the data were limited, and for the Japanese L1 participants, only Mana expressed a negative response to Kaori's speech. As with the data on difficulty, only Wai and Li expressed negative attitudes towards Kaori. However Ying was the only listener to have an overtly positive reaction to Kaori in her responses during the test.

The Oldest Old test (Jun)

On the Oldest Old test (featuring Jun), there were slightly more SPAREs and AIRDs in the data, although it was still relatively sparse. Again, though, the patterns in the data appeared broadly to fit the findings of study one. Japanese L1 listeners reported five instances in which Jun's accent or pronunciation was explicitly linked to listening difficulty. Furthermore, there were five instances of apparent intelligibility-related difficulty in their data. Although these were spread across all Japanese L1 listeners, it appeared that Takahiro in particular experienced accent-related difficulty with Jun more regularly than other listeners. The Mandarin Chinese L1 listeners, by contrast, seemed to have struggled less with Jun. Only Wai and Li directly connected pronunciation and listening difficulty in one of their comments. Two sites of apparent intelligibility-related difficulty were observed in Li and Ying's data. It is worth noting that Xiao appeared to be unaffected by the accent of either Kaori or Jun, again reporting no instances of difficulty.

Interestingly, although they appeared to experience greater levels of accent-related difficulty on the Oldest Old, there were no attitudinal responses towards Jun in the data of the Japanese L1 listeners. As with the Sleep test, only Wai and Li responded negatively to Jun's speech. This suggests that these particular listeners may have held negative attitudes towards L2 speech more generally. This notion will be explored in more detail below.

The next two sections will present the data elicited through verbal reports in a more detailed qualitative analysis. Firstly, the findings presented above regarding accent-related difficulty will be analysed further in an effort to establish the nature of accent-related difficulty experienced by test-takers. Secondly, the attitudinal responses expressed in the verbal reports will also be analysed further, and the relationship between negative attitudes and test performance will be explored.

7.5 The nature of accent-related difficulty

A qualitative analysis of the content of verbal report data revealed two types of accent- or intelligibility-related difficulty experienced by test-takers:

1. Misperception/inability to recognise key phonetic information
2. Difficulty in processing speech efficiently

In most cases, these types of reported difficulty were connected by listeners to the effect listening to an "unfamiliar" accent, even when reported by shared-L1 listeners. Each difficulty type is elaborated on below:

7.5.1 Misperception/inability to recognise key phonetic information

Across the verbal report data the clearest source of accent- or intelligibility-related difficulty was the misperception of, or inability to recognise, the key phonetic information required to answer test items ("necessary information" according to Buck and Tatsuoka [1998]). A useful example is Takahiro's report on item 26 of the Oldest Old test, where he appeared to have experienced difficulty at the perceptual level. On this item, the listener is required to complete the sentence "adaptive capacity is the ability to ..." with the phrase "overcome disease (or injury)" (see Appendix H). Excerpt 7-1 shows that Takahiro used the syntactic structure of the prompt to identify that a verb phrase is needed to complete the sentence. However he experiences confusion between what he perceives Jun to have said – "old" – and his knowledge of the appropriate word-form required:

Excerpt 7-1 (TA-OO.26)

Researcher: Okay um ... what answer did you put down?

Takahiro: I just couldn't I missed the verb [overcome] which which comes after "to" ... "t" "o" ... and it sounded like "old" (laughs) that's not a verb so I ... but after the verb she says diseases in um in something but I just lost the key the key the very important key word, the verb so ... mm

Misperceptions on this item were also common in study one – however they were equally common between more and less familiar listeners and so did not show DIF. Jun's utterance contained a labiodental approximant [ʋ] in place of a labiodental fricative [v] resulting in [ˈəʊʋəkʌm]. This led many listeners in the study one to misperceive the first syllable as "old" or "all", and a particularly common answer provided to this question was "all common diseases". In the case of Takahiro, it provides useful evidence of the misperception of necessary information for the answer leading to an incorrect response.

In his report, Takahiro did not explicitly link his listening difficulty to Jun's accent, although later in the test he made a retrospective evaluation of his listening difficulty thus:

Excerpt 7-2 (TA-OO.GC4)

Researcher: All right um any general comments at the end of Section C?

Takahiro: Mm ... I'm I'm getting the idea that ah ... she ... she's got um a bit of accent which I sometimes can't understand

Researcher: Um can you explain a bit more what ah what ... particular trouble might you be having?

Takahiro: Mm ... may(be) no ... it's not only on this question but um ... yeah I'm not really famili(ar), familiar with this kind of accent and ... mm

While Takahiro's example shows clearly how an unfamiliar accent may create difficulties at the perceptual level, data from Mana's verbal reports demonstrates that unfamiliar vocabulary may be a moderating factor. The excerpt below shows Mana's verbal report on item 12 of the Oldest Old test. This question requires the listener to extract and note down two key phrases: "(Boston) centre" and "previous surveys/research" (see Appendix H). Mana did not provide a response to this question, and in her verbal report this is attributed to word recognition difficulty – "she said 'central' something". Mana directly links her struggle to Jun's accent – "her pronunciation I guess" – and suggests that she is not familiar with the variety – "she's not Japanese ... I'm pretty sure". Yet she also raises the key role played by lexical knowledge, and its influence on her ability to deal with the unfamiliar accent:

Excerpt 7-3 (MA-OO.12)

Researcher: Okay if we go back to [item twelve][27] ... um it looks like you might have missed that one

Mana: Yeah

Researcher: Um what were you thinking during that question?

Mana: Um for first blank I thought um she would tell that place ... and with I don't know ... I really don't know with ... but I've never heard of place before ... she said "central" ... something ... so ... I didn't really get where it is

Researcher: So what difficulty do you think you were having there?

Mana: Mm: ... <u>unfamiliar word ... and ... her pronunciation I guess</u> (laughs) ... <u>because she's not ... she's not Japanese I I I'm pretty sure and ... like ... if I'm really familiar with some word I can guess but if I'm not ... I can't guess so ... and also I don't really know the spelling either ... if she's um like if speaker's non-native English speaker</u> so ...

Mana's statement that "if I'm really familiar with a word I can guess but if I'm not ... I can't guess", suggests that accent-related difficulty may be less pronounced when vocabulary is familiar. It seems logical to assume that unfamiliar vocabulary would hinder a test-taker's ability to "guess" an answer when a word is not recognised with some degree of automaticity. Indeed, the relationship between intelligibility and lexical familiarity has been well investigated within speech perception research, and it is generally held that perceptual acuity is partly dependent on whether a listener is hearing a known word (see Flege, Takagi & Mann, 1996).

Mana's comments also suggest that an unfamiliar accent curtails a test-taking strategy used when a word is not immediately recognisable – phonetic transcription. It was hypothesised in study one that, in a note-taking test of this kind, listeners may attempt to transcribe a key word which has not been automatically parsed based on the phonetic information available. In study one, this particular approach seemed to explain the high number of non-words with some phonemic relationship to the uttered word. Mana's suggestion that "I don't know the spelling either ... if speaker's non-native English speaker" alludes to the notion that transcription is made more difficult when the speaker has an unfamiliar accent. These sentiments were repeated in Mana's verbal report data for item 25 of the Oldest Old test – an item which showed strong and substantive DIF in study one (see Figure 5-17). In excerpt 7-4, Mana misperceives Jun's production of "number" as "ramber" (a common response among less familiar listeners in the DIF study):

---

27 Any references in the transcripts to question numbers (as they appeared in participants' answer papers) have been replaced with the corresponding item numbers to avoid confusion.

201

Excerpt 7-4 (MA-OO.25)

Researcher: Okay um what answer did you have there?

Mana: She said "low ramber" something ... but I don't know what this mean

Researcher: What were you thinking ah when you were listening?

Mana: Ah before I listened to this I was thinking probably this "E4" um represent sort of gene so I thought she will talk about gene mm yeah that's it

Researcher: Okay and ah what difficulty if any do you think you had there?

Mana: Mm: because um this answer I don't know what this, what that is so ... I'm not really sure and I don't know the spelling either

Mana's final comments suggest two types of difficulty resulting from her initial misperception. Firstly, she could not parse the word, evidenced by her comment, "because um this answer I don't know what this, what this is". Secondly, Mana seems to suggest that she also could not perceive the sounds well enough to transcribe what she heard – "and I don't know the spelling either". These examples are, to a certain extent, an indictment on the UTESL, which over-emphasises task types which target listening for specific details. They also help to explain the listening processes at work in the non-word responses in study one which can be understood as phonetic transcriptions.

Activating top-down knowledge

It was not always the case that a listener's inability to recognise words from the available phonetic information due to an unfamiliar accent led to a communication breakdown. There was evidence in the data that listeners drew on top-down knowledge to compensate, in a manner which would fit the principles of an interactive-compensatory mechanism (Stanovich, 1980). A clear example of this is found in Takahiro's report on item 23 of the Oldest Old test. This item – which concerned recognition of the term "environmental" (see Figure 5-16) – showed large statistical DIF in study one, and was demonstrated to be substantively related to differential intelligibility between more and less familiar listeners through an analysis of responses. Although Takahiro managed to arrive at the correct answer, he demonstrates in his verbal report that he was forced to use top-down contextual knowledge to assist in decoding Jun's pronunciation of the key term:

Excerpt 7-5 (TA-OO.23)

Researcher: All right let's go back to the first ah answer you had there ...

Takahiro: Ah "environmental factors"

Researcher: Okay what were you thinking while you were answering that one?

Takahiro: Mm ... the, I thought that was a totally different word, j(ust) it sounded totally different to "environmental" ... she has, I think she have has a bit of accent from I don't know where so: ...

Researcher: What led you to that answer?

Takahiro: Um because of the cons, in context um ... I just guessed and browsed my very thin dictionary[28] (laughs) and I thought this is the answer I should put mm

Takahiro's strategy on this item could be classified under Goh's (1998) taxonomy of cognitive listening strategies as "inferencing". Goh (1998) suggests that listeners may "fill in missing information such as ... parts of the text that they cannot hear clearly" using "context, key words, knowledge about the world, knowledge about English, and speaker's body language and visual aids" (pp.133-134). Although this instance suggests that accent-related difficulty at the perceptual level may be overcome through the activation of higher order listening skills, it also highlights that listeners may arrive at a correct answer through very different methods. Where a highly familiar listener may have been untroubled by Jun's pronunciation on this item and parsed the speech with a high degree of automaticity (as many of the more familiar listeners in study one were able to do), Takahiro relied on a different set of listening skills and strategies to overcome his unfamiliarity with the speaker's accent. This has implications for construct validity; which will be addressed further in the discussion below.

However the activation of top-down knowledge was not always a successful strategy for listeners. Excerpt 7-6 shows Akiko's report on item 15 of the Oldest Old test, a short answer question which requires the listener to note down the term "selective survival" (see Appendix H). In her report, Akiko explicitly relates her difficulty on this item to Jun's pronunciation of the key information, the first word of which ("selective") is realised in the recording as [sɪnektɪv]. She then describes her rationale for "guessing" that the uttered term was "synthetic":

Excerpt 7-6 (AK-OO.15)

Researcher: Okay um question twelve what answer did you write down there?

Akiko: "Synthetic survival"?

Researcher: Okay and what were you thinking while you were answering that one?

Akiko: Mm try to remember the sound she said before the ... similar expression

Researcher: Okay what do you, do you know the meaning of that ah particular expression?

---

28 Participants did not have access to dictionaries during the tests. Takahiro is here making reference, in a metaphorical sense, to his mental lexicon.

Akiko:	Mm actually I couldn't catch up the: ... her pronunciation "synthetic" but ... I know what "synthetic" means ... but I couldn't catch up the "survival" so ... I was just guessing
Researcher:	Okay
Akiko:	"Synthetic" ... "synthetic" is not original just ah producing isn't it ... so, so maybe because the human getting older they try to be fit fit fit, so "synthetic" ... so ...

Akiko clearly based her guess on some of the phonetic information provided in Jun's utterance; "synthetic" is a close phonemic match of [sɪnektɪv]. However she also appears to have based her guess on the broader context of the lecture: "'synthetic' is not original just ... producing ... maybe because the human getting old they try to be fit ... so 'synthetic'". It is not clear precisely how Akiko perceives the term "synthetic" as fitting the context, other than through a broad link between the concept of "producing" and of older people "getting fit". However Akiko seems aware of this lack of fit when she states earlier, "her pronunciation 'synthetic' but ... I know what 'synthetic' means". This example, then, clearly shows the utilisation of erroneous top-down reasoning because of initial difficulty at the perceptual level.

Akiko applied a similar strategy in her response to item 26 of the Oldest Old test (see Appendix H). Like Takahiro's report on this same item discussed above, Akiko experienced difficulty in decoding Jun's pronunciation of the word "overcome", and she directly attributes this difficulty to Jun's accent. Akiko uses the compensatory strategy of guessing based on context to arrive at an answer:

Excerpt 7-7 (AK-OO.26)

Researcher:	Um what did you have for number one there?
Akiko:	It's "protect body and stop disease process by naturally"
Researcher:	All right what were you thinking while you were answering that question?
Akiko:	Uh I couldn't catch up her: ... she clearly mentioned the one word but I couldn't catch up ... be accent?
Researcher:	What uh could you explain a bit more?
Akiko:	Mm ... adaptive capacity is the ability to "blah blah" but I really can't catch up the sound ... so but I can guess ... mm mm

However, unlike the previous example ("selective/synthetic") Akiko did not appear to have grasped any useful phonetic information in this instance, as evidenced by her statement "adaptive capacity is the ability to "blah blah" but I really can't catch up the sound". As such, her erroneous "guess" of "protect body and stop disease process by naturally" was purely based on knowledge of context, with no "guidance" from information provided at the perceptual level.

Akiko's case also provides evidence that the activation of top-down knowledge in this manner may affect responses on items which immediately follow. The accent-related difficulty Akiko experienced on this item, and her associated use of top-down strategies, appeared to occupy her attention to the detriment of her performance on the next item (OO27):

Excerpt 7-8 (AK-OO.27)

Researcher:	How about number two?
Akiko:	It's "amount of body performance"
Researcher:	And what were you thinking there?
Akiko:	Mm I want to ... <u>I was thinking to question one</u> so although she was giving me the example the brain something I should be, I should be written more longer sentence

The notion of a "flow-on effect" from sites of accent-related difficulty was not directly addressed in study one, but it may have useful implications for the future interpretation of accent-related DIF.

Retrospective correction of a mishearing

The data also demonstrated that a listening test is a site of "dynamic" listening – that is, there is scope for a listener to amend their hypotheses about difficult pronunciations based on their developing understanding of a speaker's phonology throughout the test. One example of this type of phenomenon was the retrospective correction of an initial mishearing in the data of Li's performance on the Oldest Old test. In excerpt 7-9, Li reports on her response to item 22, which required the answer "longevity genes" (see Appendix H). Li mishears Jun's production as "gyms", and is confused by the presence of this word in the context of factors affecting the oldest old:

Excerpt 7-9 (LI-OO.22)

Li:	With this one ah of course we don't know what kind of things we should, we will hear(d) hear so just missed it, <u>just write "gyms" but it's not right? I don't think that's right</u>
Researcher:	What do you recall hearing?
Li:	<u>A just remember "gyms" ... because she say "gyms" I say "how come why why she want to say 'gyms'?" so ... suddenly missed the rest thing</u>

Following this item, however, the term "genes" is spoken again several times in the ensuing text. Once Li was afforded the opportunity to hear Jun's production

205

of "genes" in these further contexts, she was able to retrospectively correct this initial mishearing. This is evidenced by her report item 25 in the next section:

Excerpt 7-10 (LI-OO.25)

Li:	Ah: it's "genes" … I think do some sports like "gyms" (laughs) yeah I find the answer here
Researcher:	Okay …
Li:	So the oldest old have low number of E-4 …
Researcher:	Okay what were you thinking there?
Li:	Mm: this sentence is good, yeah it's remind me again so I can fix the, this one [item 22]

This is an important observation because it provides direct evidence that a test taker's ability to deal with a speaker's pronunciation is not static. Listeners are learning how to cope with speaker accent throughout the test, and may rectify their responses to items where they were not confident of their initial "hearing".

7.5.2 Processing cost

Increased processing time was identified in the literature review as a potential source of difficulty among listeners dealing with an unfamiliar accent (Munro & Derwing, 1995b; Schmid & Yeni-Komshian, 1999), and it was hypothesised that this may have had some impact on item response processes in the findings of study one. The issue of processing time arose in the verbal report data of Li, in relation to her performance with Kaori. In the excerpt below, taken from general comments following the first two questions of the test, Li gives a strong negative evaluation of Kaori's accent before discussing the particular difficulties she believes the accent is causing her in terms of "cost time":

Excerpt 7-11 (LI-SL.GC1)

Researcher:	Okay um any general comments at this point?
Li:	I just don't like the speaker (laughs)
Researcher:	Okay … um can you explain a bit more?
Li:	Yeah because her accent, so just not familiar with the word, it just take me a long uh um maybe a few second to (get) used to it and to think about "oh is that the word?"
Researcher:	Okay …
Li:	Yeah it's just cost time you know … but if we cost time and we can't concentrate on it we just missed the information, it's not good

It is interesting to observe that Li touches closely on processing metaphors in her use of the phrase "cost time". She also provides some insight into the nature of a general sort of "cost time" when she describes her experience of listening to Kaori's accent thus: "it just takes me ... maybe a few seconds to (get) used to it and to think about "oh is that the word?"". Two points are notable about this statement. One is the notion of "adjustment" to an unfamiliar accent; the second is the relationship between this adjustment and the process of word recognition. Li does not seem to suggest that Kaori's accent is less intelligible *per se*, but rather that it requires more effort to cope with the variable, unfamiliar realisation of words. If this effort is not spent, only then will communication break down, as evidenced in Li's statement, "if we cost time and can't concentrate on it we just missed the information". In her own performance, Li obviously was able to maintain this level of concentration because she answered the two preceding items correctly.

Li also alluded to the theme of a listening "lag" and the process of adjustment in her comments at the second pause in the Sleep test. Excerpt 7-12 below shows Li's report for items 3-5 (see Appendix H), in which she was only able to identify two out of three answers:

Excerpt 7-12 (LI-SL.5)

Researcher: Okay ...

Li: Just missed one ... yeah so the first one is "produce energy" and the second one is "wastes produce" and third one ... it's maybe like a "metabolism something" I just can't ... missed it

Researcher: Um what particular difficulty do you think you had there?

Li: Ah actually it's from the beginning when she start, uh just can't (get) used to that accent I just tried to [mimes writing quickly] (laughs) like this ...

Researcher: Okay ...

Li: Actually this part is easy I know it's easy if the local people speak it I can ah write down write down but ... no, not her

Here Li appears to be taxed at a greater level by the demands of the task interacting with Kaori's unfamiliar pronunciation. She firstly claims that she "just can't (get) used to that accent", suggesting that the rapid adaptation to unfamiliar speech found to occur in Clarke and Garrett (2004) has not held in this case. She then suggests that she would not be struggling with the task demands – which require the quick notation of key information – if she were listening to "local people speak it". Thus it seems that a general "cost time" associated with listening to an unfamiliar accent might affect performance more seriously when task demands are cognitively taxing in other respects.

7.5.3 Comments on speaker clarity

There was only one instance in the data where a test-taker directly stated that they found a speaker's manner of speech easy to understand. In relation to items 24 and 25 on the Sleep test, Takahiro explicitly stated that Kaori's "way of speaking is quite clear". In context, though, this appears to have been partly related to his own familiarity with the topic of the lecture:

Excerpt 7-13 (TA-SL.25)

Researcher:	Um [item 25] what what answer did you have?
Takahiro:	Highly active
Researcher:	And [item 26]?
Takahiro:	Um "rapid eye movement"
Researcher:	And what were you thinking through that section?
Takahiro:	Um ... <u>the topic is actually quite familiar to me so ... I could pick up the words easily and also you know her way of speaking is quite clear so, yeah that's easy</u>

Takahiro's comments suggest the idea that familiarity with topic aids intelligibility. Background knowledge may indeed advantage the listener at all levels of processing – both in creating a "cognitive environment" (see Buck, 2001, p.26) of more efficient word recognition, and in providing a richer context from which to make guesses when bottom-up processing is deficient.

7.6 The nature of "online" attitudinal response

7.6.1 Negative evaluations and affective response

Negative evaluations of Kaori and Jun were confined to the verbal reports of three particular participants: Mana, Li and Wai. Within the examples provided by these listeners, three types of negative evaluative and affective response were observed. These were, firstly, judgments of speaker competence – both as an English user and as a professional; secondly, comments on the "normality" of certain pronunciation features; and thirdly, the expression of feelings of "uncomfortableness". Often these three types of response were present in the same instance. For example, in her general comments towards the end of the Sleep test, Li evaluated Kaori in the following manner:

Excerpt 7-14 (LI-SL.GC5)

Researcher:	Any general comments?
Li:	This one is easier than the first one [the Oldest Old] ... yeah <u>but the reader is not good enough</u> (laughs)
Researcher:	Okay okay can you explain a bit more?
Li:	Um just because <u>her pronunciation is very weird</u> so just need yeah try to understand what she is saying then you can gots the information from it ...

In describing Kaori's as "not good enough", Li appears to be suggesting that for the purposes of a lecture she finds Kaori's pronunciation unacceptable. This is explained with the phrase "her pronunciation is very weird", indicating that Kaori's pronunciation is not viewed as normal.

Similar views on Kaori's pronunciation were expressed by Wai in her verbal report at the first pause during the Sleep test. Wai's reponse (shown below) appears to have been "triggered" by accent-related difficulty experienced on item 2. It is notable, however, that Wai describes Kaori's accent with the same term – "weird" – as Li:

Except 7-15 (WA-SL.2)

Researcher:	Okay ... how about question two, what answer did you have there?
Wai:	Um ... the main reason um ... <u>I'm not really specific heard about what she saying I think I lost</u> it um but I think she's talking about body get tired and uh need to sleep
Researcher:	Okay, and what were you thinking while you were answering that question?
Wai:	What I'm thinking ... um ... <u>the accent's really strong</u>
Researcher:	Okay um can you talk a bit more about that?
Wai:	Accent?
Researcher:	Yeah
Wai:	I I <u>I feel it's like a Korean accent</u> ... um and ... yeah: ...
Researcher:	Okay
Wai:	<u>It's weird</u>
Researcher:	Did you have any difficulties with question two?
Wai:	Um <u>I just didn't heard clearly about what she exactly saying</u> the main reason for sleep

Wai's attitudes towards Kaori's pronunciation re-surfaced at the end of Section A of the Sleep test in her general comments on the first section:

Excerpt 7-16 (WA-SL.GC2)

Researcher: Do you have any general comments on that section?

Wai: Um ... still the ... um ... <u>the accent sort of make me feel uncomfortable</u>

Researcher: Okay um: ... can you explain that a bit further? What what aspects of the accent?

Wai: Ah ... sorry what's that?

Researcher: What ah ... what features of the accent or wh[y] why is the accent making you feel uncomfortable?

Wai: Um ... cause it's just um ... it's not very, <u>it's not ver[y] English</u> ... and uh ... yeah it's just like, <u>it just feel like abnormal stuff so you feel it's weird</u> ...

Researcher: Okay, let's continue ...

Wai: Oh and one thing ... um ... like <u>if the accent is a bit weird like those other country's accent make me feel like not very professional like the information she give to me I will not believe like trust her that ... much as some, someone sounds more professional</u> ... cause yeah it makes make much more difference ... I think

These comments are noteworthy for several of reasons. Firstly, Wai frames her reaction as an affective response: "the accent sort of make me feel uncomfortable". However Wai goes further in describing Kaori's speech as "abnormal" and "weird", also stating that "it's not ver[y] English". These statements suggest a high native-speaker orientation in judgments of correctness and acceptability. Of most importance, Wai then links Kaori's L2 accent to negative evaluations of believability, trust and professionalism. This excerpt draws clear links between judgements of competence and professionalism, perceptions of accent "normality", and listener "discomfort".

The excerpts presented above demonstrate that Wai was highly aware of Kaori's accent throughout the Sleep test. She was also very conscious of Jun's accent from the beginning of the Oldest Old test. At the first pause, she correctly identified the Jun's accent variety:

Excerpt 7-17 (WA-OO.GC1)

Researcher: Um: do you have any general comments on that section?

Wai: Um: <u>it's obviously the Chinese speaker's accent</u>

Then in the next pause she describes Jun's accent as "weird":

Excerpt 7-18 (WA-OO.GC2)

Wai: Um ... it's a ... <u>it feel, feel weird that ... like someone speak very strong Chinese accent English ... like you are Chinese and you heard that, it's funny</u>

In contrast to her comments on Kaori, Wai was somewhat milder in her response to Jun. However it is noteworthy that she saw herself as in a unique position because of her L1 background: "like you are Chinese and you heard that, it's funny".

At the very end of the Oldest Old test, Wai evaluated Jun's accent in stronger terms as "really weird" and commented directly on Jun's speaking skill as "not fluent". She also described her own feeling while listening as "very, very uncomfortable":

Excerpt 7-19 (WA-OO.GC5)

Researcher: Right, well before we finish any general comments on that section?

Wai: Ah .. I don't know why like this ... the question from question twenty-one to twenty-two ... I'm, you know some words ... um, I guess the people didn't like not very ... maybe not say them often or anything ... <u>she pronounces really weird like ... just not fluently and I found it's really weird like very very uncomfortable</u> ...

The notion of "uncomfortableness" also appeared in Mana's verbal report data for item 36 of the Sleep test. Excerpt 7-20 shows a clear example of accent-related difficulty triggering a critical appraisal of Kaori's pronunciation: "to be honest, I don't like her English". This then leads Mana to reveal a feeling of "uncomfortableness" which she claims to have experienced from the beginning of the test.

Excerpt 7-20 (MA-SL.36)

Researcher: Okay what about [item 36] uh what answer did you have there?

Mana: Um the one is "driving" ... the second one I don't really get ... I don't know ... she <u>say something something "machinery" ... but ... "using" machine or something</u> ... I don't know

Researcher: What what uh what were you thinking during that section?

Mana: Mm: ... <u>to be honest I don't like her English</u>

Researcher: Okay

Mana: (laughs) um ... <u>like personally I like native English speaker ... so mm ... sounds like uncomfortable</u>

Researcher: Okay

Mana: Mm hm

Researcher: Did you notice uh did this make you feel uncomfortable for the first time now?

Mana: <u>No from beginning</u>

Researcher: Okay ... um ... okay and that particular question ... um what particular difficulty do you think you had there?

211

Mana: Uh: I guess <u>maybe I don't have enough experience listening</u> so ... yeah: I guess that's it

The notion that a negative attitude may be triggered by a particular instance of listening difficulty seems to be supported in several of the examples discussed above. However these excerpts also provide evidence that these expressions were symptomatic of latent negative attitudes towards L2 speech more generally. For example, Mana stated: "personally I like native English speaker", expressing a clear preference for inner-circle pronunciation norms. Wai explicitly linked negative traits with "foreign" varieties: "if the accent is a bit weird like those other country's accent make me feel like not very professional", and linked the description of an accent as "weird" with the identification of the same accent as "like Korean". In this sense, it seems that attitudes towards accent expressed during a listening test are not formed by experience on that listening test, but relate to pre-existing views on the correctness and acceptability of native and non-native speech.

7.6.2 Positive evaluations and acceptability

The only positive attitudinal response within the verbal report data was Ying's appraisal of Kaori. Early in the Sleep test, Ying observed that Kaori's pronunciation was "more similar" compared to Jun's. It is not clear whether Ying means to say that she feels Kaori's accent is more similar to her own, or more *familiar* to her. However, she goes on to correctly identify Kaori's accent (correctly) as an Asian variety:

Excerpt 7-21 (YI-SL.1)

Ying:	The first is "machine"
Researcher:	Okay and ...
Ying:	The second is "continue function"
Researcher:	Okay um the first question, can you recall what you were thinking during that section?
Ying:	Uh not really but <u>I think the lady [Kaori] is, I mean pronunciation more similar for me than compared the first tape lady [Jun]</u>
Researcher:	Okay
Ying:	Yeah
Researcher:	Uh can you explain a bit more about your feelings about her pronunciation?
Ying:	I think ... uh <u>my guess if it's correct I think she's Japanese, more Asia the pronunciation I can be accept more, yeah</u>

In identifying Kaori as a speaker with an Asian – and specifically a Japanese – accent, Ying's comments seem to signal an overt preference for listening to an Asian variety. It was not clear from this excerpt what particular accent she believed Jun to hold. However these comments suggest an element of solidarity in her attitude towards Kaori's pronunciation, and this solidarity is in turn linked to greater acceptability.

7.6.3 Attitude and performance

There were a limited number of instances in the data from which it might be inferred that a negative attitude towards a speaker had affected test performance. All of these instances were found in the data provided by Wai, and all involved the same type of reported issue: being "distracted" by the speaker's accent. It has been demonstrated above that Wai held strong, negative attitudes towards the pronunciation patterns of both speakers. The examples presented here suggest a link between this pre-occupation with correctness and "normality", and her attention to test tasks.

In the first instance, Wai reported being distracted by Kaori's pronunciation early on the Sleep test. In the excerpt below, Wai is reporting on items 3-5 of the Sleep test (see Appendix H). Wai appears to have been distracted by Kaori's pronunciation of the term "growth" in the text surrounding the necessary information:

Excerpt 7-22 (WA-SL.3)

Researcher: What answer did you have, what answers did you have there in [item 3]?

Wai: In the number one um ... cause I was thought she gonna say like number one number two and number three but actually she just talking them through so I I was just um went "pih" [tone on CD sound] so I just write the last one that I remember and I try to remember before one, so at answer one I write there is something um through the skin like um yeah (laughs)

Researcher: Ah okay, and what were you thinking while you were trying to answer that that question?

Wai: Um ... I've heard she saying something like "growth level" or ... yeah I was lost (laughs)

Researcher: Um you say you were lost, what difficulties do you think you had there?

Wai: Um ... cause when I like heard she um speaking I put bit more attention on ... she pronounce "s" instead of "th" so ... it sort of like draw me uh draw my attention on some, somewhere else

This theme of distraction arose again in Wai's verbal reports during the Sleep test. At one point Wai suggested that she might have been adjusting to Kaori's pronunciation:

213

Excerpt 7-23 (WA-SL.GC3)

Wai: Mm: ... I think I get used to her accent

However, in the first part of section C, Wai again reported feeling distracted by Kaori's speech:

Excerpt 7-24 (WA-SL.28)

Wai: Mm ... mm still a bit ... I still a bit like draw my attention on the accent

Wai's comments reflect one of the observations made in Harding (2008) in which L2 listeners reported feelings of distraction when they heard certain features of pronunciation which they felt to be "incorrect" during a lecture. In that study, this phenomenon was most evident among shared-L1 listeners. However, Wai also made similar comments in relation to Jun at one point late in the Oldest Old test. The excerpt below shows Wai's report on item 28 of the Oldest Old test. Wai's response was sufficient for her to gain a correct score on this item; however she reprised the issue of distraction in her statement that Jun's pronunciation had drawn her "attention out of the topic". Of note, Wai also links this distraction to the notion of "uncomfortableness":

Excerpt 7-25 (WA-OO.28)

Researcher: What answer did you have there?

Wai: I've got um "suffering more disease than eighties"

Researcher: Okay and what were you thinking when you responded there?

Wai: Um ... this, I think this is not exactly the information that I've got in my mind

Researcher: What information do you have in your mind?

Wai: Um this is, but I feel it's not like exactly correct

Researcher: Okay, um: ... any difficulty that you can ... spot?

Wai: I still feel like um: ... but it's only listening to the, the voice without like looking people I don't feel I get information ah as good as when I actually in the situation and people talking ... and the accent also makes me a bit uncomfortable

Researcher: Can you explain a bit more about that?

Wai: Um ... some ... it's just a ... mm ... just some little pronunciation that will draw your attention out of the topic

These examples do not provide clear evidence that there was a relationship between Wai's negative attitude towards speakers and her performance on the test tasks. However they do provide some insight into understanding how such an effect might occur. Those listeners who are predisposed to look critically upon pronunciation which is non-standard may be so distracted, or indeed irritated, by a speaker with an L2 accent that their attention on a task strays. That this appeared to be a problem for only one listener may be attributed to two factors: firstly, that attitudes towards both speakers were not particularly negative among the listeners; and secondly, that a focus on task completion overrode the potential for distraction in a simulated test situation.

7.7 Post hoc comments

Following the verbal report procedure, listeners were asked to retrospectively identify the accents of the speakers they had heard on the test. After they had provided their "guesses", they were told the language backgrounds of Kaori and Jun. This provided the basis for discussion on a second question "do you have any comments on the use of accented speakers on a listening test". An analysis of the comments provided by test-takers in each of these instances is presented below.

7.7.1 Retrospective identification of Kaori and Jun

In most instances test-takers were not precisely accurate in identifying the accents that they had heard, with only five correct identifications of a speaker's L1 background. When considering a broader regional identification – an Asian variety – the listeners were correct in nine cases. Only one test-taker, Xiao, believed that one of the speakers was an Australian native speaker. The table below shows the attempts at identifying Kaori and Jun's accent by all participants:

Table 7-1: Identifications of speakers' accents

	Kaori	Jun
Mana	Asian but not Chinese not Japanese not Korean ... Thailand or something I don't know	
Akiko	More Asian country background ... Indian or Malaysian or something ... not Singaporean	Latin ... Middle East or like more Europe
Takahiro	[Did not comment]	Don't think I remember
Tomoko	Not native Austral[ian] ... I don't know ... Indian ... or something ... not sure ... Indian kind of	I don't know

Wai	Korean or Japanese but I prefer it's Korean	I feel it's definitely it's Chinese
Ying	I think it's Japanese	I don't know
Li	Japanese	Not local people ... maybe from Asia ... China or something
Xiao	like Korea accent	local ... born in Australia

These results are not surprising; studies have shown that non-native listeners find it difficult to recognise or identify accents based purely on a speech sample (Stephan, 1997; Ladegaard, 1998). Moreover, difficulties in identifying varieties may not be confined to language learners only. Lindemann (2003) also found that American English native speakers performed poorly on an identification task of Korean accented English, guessing that the speakers were Japanese, Chinese, Indian or Latino more often than Korean. It is interesting to note, however, that those listeners who did not express negative attitudes towards Kaori and Jun in the verbal reports – Akiko, Takahiro, Tomoko, Ying and Xiao – appear in most cases to have been aware that they were listening to speakers of L2 varieties. This might indicate an implicit acceptance of these speakers.

7.7.2 Perceptions of general acceptability and fairness

Test-takers' responses to the question "do you have any comments on the use of accented speakers on a listening test?" were extremely varied in nature, and could not be easily categorised. In some cases test-takers held ambivalent views about the use of accented speech, though they seemed to express a preference for native varieties. For example, Tomoko gave the following response:

Excerpt 7-26 (TO-PHC)

Tomoko: Ah: ... mm: ... ah, don't know but um ... I think easier to listen to if the person has a more Australian kind of accent, not like very Australian but you know the language that you hear on TV like those ... TV announcers and stuff ... those kind of English would be easy to listen to I think ... 'cause, yeah ... 'cause like ... I wasn't sure if it was Japanese or Chinese but I could still ... I think hear the little bit of, you know, the accent, little bit different ... just more familiar to me by TV and stuff those people, Australian people

In this excerpt, Tomoko seems to express a preference for Australian English varieties for the reason that they are "more familiar" to her by way of exposure through the media. She also suggests that listening to an Australian accent is "easier to listen to" for that reason.

Li took a position which was informed by concern for fairness if candidates are not familiar or do not share a speaker's accent, and also by the conservative approach of language testing she has experienced in mainland China:

Excerpt 7-27 (LI-PHC)

Researcher: OK ... final question ... do you have any comments on the use of accented speakers on listening tests?

Li: Ah: ... maybe ... for the Japanese student they feel ah it's very familiar with what she is talking but for the other language background student it's not fair

Researcher: OK ... um ... you heard a Mandarin Chinese speaker ...

Li: Yeah, I heard a Mandarin Chinese but still not used to that one ... because ... all um, all the listening test we heard about is from very, very traditional English language background people ... so, just used to that one ... if you suddenly changed it ... no ... no way (laughs)

Li's comments are important, because they point to the influence of the orthodox approach on attitudes towards diversity. Her opinion suggests that stakeholders are guided in their attitudes, to some extent, by their awareness of the difficulties involved in challenging traditional testing practice.

Ying also did not see the use of "foreign" accents as feasible, but she was more concerned with matters of intelligibility. She returned to the example of her difficulties understanding Indian English pronunciation, which she had touched on in the verbal reports. It emerged in her post hoc comments that Ying's boyfriend is Indian, and in the excerpt below Ying provides a narrative of learning to deal with her boyfriend's Indian accent. This narrative gives rise to a number of crucial concepts relating to the learning of accent, and to its place in the specific context of a listening test, which are discussed below.

Excerpt 7-28 (YI-PHC)

Ying: Oh: ... I I don't think it's really going to work if for the foreigners because ... I have a boyfriend, he's Indian ... used to like a year two years back when I just knowing them ... knowing to him or knowing to India, I really frustrated at at knowing about the way are talk like what I say the "drank" of "three" they say three [with trilled /r/] ... they not saying three [untrilled] ... so, it's really you need, like, to pay attention ... to recognise to work out what they are talking about ... but, like ... for the past two years and even now [university] teacher asked about it, a teacher she's also from India ... so ... every day you are hearing this kind of accents ... you start to to to adapt or used to used to the accents ... so ... you ... for me, like, the accents, you never heard before and suddenly one day you heard that ... it's quite it's especially in the exam it's quite annoyed for you because you not familiar with that, you don't know the word actually you know the word but you don't know ... if ... the way they pronounced you don't know the word and even maybe, you just ... don't know the sentence ... so ... we can't ... so for if the exam is more important to test the things how much we understand ... it's not like how much accents we can pick up ... it's quite tricky, yeah

Firstly, in describing her experience with Indian English, Ying describes feelings of initial "frustration" in encountering the new accent, and recalls the need to "pay attention" in order to "recognise" what is being uttered. Ying's narrative goes on to describe how she "adapted to" or "got used to" that particular accent, but suggests that it took a long period of regular contact (with more than one speaker) to build up a real familiarity with Indian English. The overarching theme of this embedded narrative appears to be that one *can* "get used to" an accent, but sufficient time is required, and there will be greater affective and cognitive strain in early encounters. These notions appear to feed into Ying's appraisal of the general use of diverse accented speakers in listening assessment. Ying envisages an assessment situation in which a test taker is presented with an unfamiliar accent as analogous to her own early encounters with Indian English – having the potential to cause negative affect and difficulty at the perceptual level. Importantly, while Ying perceives this ability to "pick up" an accent as a real phenomenon, she also views it as a distinct dimension of listening ability which should not necessarily be tested alongside general listening comprehension: "so for if the exam is more important to test the things how much we understand ... it's not like how much accents we can pick up".

Mana's opinion takes up her concern – expressed in the verbal reports – over the heightened difficulty of listening to accents when technical vocabulary is involved. For this reason she saw the use of accents as acceptable for "general" topics, but not for specific purpose tests:

Excerpt 7-29 (MA-PHC)

Mana: Mm: ... if it's a general thing, general topic it's okay ... but if it's specific like medical or I don't know I guess something specific um ... stuff I think it's not very good to use

Researcher: Mm: why why those particular situations?

Mana: Cause I can't guess the words and I don't ... sometimes if I don't know the, this word and I don't know the expression so I can't understand what they're talking, what they're explaining

As well as concerns over familiar topics and vocabulary, Mana also raised the question of familiarity with speakers or accents in relation to test fairness:

Excerpt 7-30 (MA-PHC)

Mana: Mm: ... I: don't know it really depends on the student too ... if we thinks familiar to these speakers, I guess it's okay but I if we feel unfamiliar it's ... suddenly it's unfair

These comments echo those of several of the participants in Harding (2008) who perceived prior access to speakers or varieties as a vital issue of fairness in the use of diverse accents in listening assessment. It is worth noting, however, that Mana uses the verbs "think" and "feel" when talking about the importance of familiarity. This might be interpreted to mean that whether or not a speaker has a familiar accent, if the candidate *believes* the speaker to have an unfamiliar accent, then the candidate will think the test unfair.

Turning now to slightly more positive views, given her responses throughout the verbal reports, Wai was surprisingly circumspect when asked about the fairness of using accented speakers in listening assessment more generally. Although she experienced a strong negative affect while listening to both Kaori and Jun, her response in the interview indicated she was aware of the communicative needs of students who wish to function in a metropolitan, Australian setting:

Excerpt 7-31 (WA-PHC)

Wai: I don't think it's unfair cause it does exist in the real life ... um ... but for listening test, what I think ... I don't know ... it's very ... ah it's um well it's quite interesting cause never thought about that before ... think it should be standard, like standard English but in Australia the situation which is happened very often that um got accent ... ah ... I I don't know, I think I think maybe if, maybe if got five different testing maybe one or two? Like accent language testing maybe it's all right, I'm not really sure

In her "off-the-cuff" opinion, Wai suggests that maybe one or two voices out of five might be non-standard accents, a concern which echoes the comments of participants in Harding (2008) in which an even representation of relevant accents was considered to be fair in the context of diverse accents in listening assessment.

Despite his difficulties with Jun's accent, Takahiro was in support of the inclusion of diverse accents in listening assessment. This opinion appears to be based on Takahiro's experience living and working in Australia where, he says, "I really need to listen to someone who ... have different language backgrounds":

Excerpt 7-32 (TA-PHC)

Takahiro: Um, well ... I think it, well ... it's good idea to have ... you know, people with different accents because ... we still speak the same language and ... specially in Australia, yeah ... I really need to listen to someone who are from, you know ... have have different backgrounds ... mm ... but ... um ... like, the other day I had a chat with my classmate who just had had IELTS test ... couple of month couple of weeks ago, and she had a big challenge in listening section because the speaker was strongly, um ... the speaker had very strong cockney accent ... and her listening skills much better than mine

Yet while Takahiro agrees with the necessity for becoming acquainted with different accents, he also acknowledges that different accents in stimuli can present a challenge in listening assessment, as evidenced by the embedded narrative of his friend's difficulty taking IELTS. What is most interesting about his comment during this story is not so much that his friend experienced accent-related difficulty during a listening test, but that the "difficult" accent was a "very strong cockney accent" – in other words, a native speaker variety. Takahiro's comments again highlight that perceptions of accent-related difficulty are not limited to, or indeed regularly connected with, L2 varieties.

According to Xiao, if difficulty can be managed, then there is no need to refrain from using diverse accents in listening assessment – in fact this can lead to a "fun" experience:

Excerpt 7-33 (XI-PHC)

Xiao: Yeah I feel more relaxed with the accent one ... truly ... as long as it doesn't affect my test ... it's fun

Researcher: Do you think it's fair or unfair or neither?

Xiao: Not at all ... it doesn't matter

However Akiko's response to this question might be taken as the richest and most detailed rationale for the use of L2 accents in listening assessment. Her mild reaction to both speakers may be explained by previous experience with speakers of diverse accents in the Australian community, and a subsequent perception that dealing with accent is a vital dimension of real-world listening comprehension. This attitude was expressed through a long turn in the interview during which Akiko reflected on several occasions in which she had experienced accent-related difficulty in comprehending speakers from a range of language backgrounds:

Excerpt 7-34 (AK-PHC)

Akiko: Yeah ... actually it's really good ... good to be familiar with someone who has accent because ... because when I study in Japan I always study with the American accent or Australian English accent ... I never ever came across someone who has Indian or Chinese accent ... and when I come to Australia, I suffer a lot ... I couldn't understand any single word from Indian ... and ... anything like, ah ... when I just arrive here I need the mobile so I ... I wanted to activate my [phone company] prepaid and I ring to [phone company], everyone was Indian and I couldn't understand anything ... you know it was "oh!" ... I was talking to myself, "does he speaking English ... or what language?" Yeah, seriously and then, and then after that when I go shopping or something it it was ... maybe he come from Turkey or something, I couldn't understand anything ... and I don't wanna be rude to them and I said "mm?" "mm?" yeah (laughs) and then someone from New Zealand people ... and I have one lecturer who come from New Zealand ... and then ... when I was take ... because I was taking with the human anatomy and he was explain all the muscle name and he said "pip" ... "pip" ... this "pip" area ... and I was like, oh mm: "pip" ... which part of the body? Which part of the body? And I asked my friend, where is the pip? He said "hip" ... Ah: and then the some lecturer is from France ... he said he all the time ... I was taking one of his ... some ... communication class and he was something explain "internal par" ... "internal par" ... and again I was like "par" ... what is the word "par"? And then I ask do you know what is "par" mean? And he said "power" and "ah:" so, actually it's really good to be accommodate because in all over the world people speak with accent ... but I wasn't really aware of that when I was preparing to come to Australia, so I think it's really good ... good to be familiar with ... little by little because obviously in the worldwide Chinese people ... majority is the Chinese people ... in the ten years people maybe speak ... maybe we hardly ever listen pure English any more ... so I think it's really nice, mm

Within this collection of short narratives on Akiko's experiences with accent-related problems, two other features are worthy of attention. The first is the thread running through these stories that it is both good and necessary to become familiar with diverse accents in an Australian context. To this end, Akiko makes the following statements at various points throughout the excerpt: "actually it's really good ... good to be familiar with someone who has accent"; "I never ever came across someone who has an Indian or Chinese accent ... and when I come

221

to Australia, I suffer a lot"; "actually it's really good to accommodate because … all over the world people speak with accent"; "I think it's really good … good to be familiar with [accent] little by little"; "I think it's really nice".

The second feature is the image of the range of communicative situations faced by international students in Australia which is drawn by Akiko's discourse. Her comments here provide a first-hand account which supports Canagarajah's theoretical description of the language varieties prospective students may encounter in globalised, metropolitan settings:

> By the same token, standard British or American English is not sufficient for a person moving to the United Kingdom or the United States for higher education or employment. Students moving from Sri Lanka to New York City for graduate studies will find that they need an awareness of Black English or Caribbean varieties for the neighborhood in which they will live; they need a sensitivity to Indian and Chinese varieties of English to understand some of their professors; they need the ability to negotiate certain regional varieties within the United States – such as Brooklynese or Texan English – depending on the people and activities with whom they hope to engage.
> (Canagarajah, 2006, pp.236-237)

Like the hypothetical Sri Lankan student in Canagarajah's example, Akiko has encountered a range of accents, and has needed to develop skills in order to surmount any communicative difficulties this has raised. It would seem that Akiko's previous experience with accented speakers, her current context (as a student in an Australian university), and her views on the use of accented speakers in listening assessment are inextricably connected.

7.8 Summary

The findings from the initial analysis of SPAREs and AIRD addressed research questions 1(a), 1 (b) and 2(a). Firstly, they demonstrated that accent-related difficulty was reported by test-takers during the Sleep test and the Oldest Old test, but that it was not widespread across either test. Secondly, the data suggested that even in this very small sample, accent-related difficulty appeared to be more pronounced for non-shared-L1 listeners. Thirdly, the initial findings suggest that attitudinal responses towards speakers and accents were not routinely expressed by test-takers, and appeared to be more related to individual listeners than to either speaker. These observations appeared to fit study one's broad finding that less familiar listeners may experience accent-related difficulty on certain test items. They also reflected the finding of study two that attitudes were not routinely negative towards Kaori and Jun among L2 listeners.

These initial observations were given greater substance in the qualitative analysis of verbal reports. Firstly, research question 1(c) was addressed through an analysis of test-takers' reports throughout both tests which demonstrated the nature of accent-related difficulty. Observed accent-related difficulty on both listening tests was divided into two types: misperception/inability to recognise key phonetic information, and difficulty in processing speech efficiently. In the first case, misperception, or an inability to recognise key phonetic information, was shown to be the most common type of difficulty related to dealing with an unfamiliar accent. In some cases perceptual difficulty with an unfamiliar accent appeared to be heightened if vocabulary was also unfamiliar. In the second case, a general processing lag while listening to an unfamiliar accent was reported by one listener, and it was suggested that a particularly demanding task – such as note-taking while listening – may exacerbate any such processing cost. These findings corroborated, to a certain extent, speculation in study one concerning the underlying reasons for accent-related difficulty among some less familiar listeners.

In addition, the analysis provided novel observations about test-takers' strategies for dealing with perceptual problems. In the first case, listeners were shown to be able to draw on top-down knowledge to compensate for perceptual difficulty. Although this did not always lead to an accurate response, it nevertheless provided evidence for an interactive-compensatory process in dealing with difficulty at the level of word recognition (see Stanovich, 1980). In the second case, it was shown that a listening test may be a site of "dynamic" perceptual learning in the sense that a listener may retrospectively correct an initial misperception as they gain more experience with a speaker's realisation of a particular term. The potential impact of background knowledge on perceptions of comprehensibility was also raised in one shared-L1 listener's report of accent-related listening ease. Although the listener in this case spoke positively of the lecturer's "way of speaking", he also revealed that the topic was familiar suggesting that background knowledge may have some bearing on how well-disposed listeners are to dealing with accent in a listening test situation.

The findings from the qualitative analysis of "online" attitudinal response addressed research questions 2(b) and 2(c). Limited examples of negative evaluation and affective response were found in the verbal report data. Of those few instances that were observed, it was shown that negative reactions towards accents were framed in terms of judgements of correctness and professionalism, perceptions of "normality" and feelings of "uncomfortableness". These themes were remarkably similar in the responses of three different listeners. Although negative reactions were often triggered by instances of accent-related difficulty, these appraisals appeared to be expressions of latent negative attitudes towards L2 accents more generally among individuals, and were not necessarily formed during the test itself.

A positive evaluation of Kaori was observed in Ying's data. It was noted that this individual listener found Kaori's accent more acceptable *because* it was identified as an Asian variety. Reflecting on the findings of study two, this data would support the interpretation that an L1 group interaction on the social attractiveness measure was related to solidarity.

With regard to research question 2(c), a relationship between negative attitudes towards accent and test performance was shown to potentially manifest in being distracted or irritated by a speaker's pronunciation (cf. Fayer & Krasinski, 1987). However there was no clear evidence of a particularly detrimental effect on actual test performance.

Finally, listeners' post hoc comments revealed a number of interesting opinions regarding the speakers, and the use of accented speech on listening comprehension tests more broadly. Firstly, in addressing research question 3(a), listeners were shown to be moderately accurate in identifying the accents of Kaori and Jun. However it was noted that most listeners were aware that they were listening to speakers with L2 accents of some kind. With regard to research question 3(b), listeners also varied in the extent to which they felt it was acceptable and fair to use diverse accented speakers in listening assessment. Comments reflected the range of opinions noted in Harding (2008), where test-takers tended to frame their responses around perspectives of their immediate communicative needs in an Australian metropolitan setting. Some interesting findings also emerged concerning listeners' prior experiences with adjusting to accent, and their awareness of the conservatism of testing approaches in their own countries.

Overall, the findings of this study provide data which both complement the findings of studies one and two, and also enrich those findings. Investigating the nature of listening to speakers with L2 accents from the perspective of test-takers afforded a range of insights that were not possible through the quantitative methods used primarily in studies one and two. The voices of test-takers help to fill gaps concerning the nature of accent-related difficulty (as experienced), and the manner in which attitudinal responses might be activated throughout the listening test event. At the same time, the findings from this study need to be treated with caution. A range of limitations with verbal report data were raised in the methodological considerations; and the questions over veridicality and reactivity apply to the data presented above.

Chapter 8: Summary and implications

8.1 Summary

8.1.1 Review of approach and methods

This book began with the premise that there exists a strong theoretical rationale for the broader representation of accent varieties in listening input. However a number of key concerns regarding the use of L2 speech in English language listening assessment underlie the orthodox approach of using primarily inner-circle accents. A general research aim was then stated: to address specific concerns with empirical evidence to evaluate the extent to which they represented threats to validity, and also to establish under what conditions, and through what preparatory measures, an EAP test featuring speakers with L2 accents may be feasible.

After gaining a more thorough understanding through a review of literature, a research plan was set out to provide empirical evidence in order to evaluate these concerns, which were transformed into four questionable assumptions, akin to a set of hypotheses. The research design was in three stages. In the first stage, test materials were identified, and highly-intelligible speakers were selected to re-record existing UTESL listening sub-tests. This rigorous process of speaker selection yielded a set of test materials featuring three speakers – Henry, an Australian English native speaker; Kaori, a Japanese L1 speaker; and Jun, a Mandarin Chinese L1 speaker. These materials were used as the basis to investigate the questionable assumptions in three linked studies which formed the second stage of research.

In the first study, a differential item functioning analysis was performed to investigate the potential for a shared-L1 or familiarity advantage. Statistical DIF findings were explored at a micro-level through an analysis of test-taker responses. In the second study, attitudes towards speakers were investigated through the verbal-guise technique. The relationship between an individual's attitude towards a speaker, and their subsequent performance on a test featuring that speaker, was also explored. The third study served to triangulate, and expand upon, the findings of the first and second study through an in-depth study of a small sample of test-takers' verbal reports while completing test materials. This study yielded data which complemented studies one and two, and provided a richer understanding of the topic from the test-taker's perspective.

Stage three of the research design is presented in the current chapter (see Figure 3-1: Stages of research in Chapter 3).

8.1.2 Key findings from three studies

The key findings from the three studies presented in this book are summarised below. They are organised around the questionable assumptions which were articulated in Chapter 3, with the first two assumptions considered together, and the second two assumptions considered together. Detailed discussions of each of these findings in relation to specific research questions were presented in relevant chapters (indicated).

Familiarity, shared-L1 and listening performance

Assumption 1:	Test-takers of otherwise equivalent ability will not perform differentially on an EAP listening test featuring a highly-intelligible speaker with an L2 accent, irrespective of whether or not they share the speaker's L1.

Assumption 2:	Test-takers of otherwise equivalent ability will not perform differentially on an EAP listening test featuring a highly-intelligible speaker with an L2 accent, irrespective of whether or not they are highly familiar with the speaker's accent.

Finding (1): In the case of the Sleep test, it was possible to use a highly-intelligible speaker with an L2 accent on a listening test without a clear advantage at the score level for shared-L1 or highly-familiar listeners. (Chapter 5)

Finding (2): In the case of the Oldest Old test, shared-L1 and highly-familiar listeners were advantaged on listening test items when certain conditions were present relating to task demands, speaker pronunciation, and the linguistic demands of the text. (Chapter 5)

Finding (3): When an unfamiliar accent was implicated in listening difficulty, the difficulty was of two types: misperception/inability to recognise phonetic information, or difficulty in processing speech efficiently. (Chapter 7)

Finding (4): Listeners were shown to use various compensatory strategies to deal with difficult pronunciation, although these were not always successful. (Chapter 7)

Attitudes and acceptability

Assumption 3:	Test-takers will not, overall, hold negative attitudes towards highly-intelligible speakers with L2 accents used on an EAP listening test.

Assumption 4:	Test-taker attitudes towards diverse accented speakers will not affect their performance on a listening test featuring that speaker.

Finding (5): Listeners exhibited generally positive attitudes towards highly-intelligible speakers with L2 accents on measures of lecturer competence and social attractiveness. Evaluations of lecturer competence were strongly speaker determined, whereas evaluations of social attractiveness varied according to listener background factors. (Chapter 6)

Finding (6): Listeners expressed a range of views regarding the acceptability and fairness of using "accented" speakers on listening assessment. These views appeared to relate to test-takers' perceptions of their current communicative needs, and their previous experience with diverse accents. (Chapter 7)

Finding (7): There was no clear relationship between attitudes towards speakers (as measured by a speaker evaluation instrument) and subsequent performance on a listening test featuring that speaker. (Chapter 6)

Finding (8): Individual listeners held strong attitudes or experienced strong affective responses towards speakers but these very rarely interfered directly with comprehension. When "interference" did occur, it appeared that the listener was distracted from a task by features of the speaker's pronunciation. (Chapter 7)

8.1.3 Contribution to the field

As Chapters 1 and 2 made clear, there has been little empirical research conducted on the use of speakers with different accents – whether L2, regional or standard varieties – on second language listening assessment. Of those studies which had been conducted, principally Major et al. (2002; 2005), the focus had primarily been the effect of different accents on different listener groups, and findings had been inconclusive. At the same time, there has been growing discussion on the merits of including different accent varieties on international

English language proficiency tests. For example, as recently as May 2008, Geranpayeh and Taylor raised the issue of speaker accent in their article entitled "Examining listening: developments and issues in assessing second language listening" where they wrote, "inclusion of more accented varieties on context, cognitive and consequential validity grounds has to be carefully balanced against the risk of introducing test bias which is well recognised as a threat to test validity" (2008, p.4).

This research, it is hoped, has provided some useful, empirical evidence that serves a pragmatic view of the use of speakers with L2 accents in listening assessment. One of the chief contributions of the findings presented above is that a deterministic view of the effects of familiarity or a shared-L1 is not tenable. When more familiar listeners are advantaged on a certain item because of greater experience with a given accent, there are complex factors at work; not least of which are the moderating variables of the test task, the text, and other scaffolds from which a test-taker might derive meaning, and so deal with a breakdown at the perceptual level. In this sense, this study has shown that approaching the issue of the "effect of accent" by testing the existence of a "universal" effect which would either support or refute any future policy is not fruitful. More promising is the thick description of the relationship between listener factors, speaker factors, test factors, and external social factors, as this builds theory which can be directly applied in practical situations. In attempting this, the next section proposes three models for the use of diverse accented speakers in listening assessment.

8.2 Three models for the use of speakers with L2 accents in listening assessment

The findings of this research project have implications for the future development of listening tests both in EAP contexts, and also in ESP and more general contexts. Key findings from the studies presented above may help to inform policy on the development of listening test materials in situations where it is felt that the inclusion of diverse accents – including L2 varieties – is warranted, or where the orthodox approach has been challenged. Three approaches are therefore proposed in which the use of accented speakers may be "managed" or made feasible within the particular constraints of test development:

- The weak ELF approach
- The strong ELF approach
- The local Englishes approach

These three approaches are presented in greater detail below.

8.2.1 The weak ELF approach

Overview

The "weak ELF approach" is so named because it presents a surface-level only approach to the inclusion of diverse accents in listening assessment. Principally, this approach would be desirable in contexts where L2 accents were warranted on authenticity grounds, but where test developers did not want to introduce greater levels of accent-related difficulty into their construct. To achieve this, highly-intelligible speakers with L2 accents would be selected (as in this study), and recordings would be carefully monitored to ensure that pronunciation remained highly-intelligible across all stimuli. This process would pre-emptively mitigate, to the greatest extent possible, the potential for intelligibility breakdowns. Importantly, it would also reduce the potential for shared-L1 or familiarity effects. At the same time, test developers would be introducing "tolerance of variety" into their construct in the sense that listeners would be required to deal with their attitudinal or affective response to a range of accents. The resulting test would be comparable to the Sleep test used in this study, which evoked a range of attitudinal and affective responses to the speaker, but which did not show any tangible performance disadvantage for less familiar listeners.

Construct implications

The primary benefit of this approach is in the slight broadening of the listening construct to model elements of "ability for use", a notion raised in the introductory chapter. In this sense, the approach offers a weakened version of Alptekin's (2002) intercultural communicative competence; it requires that listeners cope with or tolerate non-standard phonological features of L2 accents which remain salient in highly intelligible speakers, but not that they negotiate significant accent-related difficulty in their perception of the code. The chief limitation of the weak ELF approach, then, is expressed precisely in its title: it is a weak, and to a certain extent, artificial representation of the real-life linguistic demands of candidates who would wish to, for example, study in an inner-circle context. This problem of selecting highly intelligible speakers was expressed by Mana in Chapter 7 thus:

> I think they are better than my lecturers (laughs) ... some of my lecturers are non-native English speakers ... so I feel, I often feel difficult.

The weak approach only goes halfway towards capturing the real accent demands of the TLU domain.

Potential contexts

The clearest context of use for the weak ELF approach is in general, academic or specific purposes English language testing where the TLU domain may include L2 speakers, but no specific accent can be identified as particularly salient. This could include low to medium-stakes assessments such as UTESL, but also high-stakes assessments such as IELTS, TOEFL, TOEIC, the Pearson Test of English or the Occupational English Test.

Considerations in test development

Speaker selection

In taking the weak ELF approach, the speaker selection, or intelligibility screening, stage becomes of crucial concern. The speaker selection methods outlined in this study are not the most practical, nor are they the most careful. Future research is required to find an efficient and accurate intelligibility screening tool which selects speakers with a high level of general intelligibility for listeners from a range of L1 backgrounds. While it may also be desirable in high-stakes testing situations to carefully monitor speakers' pronunciation of technical or unfamiliar language in the recording studio, working *in situ* with speakers in this way would perhaps only be possible in situations where listening input is scripted, and professional speakers or actors are asked to read prepared materials. In situations where naturalistic input is recorded by authentic speakers – such as the case of the Occupational English Test used in Australia, where real health professionals record consultations and short talks – it would not only be difficult to manage, but would be potentially offensive to those speakers who had been asked to speak for the test. In such situations, a speaker selection process itself may also not be practicable, and impressionistic judgments of general intelligibility alone would have to suffice.

Text selection and item writing

The potential for a shared-L1 or familiarity effect may also be minimised at the item writing stage. Chapter 5 of this book demonstrated that DIF may be prevalent when items focus on bottom-up listening skills, or when surrounding text is particularly technical. This was supported in the third study, where listeners reported accent-related difficulty on tasks where they were required to locate specific detail (and when the input was not ideal). In this sense, the weak ELF approach may be more suited to items that test higher order listening skills, or to task types that provide more scaffolding to listeners – such as multiple choice tasks – than note-taking style tasks, where listeners are entirely reliant on the input to draw information. In terms of text, a general topic would be preferable; specialist vocabulary should be minimised (even if is not required for item response). Ideally, to minimise the potential for DIF, texts would be graded to a particular level. With such restrictions on these other important aspects of construct representation it would seem likely that an L2 accent might only feature in limited sections of a listening paper.

Monitoring

DIF analyses at the trial stage would be a useful check to ensure that shared-L1 or familiarity effects had indeed been minimised through the speaker selection process, and through considerations at the text preparation and item writing stages. Alternatively, a small number of unfamiliar listeners might be drawn on to conduct verbal report trials in order to identify any particularly problematic items.

8.2.2 The strong ELF approach

Overview

Rather than selecting highly-intelligible speakers, the "strong" ELF approach would select speakers whose intelligibility was not optimal (but not so severe that it led to communication breakdown). These speakers might be, for example, lower proficiency L2 speakers such as those not chosen for this study, but who featured in Chapter 4. The aim of such a test would be to provide test-takers with some level of scaffolding to enable them to utilise top-down strategies to deal with problems at the perceptual level, as was demonstrated among some listeners in study three.

Construct implications

The strong ELF model represents a deep-level approach to the use of L2 accents in listening assessment. Indeed, it is this approach that fits Canagarajah's (2006) advocacy of a "new level of proficiency" which was raised in Chapter 1:

> One should be able to inductively process the underlying system in the varieties one encounters in social interactions. One should draw on intuitive skills to develop relative communicative competence in new varieties according to one's needs. Therefore, tests should examine a candidate's ability to discern the structure, pattern, or rules from the available data of a given language.
> (Canagarajah, 2006, p.237)

In contrast to the weak approach, this strong approach would involve the test developers specifically introducing a level of accent-related difficulty into the construct, to which a candidate would be expected to adapt based on the limited phonological data available. It is called the strong ELF approach because it is assessing, in part, a listener's ability to deal with potential communication breakdown. As with the weak approach, tolerance of variety is also introduced – perhaps to an even greater degree. This approach, then, broadens the construct to include elements of sociolinguistic competence as well as strategic competence, as defined by Canale and Swain (1980): "verbal and non-verbal communication strategies that may be called into action to compensate for breakdowns in communication due to performance variables or to insufficient competence" (p.30).

Potential contexts

Potential contexts of use may be any test of general English language proficiency that wishes to add this aspect "dealing with accent". For example, the strong ELF approach is already being taken – to a certain extent – with varieties of native speaker accent in the Common European Framework of Reference. For example, the descriptor for C2 listening says that a learner at this level has,

> no difficulty in understanding any kind of spoken language, whether live or broadcast, even when delivered at fast native speed, provided [he/she has] some time to get familiar with the accent.

With respect to the ability to deal with various L2 accents, the strong ELF approach would most clearly be of relevance in situations where English as a Lingua Franca competencies are directly of interest.

Considerations in test development

Speaker selection

Speaker selection would be of crucial concern in the strong ELF approach, but for very different reasons than for the weak approach. In selecting appropriate speakers, it would be necessary to find speakers who posed some level of difficulty to a range of listeners from different L1 backgrounds. The fundamental problem of the strong ELF approach is that it might be more prone to DIF because a threshold level of general intelligibility is not required. As this research has demonstrated, one of the conditions for accent-related DIF (or more specifically, differential intelligibility) appears to be when a listener departs from the lingua franca core in a particular pronunciation, and where this pronunciation also bears some documented characteristic of a particular variety – such as Jun's production of "number" as "lumber". There are two potential methods of combating this threat of DIF through the broader process of speaker selection. One would be to follow Buck (2001) in ensuring that the accent is equally unfamiliar for all listeners. This may prove difficult in large-scale international tests, but might be manageable in assessment contexts where the test-taker population is fairly homogeneous. The second method would be to include as broad a range of accents as possible on a range of short tasks. This way, any DIF might be balanced out between different listener groups.

Text selection and item writing

The selection of specific texts and the use of particular item types are also of crucial importance in the strong ELF approach. Because it is assumed that perceptual information may not be optimal for listeners, there would need to be a certain level of scaffolding in place for listeners to gain a "foothold" in dealing with an unfamiliar accent. In this sense, texts including technical or complex vocabulary might not be suitable. A context-rich text will be necessary to give listeners the best chance of "filling in" gaps at the perceptual level. Likewise, items which test gist, which ask listeners to synthesise information, or which give listeners a greater level of support in visual cues on the answer paper may be preferred. It is assumed that a strong ELF approach may not be feasible on a note-taking, lecture comprehension style test.

Monitoring

As with the weak ELF approach, DIF analyses at the trial stage would be necessary to check for a shared-L1 or familiarity advantage. Also, verbal reports might be used to establish cognitive validity (see Weir, 2005); that is to establish that the presence of an unfamiliar or less intelligible accent is, in fact, leading test-takers to activate compensatory strategies in the sense hypothesised.

8.2.3 The local Englishes approach

Overview

The primary rationale for the inclusion of L2 accents in the local Englishes approach is grounded in authenticity. The direct representation of TLU-domain relevant accents means that issues of speaker selection are less relevant than in the two previous approaches. Put simply: any variation in an authentic speaker is considered directly construct relevant. This approach validates the role of local Englishes (e.g., Japanese English, Hong Kong English, Indian English), by viewing the TLU domain as the vital consideration in choice of speaker.

Construct implications

Under the local Englishes approach, there are no particular construct implications in the use of speakers with L2 accents. As mentioned above, the test-taker's ability to deal with a certain accent is considered entirely construct relevant. In a sense, the local Englishes approach is the default position for many tests currently in use. For example, the UTESL – used in this research – might be viewed as taking up the local Englishes approach in its default use of

Australian accented speech in its standard recordings. There is an implicit acknowledgement that the ability to deal with the Australian accent, in particular, is directly relevant to the purpose of the test, which is to measure academic listening proficiency in the environment of tertiary education in Australia. However the local Englishes approach may be broadened even within inner-circle situations, based on evidence of one or several *specific* accents which are deemed relevant to the needs of test-takers in a given context.

Potential contexts

A local Englishes approach would be most useful in a situation where the domain of target language use includes one or more easily identifiable accents or varieties which may typically be considered "non-standard". An example would be an entry exam to an English-medium university in Singapore or Hong Kong where the vast majority of teachers/students may have a particular type of accent. However a case may also be made for a local Englishes approach in inner-circle contexts where particular accents can be easily identified through a needs analysis. A local Englishes approach may also be integrated into a large-scale international test whereby local speakers are used in local administrations – i.e., a Japanese speaker is used in Japanese administrations and so on.

Considerations in test development

Speaker selection

Careful speaker selection to screen for intelligibility is less important in this approach. The principal consideration is the selection of authentic speakers, both in terms of their variety and also in terms of their performance quality for the role they are purporting to represent on the test.

Text selection and item writing

There are no special considerations for text selection and item writing under the local Englishes approach. Texts should be selected which are construct-relevant, with no specific need to provide "footholds" for listeners to cope with the demands of speaker accent. A full repertoire of task types may be utilised.

Monitoring

Ongoing validation studies with respect to construct validity should be conducted, but with no particular focus on the issues surrounding speaker accent. Studies may be required in order to identify and describe the characteristics of an "authentic" accent in a given context.

8.3 Suggestions for further research

During the course of researching this book, a number of avenues for further research became clear. These are discussed below.

Needs analysis of university accents

Although Chapter 1 provided a theoretical argument, and some evidence, to support the notion that accent heterogeneity is commonplace in inner-circle academic institutions, there is very little "hard data" on the nature or prevalence of particular accents in different institutional contexts. For those large-scale corpora of academic spoken which have been collected in recent years to assist in the development of listening materials representative of the academic domain (e.g. Biber et al., 2004), the focus has largely been on lexical, grammatical and discourse features. In many ways, phonological features have been a forgotten element in the development of authentic materials. One way to address this gap in knowledge would be to conduct a large-scale accent survey, as a type of needs analysis, among various faculties in universities within a given context. This may take the form of an accent survey of academics at a particular university; or it may focus on a particular field, for example, a survey of engineering faculties across several institutional sites. Such a survey would provide evidence to judge the degree to which L2 accents should be incorporated into academic listening assessment. It would also provide useful data on the types of accent most prevalent in particular contexts.

Speaker selection

As discussed above, the weak ELF approach relies, to a certain extent, on the adequacy of the speaker selection process in identifying speakers who will have a high general intelligibility across different listener groups. This may be accomplished through an intelligibility screening procedure similar to the one used in this study, which is based on the methods developed by Munro and Derwing (1995a; 1997). However two problems exist with this procedure. Firstly, as the current study has demonstrated, a speaker may be identified as having a high general intelligibility, but still be differentially intelligible to listener groups with greater or lesser accent-familiarity at certain points during a test. Secondly, this procedure is laborious, and probably unworkable in a regular test development situation. Although the alternative method of allowing judges to assess a speaker's intelligibility impressionistically may be susceptible to selection based on mildness of accent rather than level of intelligibility, it seems likely that some sort of judgment or rating – with raters representing different language varieties – would be most feasible. For a low-stakes testing situation, a standardised rating procedure might be sufficient. In a high-stakes situation, this might be teamed with a post-hoc analysis of a selected speaker's phonological patterns in natural speech to identify any particular features which might be problematic at the recording stage. Further research is required to assess the suitability of such measures in comparison with transcription task approaches to measuring intelligibility.

Replication in different contexts

A third area for further research is in replicating the studies above with different accents, in different contexts, or with different modes of language use. On the first two points, one limitation of the current study was that both accents were from the same geographical region. A second, more pressing, limitation was that all of the participants who took part had been living in an Australian city, and had received varying degrees of exposure to a wide range of accents. This may have reduced any potential shared-L1 or familiarity effects in the DIF analysis. It may also have had some impact on the measured attitudes in study two, and on the responses concerning acceptability and fairness in study three. It would be interesting to see if the findings were similar for listeners in EFL contexts, and to use other expanding-circle accents that were very different from one another. A replication of this study with speakers and listeners in the outer-circle would also be useful, and may perhaps reveal some different patterns in attitudes towards shared-accent varieties. Finally, this book has concentrated on listening assessment, however the impact of non-standard variation on the testing of other skills, particularly reading, would also be worthy of investigation with methods replicated from this study.

The ability to adapt to accent

A final area which was mentioned briefly in study three relates to a test-taker's ability to adapt to accent "rapidly" during a listening test. As shown in the literature review, recent research (Clarke & Garrett, 2004) has established that native listeners are able to adapt to a "foreign" accent in a very short amount of time. The degree to which this adaptation might also occur for second language listeners is not established. However, an understanding of this phenomenon would have implications for an understanding of the ways in which a test-taker might engage in "perceptual learning" throughout the listening test event, and would deepen current understandings of the construct. This may be accomplished through psycholinguistic methods, or through verbal reports over extended stretches of discourse.

8.4 Concluding remarks

Research has begun to emerge which suggests that exposure to multiple varieties of speech improves perception of novel talkers of those varieties (Bradlow and

Bent, 2003). This is taken further by Clopper and Pisoni (2004), who claim that although listening to an unfamiliar speaker creates initial difficulty, exposure to a range of different varieties allows listeners to develop "robust perceptual learning", leading to the development of "abstract, talker-independent representations of dialect variation" (p.229). There have also been a number of programs of research which have looked at teaching world Englishes, and these have generally found that attitudes change as knowledge of language varieties increases (see Derwing, Rossiter & Munro, 2002; Kubota, 2001; Morrison & White, 2005). The implication of these lines of research is that, pedagogically, it is of benefit for language learners to have experience with varieties of accent. Not only does it increase a listener's perceptual abilities, but it also fosters positive attitudes towards different varieties. Exposure to speech variability needs to be considered in the teaching of L2 listening as akin to exposing learners to different genres of text, or to different modalities of communication.

If it is the case that teaching accent diversity is pedagogically sound, the question remains, can language testing play a role in advocating diversity of accent? At the crux of this matter is the potential for positive washback. An example helps to put this in perspective. After the TOEFL iBT was rolled out some years ago, one new feature on the listening section was the introduction of British and Australian English accents where previously there had only been standard North American varieties. An online brochure for King George International College (a language school in Canada) which was designed to inform prospective students of how their curriculum had changed in the wake of the new demands of the TOEFL iBT, clearly shows washback in action. In discussing changes to the listening section, under the heading "how will it affect teaching?", the brochure states:

- Note-taking skill will be practiced.
- British and Australian accents will be introduced.

(King George International College. n.d.)

While discussion continues over the acceptability of the norms of different varieties in speaking and writing assessment, the issue of L2 accents in the input of listening assessment may be one way in which language testing can take a leading role in the EIL debate, and help push the enterprise of language teaching in a more progressive direction. This research has shown that it is feasible to represent the accents of new and emerging L2 varieties in listening assessment without compromising the chief concern for validity. On many levels, it is an ethical course of action for testing to embrace now the use of speakers with L2 accents in listening assessment.

References

Abbott, M. L. (2007). A confirmatory approach to differential item functioning on an ESL reading assessment. *Language Testing, 24* (1), 7-36.

AEI [Australian Education International] (2008). International student enrolments in higher education in 2007. *Research Snapshot, 31.* Retrieved July 15th, 2008, from http://aei.gov.au/AEI/PublicationsAndResearch/Snapshots/31SS08_pdf

Al-Kahtany, A. H. (1995). Dialectal ethnographic "cleansing": ESL students' attitudes towards three varieties of English. *Language and Communication, 15* (2), 165-180.

Alptekin, A. (2002). Towards intercultural communicative competence in ELT. *ELT Journal, 56* (1), 57-64.

Anderson, A., & Lynch, T. (1988). *Listening.* London: Oxford University Press.

Anderson-Hsieh, J., & Koehler, K. (1988). The effect of foreign accent and speaking rate on native speaker comprehension. *Language Learning, 38* (4), 561-613.

Anderson-Hsieh, J., Johnson, R., & Koehler, K. (1992). The relationship between native speaker judgments of nonnative pronunciation and deviance in segmentals, prosody, and syllable structure. *Language Learning, 42* (4), 529-555.

Angoff, W. H. (1993). Perspectives on differential item functioning methodology. In P. W. Holland & H. Wainer (Eds.), *Differential item functioning* (pp. 3-24). Hillsdale: Lawrence Erlbaum Associates.

Arnold, J. (2000). Seeing through listening comprehension exam anxiety. *TESOL Quarterly, 34* (4), 777-786.

Bachman, L. F. (1990). *Fundamental considerations in language testing.* Oxford: Oxford University Press.

Bachman, L. F. (2004). *Statistical analyses for language assessment.* Cambridge: Cambridge University Press.

Bachman, L. F., & Palmer, A. S. (1996). *Language testing in practice: Designing and developing useful language tests*. Oxford: Oxford University Press.

Baldwin, W. (2000). Information no one else knows: The value of self report. In A. A. Stone, J. S. Turkkan, C. A. Bachrach, J. B. Jobe, H. S. Kurtzman, & V. S. Cain (Eds.), *The science of self report: Implications for research and practice* (pp. 3-8). Mahwah, NJ: Lawrence Erlbaum.

Bambgose, A. (1992). Standard Nigerian English: Issues of identification. In B. B. Kachru (Ed.), *The other tongue: English across cultures* (pp. 148-161). Urbana; Chicago: University of Illinois Press.

Bambgose, A. (1998). Torn between the norms: Innovation in world Englishes. *World Englishes, 17*, 1-14.

Bamford, J., & Wilson, I. (1979). Methodological considerations and practical aspects of the BKB sentence lists. In J. Bench & J. Bamford (Eds.), *Speech-hearing tests and the spoken language of hearing-impaired children* (pp. 148-187). London: Academic Press.

Bayard, D., Weatherall, A., Gallois, C., & Pittam, J. (2001). Pax Americana? Accent attitudinal evaluations in New Zealand, Australia and America. *Journal of Sociolinguistics, 5* (1), 22-49.

Bejar, I., Douglas, D., Jamieson, J., Nissan, S., & Turner, J. (2000). *TOEFL 2000 listening framework: A working paper*. Princeton, New Jersey: Educational Testing Service.

Bent, T., & Bradlow, A. R. (2003). The interlanguage speech intelligibility benefit. *Journal of the Acoustical Society of America, 114* (3), 1600-1610.

Best, C. T. (1995). A direct-realist view of cross-language speech perception. In W. Strange (Ed.), *Speech perception and linguistic experience: Issues in cross-cultural research* (pp. 171-204). Baltimore: York Press.

Bhatt, R. M. (2001). World Englishes. *Annual Review of Anthropology, 30*, 527-550.

Bilbow, G. T. (1989). Towards an understanding of overseas students' difficulties in lectures: A phenomenographic approach. *Journal of Further and Higher Education, 13* (2), 85-99.

Bond, Z. S. (1999). *Slips of the ear: Errors in the perception of casual conversation.* San Diego, California: Academic Press.

Bond, Z. S. (2005). Slips of the ear. In D. B. Pisoni & R. E. Remez (Eds.), *The handbook of speech perception* (pp. 290-310). Oxford: Blackwell Publishing.

Bourdieu, P. (1977). The economics of linguistic exchanges. *Social Science Information, 16*, 645-668.

Bradlow, A., & Bent, T. (2002). The clear speech effect for non-native listeners. *Journal of the Acoustical Society of America, 112* (1), 272-284.

Bradlow, A., & Bent, T. (2003). Listener adaptation to foreign accented English. In M. J. Sole, D. Recasens & J. Romero (Eds.), *Proceedings of the 15th International Congress of Phonetic Sciences* (pp. 2881-2884). Barcelona, Spain, 2003.

Bradlow, A., & Bent, T. (2008). Perceptual adaptation to non-native speech. *Cognition, 106* (2), 707-729.

Bradlow, A., Torretta, G., & Pisoni, D. (1996). Intelligibility of normal speech: 1. Global and fine-grained acoustic-phonetic talker characteristics. *Speech Communication, 20*, 255-272.

Brennan, E. M., & Brennan, J. S. (1981). Accent scaling and language attitudes: Reactions to Mexican-American English speech. *Language and Speech, 24*, 207-221.

Bresnahan, M. J., Ohashi, R., Nebashi, R., Liu, W. Y., & Shearman, S. M. (2002). Attitudinal and affective response toward accented English. *Language and Communication, 22*, 171-185.

Brindley, G. (1998). Assessing listening abilities. *Annual Review of Applied Linguistics, 18*, 171-191.

Brindley, G., & Slatyer, H. (2002). Exploring task difficulty in ESL listening assessment. *Language Testing, 19* (4), 369-394.

Brodkey, D. (1972). Dictation as a measure of mutual intelligibility: A pilot study. *Language Learning, 22* (2), 203-220.

Brown, G. (1990). *Listening to spoken English*. London; New York: Longman.

Brown, G. (1995). *Speakers, listeners, and communication*. Cambridge: Cambridge University Press.

Brown, K. (1968). Intelligibility. In A. Davies (Ed.), *Language testing symposium* (pp. 180-191). Oxford: Oxford University Press.

Brown, A., & Lumley, T. (1998). Linguistic and cultural norms in language testing: A case study. *Melbourne Papers in Language Testing, 7* (1), 80-96.

Brutt-Griffler, J., & Samimy, K. K. (2001). Transcending the nativeness paradigm. *World Englishes, 20* (1), 99-106.

Buck, G. (1990). *The testing of second language listening comprehension*. Unpublished doctoral dissertation, University of Lancaster, United Kingdom.

Buck, G. (1991). The testing of listening comprehension: An introspective study. *Language Testing, 8* (1), 67-91.

Buck, G. (2001). *Assessing listening*. Cambridge: Cambridge University Press.

Buck, G., & Tatsuoka, K. (1998). Application of the rule-space procedure to language testing: Examining attributes of a free response listening test. *Language Testing, 15* (2), 119-157.

Burns, R. B. (1997). *Introduction to research methods*. Melbourne: Addison Wesley Longman.

Cambridge ESOL (2008). *IELTS teaching resource*. Retrieved March 1, 2008 from http://www.cambridgeesol.org/teach/ielts/listening/aboutthepaper/overview.htm

Canale, M., & Swain, M. (1980). Theoretical bases of communicative approaches to second language teaching and testing. *Applied Linguistics, 1* (1), 1-47.

Canagarajah, S. (2006). Changing communicative needs, revised assessment objectives: Testing English as an international language. *Language Assessment Quarterly, 3* (3), 229-242.

Cargile, A. C. (1997). Attitudes toward Chinese-accented speech: An investigation in two contexts. *Journal of Language and Social Psychology, 16*, 434-444.

Cargile, A. C. (2002). Speaker evaluation measures of language attitudes: Evidence of information-processing effects. *Language Awareness, 11*, (3), 178-191.

Cargile, A. C., & Bradac, J. J. (2001). Attitudes toward language: a review of speaker-evaluation research and a general process model. In W. B. Gudykunst (Ed.), *Communication Yearbook 25* (pp. 347-382). Mahwah, New Jersey: Lawrence Erlbaum Associates.

Cargile, A. C., & Giles, H. (1997). Understanding language attitudes: Exploring listener affect and identity. *Language and Communication, 17* (3), 195-217.

Cargile, A. C., & Giles, H. (1998). Language attitudes toward varieties of English: An American-Japanese context. *Journal of Applied Communication Research, 26*, 338-356.

Chang, J. (2001). Chinese speakers. In M. Swan and B. Smith (Eds.), *Learner English: A teacher's guide to interference and other problems* (pp. 310-324). Cambridge: Cambridge University Press.

Chiba, R., Matsuura, H., & Yamamoto, A. (1995). Japanese attitudes toward English accents. *World Englishes, 13* (1), 77-86.

Chishanga, T., & Kamwangamalu, N. M. (1997). Owning the mother tongue: The English language in South Africa. *Journal of Multilingual and Multicultural Development, 18*, 89-99.

Clark, H. H., & Clark, E. (1977). *Psychology and language*. New York: Harcourt, Brace, Jovanovich.

Clarke, C. M. (2000). Perceptual adjustment to foreign-accented English. *Journal of the Acoustical Society of America, 107* (5), 2856.

Clarke, C. M., & Garrett, M. F. (2004). Rapid adaptation to foreign-accented English. *Journal of the Acoustical Society of America, 116* (6), 3647-3658.

Clauser, B. E., & Mazor, B. M. (1998). Using statistical procedures to identify differentially functioning test items. *Educational Measurement: Issues and Practice, 17* (1), 31-44.

Clopper, C. G., & Pisoni, D. B. (2004). Effects of talker variability on perceptual learning of dialects. *Language and Speech, 47* (3), 207-239.

Cohen, A. (1987). Using verbal reports in research on language learning. In K. Faerch & G. Kasper (Eds.), *Introspection in second language research* (pp. 82-95). Philadelphia: Multilingual Matters.

Cohen, A. (1996). Verbal reports as a source of insights into second language learner strategies. *Applied Language Learning, 7*, 5-24.

Cohen, A. (1998). *Strategies in learning and using a second language*. London: Longman.

Cohen, J. (1988). *Statistical power analysis for the behavioral sciences*. Hillsdale, NJ: Erlbaum.

Creswell, J. W., & Plano Clark, V. L. (2007). *Designing and conducting mixed methods research*. Thousand Oaks, California: SAGE publications.

Crystal, D. *The Cambridge Encyclopedia of the English language*. Cambridge: Cambridge University Press.

Dailey, R. M., Giles, H., & Jansma, L. L. (2005). Language attitudes in an Anglo-Hispanic context: The role of the linguistic landscape. *Language and Communication, 25*, 27-38.

Dalton-Puffer, C., Kaltenboeck, G., & Smit, U. (1997). Learner attitudes and L2 pronunciation in Austria. *World Englishes, 16*, (1), 115-128.

Davies, A. (2003). *The native speaker: Myth and reality*. Clevedon: Multilingual Matters.

Davies, A., Brown, A., Elder, C., Hill, K., Lumley, T., & McNamara, T. (1999). *Dictionary of language testing*. Cambridge: Cambridge University Press.

Davies, A., Hamp-Lyons, L., & Kemp, C. (2003). Whose norms? International proficiency tests in English. *World Englishes, 22* (4), 571-584.

Derwing, T. M. (2003). What do ESL students say about their own accents? *Canadian Modern Language Review, 59* (4), 547-566.

Derwing, T. M., & Munro, M. J. (1997). Accent, intelligibility and comprehensibility: Evidence from four L1s. *Studies in Second Language Acquisition, 19*, 1-16.

Derwing, T. M., Munro, M. J., & Wiebe, G. (1998). Evidence in favor of a broad framework for pronunciation instruction. *Language Learning, 48* (3), 393-410.

Derwing, T. M., Rossiter, M. J., & Munro, M. J. (2002). Teaching native speakers to listen to foreign-accented speech. *Journal of Multilingual and Multicultural Development, 23* (4), 245-259.

Donoghue, J. R., & Allen, N. L. (1993). Thin versus thick matching in the Mantel-Haenszel procedure for detecting DIF. *Journal of Educational Statistics, 18* (2), 131-154.

Dorans N. J. (1989). Two new approaches to assessing differential item functioning: Standardization and the Mantel-Haenszel method. *Applied Measurement in Education, 2* (3), 217-233.

Dorans, N. J., & Holland, P. W. (1993). DIF detection and description: Mantel-Haenszel and standardization. In P. W. Holland & H. Wainer (Eds.), *Differential item functioning* (pp. 35-66). Hillsdale: Lawrence Erlbaum Associates.

Dunkel, P., Henning, G., & Chaudron, C. (1993). The assessment of an L2 listening comprehension construct: A tentative model for test specification and development. *The Modern Language Journal, 77* (2), 180-191.

Edwards, J. R. (1982). Language attitudes and their implications among English speakers. In E. B. Ryan & H. Giles (Eds.), *Attitudes towards language variation: Social and applied contexts* (pp. 20-33). London: Edward Arnold.

Eisenstein, M. (1983). Native reactions to non-native speech: A review of empirical research. *Studies in Second Language Acquisition, 5* (2), 160-176.

Elder, C. (1996). The effect of language background on "foreign" language test performance: The case of Chinese, Italian and Modern Greek. *Language Learning, 46* (2), 233-282.

Elder, C. (1997). *The background speaker as learner of Italian, Modern Greek & Chinese: Implications for foreign language assessment.* Unpublished doctoral dissertation, The University of Melbourne.

Ericsson, K., & Simon, H. (1993). *Protocol analysis: Verbal reports as data* (2nd ed.). Cambridge, MA: MIT Press.

Esling, J. H. (1998). Everyone has an accent except me. In L. Bauer & P. Trudgill (Eds.), *Language Myths* (pp. 169-175). London: Penguin Books.

ETS [Educational Testing Service] (2000) *TOEFL® Test Preparation Kit (2nd edition).* Princeton, NJ: ETS.

ETS [Educational Testing Service] (2005). *TOEFL iBT Tips: How to prepare for the next generation TOEFL test and communicate with comfort.* Princeton, NJ: ETS.

Faerch, C. and Kasper, G. (1987). From product to process – introspective methods in second language research. In C. Faerch & G. Kasper (Eds.), *Introspection in second language research* (pp. 5-23). Clevedon: Multilingual Matters Ltd.

Fayer, J. M., & Krasinski, E. K. (1987). Native and nonnative judgments of intelligibility and irritation. *Language Learning, 37* (3), 313-326.

Ferne, T., & Rupp, A. A. (2007). A synthesis of 15 years of research on DIF in language testing: Methodological advances, challenges and recommendations. *Language Assessment Quarterly, 4* (2), 113-148.

Fidalgo, A. M., Ferreres, D., & Muñiz, J. (2004). Utility of the Mantel-Haenszel procedure for detecting differential item functioning with small samples. *Educational and Psychological Measurement, 64* (6), 925-936.

Field, J. (2003). Promoting perception: Lexical segmentation in L2 listening. *ELT Journal, 57* (4), 325-334.

Field, J. (2004). An insight into listeners' problems: Too much bottom-up or too much top-down? *System, 32* (3), 363-377.

Field, J. (2005). Intelligibility and the listener: The role of lexical stress. *TESOL Quarterly, 39* (3), 399-424.

Flege, J. E. (1984). The detection of French accent by American listeners. *Journal of the Acoustical Society of America, 76* (3), 692-707.

Flege, J. E. (1988). Factors affecting degree of perceived foreign accent in English sentences. *Journal of the Acoustical Society of America, 84* (1), 70-79.

Flege, J. E., & Fletcher, K.L. (1992). Talker and listener effects on degree of perceived foreign accent. *Journal of the Acoustical Society of America, 91* (1), 370-389.

Flege, J. E., Munro, M. J., & MacKay, I. R. A. (1995). Factors affecting strength of perceived foreign accent in a second language. *Journal of the Acoustical Society of America, 97* (5), 3125-3134.

Flege, J. E., Takagi, N., & Mann, V. (1996). Lexical familiarity and English-language experience affect Japanese adults' perception of /ɹ/ and /l/. *Journal of the Acoustical Society of America, 99* (2), 1161-1173.

Flowerdew, J. (1994). Research of relevance to second language lecture comprehension – an overview. In J. Flowerdew (Ed.), *Academic listening* (pp. 7-29). New York: Cambridge University Press.

Francis, A. L., & Nusbaum, H. C. (1999). The effect of lexical complexity on Intelligibility. *International Journal of Speech Technology, 3*, 15-25.

Freed, B. F., Dewey, D. P., Segalowitz, N., & Halter, R. (2004). The language contact profile. *Studies in Second Language Acquisition, 26*, 349-356.

Fulcher, G. &, Davidson, F. (2007). *Language testing and assessment: An advanced resource book*. London: Routledge.

Gallois, C., & Callan, V. J. (1989). Attitudes to spoken Australian English: Judgments of ingroup and ethnic outgroup speakers. *Australian Journal of Linguistics, 9*, 149-160.

Garrett, P., Coupland, N., & Williams, A. (2003). *Investigating Language Attitudes*. Cardiff: University of Wales Press.

Gass, S., & Mackey, A. (2000). *Stimulated recall methodology in second language research*. Mahwah, New Jersey: Lawrence Erlbaum Associates.

Gass, S., & Mackey, A. (2007). *Data elicitation for second and foreign language research*. Mahwah, New Jersey: Lawrence Erlbaum Associates.

Gass, S., & Varonis, E. M. (1984). The effect of familiarity on the comprehensibility of nonnative speech. *Language Learning, 34* (1), 65-89.

Geranpayeh, A., & Taylor, L. (2008). Examining listening: Developments and issues in assessing second language listening. *Cambridge ESOL: Research Notes, 32*, 2-4.

Giles, H., & Billings, A. C. (2004). Assessing language attitudes: Speaker evaluation studies. In A. Davies & C. Elder (Eds.), *The handbook of Applied Linguistics* (pp. 187-209). Malden, MA: Blackwell.

Giles, H., & Sassoon, C. (1983). The effect of speaker's accent, social class background and message style on British listeners' social judgments. *Language and Communication, 3*, 305-313.

Gill, M. M. (1994). Accent and stereotypes: Their effect on the perceptions of teachers and lecture comprehension. *Journal of Applied Communication Research, 22*, 349-361.

Goh, C. C. M. (1998). How ESL learners with different listening abilities use comprehension strategies and tactics. *Language Teaching Research, 2* (2), 124-147.

Goh, C. C. M. (1999). How much do learners know about the factors that influence their listening comprehension? *Hong Kong Journal of Applied Linguistics, 4* (1), 17-41.

Goh, C. C. M. (2000). A cognitive perspective on language learners' listening comprehension problems. *System, 28*, 55-75.

Green, A. (1998). *Verbal protocol analysis in language testing research: A handbook*. Cambridge, UK: Cambridge University Press.

Gruba, P. (1999). *The role of digital video media in second language listening comprehension*. Unpublished doctoral dissertation, University of Melbourne, Australia.

Gundersen, D. F. & Perrill, N. K. (1989). Extending the 'Speech Evaluation Instrument' to public speaking settings. *Journal of Language and Social Psychology, 8* (1), 59-61.

Hahn, L. D. (2004). Primary stress and intelligibility: research to motivate the teaching of suprasegmentals. *TESOL Quarterly, 38* (2), 201-223.

Hall, S. (1997). The local and the global: Globalization and ethnicity. In A. D. King (Ed.), *Culture, globalization, and the world system* (pp. 19–40). Minneapolis: University of Minnesota Press.

Hambleton, R. K. (2006). Good practices for identifying differential item functioning. *Medical Care, 44* (11), 182-188.

Harding, L. (2008). Accent and academic listening assessment: A study of test-taker perceptions. *Melbourne Papers in Language Testing, 13* (1), 1-33.

Hasan, A. S. (2000). Learners' perceptions of listening comprehension problems. *Language, Culture and Curriculum, 13* (2), 137-153.

Higgins, C. (2003). "Ownership" of English in the outer circle: An alternative to the NS-NNS dichotomy. *TESOL Quarterly, 37* (4), 615-644.

Holland, P. W., & Wainer, H. (Eds.) (1993). *Differential item functioning.* Hillsdale: Lawrence Erlbaum Associates.

Hughes, A. & Trudgill, P. (1996). *English accents and dialects: an introduction to social and regional varieties of English in the British Isles*. New York: Arnold.

Hung T. T. N. (2000). Towards a phonology of Hong Kong English. *World Englishes, 19* (3), 337-356.

Hustad, K. C. (2006). A closer look at transcription intelligibility for speakers with dysarthria: Evaluation of scoring paradigms and linguistic errors made by listeners. *American Journal of Speech-Language Pathology, 15* (3), 268-277.

Hymes, D. (1972). On communicative competence. In J. B. Pride & J. Holmes (Eds.), *Sociolinguistics* (pp. 269-293). Harmondsworth: Penguin.

IELTS [International English Language Testing System] (2007). *IELTS Handbook*. British Council, IDP: IELTS Australia, University of Cambridge ESOL Examinations.

Jenkins, J. (2000). *The phonology of English as an international language*. Oxford: Oxford University Press.

Jenkins, J. (2006a). The spread of EIL: A testing time for testers. *ELT Journal, 60* (1), 42-50.

Jenkins, J. (2006b). The times they are (very slowly) a-changin'. *ELT Journal, 60* (1), 61-62.

Jenkins, J. (2007). *English as a Lingua Franca: Attitude and identity*. Oxford: Oxford University Press.

Jesney, K. (2004). *The Use of global foreign accent rating in studies of L2 acquisition*. Calgary, AB: University of Calgary Language Research Centre Reports.

Johnson, R. B., & Onwuegbuzie, A. J. (2004). Mixed methods research: A research paradigm whose time has come. *Educational Researcher, 33* (7), 14-26.

Kachru, B. B. (1983). *The Indianization of English*. Delhi: Oxford University Press.

Kachru, B. B. (1985). Standards, codification, and sociolinguistic realism: The English language in the outer circle. In R. Quirk & H. Widdowson (Eds.), *English in the world: Teaching and learning the language and literatures* (pp. 11-30). Cambridge: Cambridge University Press.

Kachru, B. B. (1997). World Englishes 2000: Resources for research and teaching. In L. E. Smith & M. L. Forman, (Eds.), *World Englishes: Selected Essays* (pp. 209-251). Honolulu: University of Hawaii and the East-West Centre.

Kane, M. (1992). An argument-based approach to validity. *Psychological Bulletin, 112*, 527–535.

Kane, M. (2006). Validation. In R. L. Brennan (Ed), *Educational measurement (4th edition)*. Washington, DC: American Council on Education/Praeger.

Kennedy, G. (1978). *The testing of listening comprehension.* Singapore: Singapore University Press.

King George International College (n.d.). *Next Generation TOEFL ("NGT") or "IBT" (Internet-based Test) Test.* Retrieved September 8 2008 from http://www.kgic.ca/op_toefl.htm

Kirkpatrick, A. (2007a). *World Englishes: Implications for international communication and English Language Teaching.* Cambridge: Cambridge University Press.

Kirkpatrick, A. (2007b). The communicative strategies of ASEAN speakers of English as a lingua franca. In D. Prescott, A. Kirkpatrick, I. Martin & A. Hashim (Eds), *English in Southeast Asia: Literacies, literatures and varieties* (pp. 121-139). Cambridge: Cambridge Scholars Press.

Kristjansson, E., Aylesworth, R., & McDowell, I. (2005). A comparison of four methods for detecting differential item functioning in ordered response items. *Educational and Psychological Measurement, 65*, 935-953.

Kubota, R. (2001). Teaching world Englishes to native speakers of English in the USA. *World Englishes, 20* (1), 47-64.

Kunnan, A.J. (2004). Test fairness. In M. Milanovic & C. Weir (eds.) *Studies in Language Testing 18: European Language Testing in a Global Context* (pp. 27-48). Cambridge: Cambridge University Press.

Ladegaard, H. J. (1998). National stereotypes and language attitudes: The perception of British, American and Australian language and culture in Denmark. *Language and Communication, 18*, 251-274.

Lambert, W. E., Hodgson, R., Gardner, R. C., & Fillenbaum, S. (1960). Evaluational reactions to spoken languages. *Journal of Abnormal and Social Psychology, 60*, 44-51.

Lane, H. (1963). Foreign accent and speech distortion. *The Journal of the Acoustical Society of America, 35,* 451-453.

Lindemann, S. (2002). Listening with an attitude: A model of native-speaker comprehension of non-native speakers in the United States of America. *Language in Society, 31*, 419-441.

Lindemann, S. (2003). Koreans, Chinese or Indians? Attitudes and ideologies about non-native English speakers in the United States. *Journal of Sociolinguistics, 7* (3), 348-364.

Lippi-Green, R. (1997). *English with an accent: Language, ideology, and discrimination in the United States.* London; New York: Routledge.

Llurda, E. (2004). Non-native-speaker teachers and English as an International Language. *International Journal of Applied Linguistics, 14* (3), 314-323.

Llurda, E. (2005). Native-speaker reactions to non-native speech: A review. *Syntagma, 7*, 43-51.

Lowenberg, P. (2002). Assessing English proficiency in the Expanding Circle. *World Englishes*, 21, 3: 431-435.

Lumley, T., & Brown, A. (2005). Research methods in language testing. In E. Hinkel (Ed.), *Handbook of research in second language teaching and learning* (pp. 833-856). Mahwah, New Jersey: Lawrence Erlbaum Associates.

Lynch, T. (1994). Training lecturers for international audiences. In J. Flowerdew (Ed.), *Academic listening* (pp. 269-289). New York: Cambridge University Press.

Lynch, T. (2002). Listening: Questions of level. In R. B. Kaplan (Ed.), *Oxford handbook of applied linguistics* (pp. 39-48). Oxford: Oxford University Press.

Mackey, A., & Gass, S. (2005). *Second language research: Methodology and design.* Mahwah, New Jersey: Lawrence Erlbaum Associates.

Magen, H. S. (1998). The perception of foreign-accented speech. *Journal of Phonetics, 26*, 381-400.

Major, R. C., Fitzmaurice, S. F., Bunta, F., & Balasubramanian, C. (2002). The effects of nonnative accents on listening comprehension: Implications for ESL assessment. *TESOL Quarterly, 36* (2), 173-190.

Major, R. C., Fitzmaurice, S. F., Bunta, F., & Balasubramanian, C. (2005). Testing the effects of regional, ethnic and international dialects of English on listening comprehension. *Language Learning, 55* (1), 37-69.

Markham, P. L. (1988). Gender and the perceived expertness of the speaker in ESL listening recall. *TESOL Quarterly, 22* (3), 397-406.

Matsuura, H., Chiba, R. & Fujieda, M. (1999). Intelligibility and comprehensibility of American and Irish Englishes in Japan. *World Englishes, 18* (1), 49-62.

Matsuura, H., Chiba, R., & Yamamoto, A. (1994). Japanese college students' attitudes towards non-native varieties of English. In D. Graddol & J. Swann (Eds.), *Evaluating Language* (pp. 52-61). Clevedon: Multilingual Matters.

Mauranen, A. (2003). The corpus of English as a lingua franca in academic settings. *TESOL Quarterly, 37* (3), 513-527.

Maxcy, S. J. (2003). Pragmatic threads in mixed methods research in the social sciences: The search for multiple modes of inquiry and the end of the philosophy of formalism. In A. Tashakkori & C. Teddlie (Eds.), *Handbook of mixed methods in social and behavioral research* (pp. 51-89). Thousand Oaks, California: SAGE Publications.

McClelland, J. L., & Elman, J. L. (1986). The TRACE model of speech perception. *Cognitive Psychology, 18* , 1-86.

McGraw, K. O. & Wong, S. P. (1996). Forming inferences about some intraclass correlation coefficients. *Psychological Methods, 1* (1), 30-46.

McKenzie, R. M. (2008). Social factors and non-native attitudes towards varieties of spoken English: a Japanese case study. *International journal of Applied Linguistics, 18* (1), 63-88.

McNamara, T. F. (1996). *Measuring second language performance*. London; New York: Longman.

McNamara, T. F., & Roever, C. (2006). *Language testing: The social dimension*. Oxford, England: Basil Blackwell.

Messick, S. (1989). Validity. In R. J. Linn (Ed.), *Educational Measurement* (pp. 13-103). New York: Macmillan.

Morrison, R., & White, M. (2005). Nurturing global listeners: increasing familiarity and appreciation for world Englishes. *World Englishes, 24* (3), 361-370.

Morse, J. M. (1991). Approaches to qualitative-quantitative methodological triangulation. *Nursing Research, 40*, 120-123.

Mulac, A. (1998). The gender-linked language effect: Do language differences really make a difference? In D. J. Canary & K. Dindia (Eds.), *Sex differences and similarities in communication* (pp. 127-153). Mahwah, NJ: Erlbaum.

Muñiz, J., Hambleton, R. K., & Xing, D. (2001). Small sample studies to detect flaws in item translations. *International Journal of Testing, 1* (2), 115-135.

Munro, M. J. (2008). Foreign accent and speech intelligibility. In J. G. Hansen Edwards & M. L. Zampini (Eds.), *Phonology and Second Language Acquisition* (pp. 193-218). Amsterdam: John Benjamins.

Munro, M. J., & Derwing, T. M. (1994). Evaluations of foreign accent in extemporaneous and read material. *Language Testing, 11* (3), 253-266.

Munro, M. J., & Derwing, T. M. (1995a). Foreign accent, comprehensibility, and intelligibility in the speech of second language learners. *Language Learning, 45* (1), 73-97.

Munro, M. J., & Derwing, T. M. (1995b). Processing time, accent and comprehensibility in the perception of native and foreign accented speech. *Language and Speech, 38* (3), 289-306.

Munro, M. J., Derwing, T. M., & Morton, S. L. (2006). The mutual intelligibility of L2 speech. *Studies in Second Language Acquisition, 28* (1), 111-131.

Norris, D., McQueen, J. M., & Cutler, A. (2000). Merging information in speech recognition: Feedback is never necessary. *Behavioural and Brain Sciences, 23*, 299-370.

Norton, B. (1997). Language, identity, and the ownership of English. *TESOL Quarterly, 31* (3), 409-429.

Ockey, G. J. (2007). Construct implications of including still image or video in computer-based listening tests. *Language Testing, 24* (4), 517-537.

Ogier, J. (2005). Evaluating the effect of a lecturer's language background on a student rating of teaching form. *Assessment and evaluation in higher education, 30* (5), 477-488.

O'Malley, J.M., Chamot, A., & Kupper, L. (1989). Listening comprehension strategies in second language acquisition. *Applied Linguistics, 10* (4), 418–37.

Ortmeyer, C., & Boyle, J. P. (1985). The effect of accent differences on comprehension. *RELC Journal, 16* (2), 48-53.

Osgood, C. E., Suci, G. J., & Tannenbaum, P. H. (1957). *The measurement of meaning*. Urbana: University of Illinois Press.

Pallant, J. (2002). *SPSS survival manual*. NSW: Allen and Unwin.

Peng, L., & Setter, J. (2000). The emergence of systematicity in the English pronunciations of two Cantonese-speaking adults in Hong Kong. *English World-Wide, 21* (1), 81-108.

Peirce, C. S. (1878). How to make our ideas clear. *Popular Science Monthly, 12*, 286-302.

Peterson, P. W. (2001). Skills and strategies for proficient listening. In M. Celce-Murcia (Ed.) *Teaching English as a Second or Foreign Language* (pp. 87-100). Boston: Heinle & Heinle.

Pickering, L. (2006). Current research on intelligibility in English as a Lingua Franca. *Annual Review of Applied Linguistics, 26*, 219-233.

Piske, T., MacKay, I. R. A., & Flege, J. E. (2001). Factors affecting degree of foreign accent in an L2: a review. *Journal of Phonetics, 29*, 191-215.

Pisoni, D. B. (1997). Some thoughts on "normalization" in speech perception. In K. Johnson & J. Mullenix (Eds.), *Talker variability in speech processing* (pp. 9-32). San Diego: Academic Press.

Quirk, R. (1982). International communication and the concept of Nuclear English. In C. J. Brumfit (Ed.), *English for international communication* (pp. 15-28). Oxford: Pergamon Press.

Rajadurai, J. (2007). Intelligibility studies: A consideration of empirical and ideological issues. *World Englishes, 26* (1), 87-98.

Read, J. (2002). The use of interactive input in EAP listening assessment. *Journal of English for Academic Purposes, 1*, 105-119.

Richards, J. (1983). Listening comprehension: Approach, design, procedure. *TESOL Quarterly, 17*, 219-240.

Riney, T. J., Takagi, N., & Inutska, K. (2005). Phonetic parameters and perceptual judgments of accent in English by American and Japanese listeners. *TESOL Quarterly, 39* (3), 441-466.

Roever, C. (2007). DIF in the assessment of second language pragmatics. *Language Assessment Quarterly, 4* (2), 165-189.

Rost, M. (1990). *Listening in language learning*. New York: Longman.

Rost, M. (1994). On-line summaries as representations of lecture understanding. In J. Flowerdew (Ed.), *Academic listening* (pp. 93-128). New York: Cambridge University Press.

Rost, M. (2002). *Teaching and researching listening*. Harlow: Longman.

Rubin, D. L. (1992). Nonlanguage factors affecting undergraduates' judgments of nonnative English-speaking teaching assistants. *Research in Higher Education, 33*, 511-531.

Ryan, E. B., Hewstone, M., & Giles, H. (1984). Language and intergroup attitudes. In J. Eiser (Ed.), *Attitudinal judgment* (pp. 135-160). New York: Springer.

Ryan, E. B. & Sebastian, R. J. (1980). The effects of speech style and social class background on social judgments of speakers. *British Journal of Social and Clinical Psychology, 19*, 229-233.

Ryan, K. & Bachman, L. F. (1992). Differential item functioning on two tests of EFL proficiency. *Language Testing, 9*, 12-19.

Schmid, P. M. & Yeni-Komshian, G. H. (1999). The effects of speaker accent and target predictability on perception of mispronunciations. *Journal of Speech, Language, and Hearing Research, 42*, 56-64.

Seidlhofer, B. (2001). Closing a conceptual gap: The case for a description of English as a lingua franca. *International Journal of Applied Linguistics, 11*, 133–58.

Seidlhofer, B. (2005). English as a lingua franca. *ELT Journal*, 59, 4: 339-341.

Shohamy, E. (2004). Assessment in multicultural societies: Applying democratic principles and practices to language testing. In B. Norton & K. Toohey (Eds.), *Critical pedagogies and language learning* (pp. 72-92). Cambridge; New York: Cambridge University Press.

Smith, L. E., & Bisazza, J. A. (1982). The comprehensibility of three varieties of English for college students in seven countries. *Language Learning, 32* (2), 259-269.

Smith, L. E., & Nelson, C. E. (1985). International intelligibility of English: directions and resources. *World Englishes, 3*, 333-342.

Smith, L. & Rafiqzad, K. (1983). English for cross-cultural communication: the question of intelligibility. In L.E. Smith (ed.) *Readings in English as an international language* (pp.49-58). Oxford: Pergamon Press.

Southwood, H. M & Flege, J. E. (1999). Scaling foreign accent: Direct magnitude estimation versus interval scaling. *Clinical linguistics and phonetics, 13* (5), 335-349.

Stanovich, K. E. (1980). Toward an interactive-compensatory model of individual differences in the development of reading fluency. *Reading Research Quarterly, 16*, 32-71.

Stephan, C. (1997). The unknown Englishes? Testing German students' ability to identify varieties of English. In E. W. Schneider (Ed.), *Englishes around the world* (pp. 93-109). Amsterdam: John Benjamins.

Stibbard, R. M., & Lee, J. (2006). Evidence against the mismatched interlanguage speech intelligibility benefit hypothesis. *Journal of the Acoustical Society of America, 120* (1), 433-442.

Strange, W. (1995). Cross-language studies of speech perception: a historical overview. In W. Strange (Ed.), *Speech perception and linguistic experience: Issues in cross-cultural research* (pp. 3-45). Baltimore: York Press.

Strevens, P. (1956). English overseas: Choosing a model of pronunciation. *ELT Journal, X* (4), 123-131.

Strevens, P. (1983). What is Standard English? In L. E. Smith (Ed.), *Readings in English as an international language* (pp. 87-93). Oxford: Pergamon Press.

Tajfel, H., & Turner, J. (1986). The social identity theory of intergroup behavior. In S. Worchel & W. Austin (Eds.), *Psychology of intergroup relations* (pp. 7-24). Chicago: Nelson-Hall.

Tartter, V. C. (1998). *Language and its normal processing*. Thousand Oaks; London; New Delhi: Sage Publications.

Tashakkori, A., & Teddlie, C. (1998). *Mixed methodology: Combining qualitative and quantitative approaches (Applied Social Research Methods, No. 46)*. Thousand Oaks, CA: Sage Publications.

Tauroza, S., & Luk, J. (1997). Accent and second language listening comprehension. *RELC Journal, 28* (1), 54-71.

Taylor, L. (2006). The changing landscape of English: implications for language assessment. *ELT Journal, 60* (1), 51-60.

Teddlie, C., & Tashakkori, A. (2003). Major issues and controversies in the use of mixed methods in the social and behavioral sciences. In A. Tashakkori & C. Teddlie (Eds.), *Handbook of mixed methods in social and behavioral research* (pp. 3-50). Thousand Oaks, California: SAGE Publications.

Thompson, I. (2001). Japanese speakers. In M. Swan and B. Smith (Eds.), *Learner English: A teacher's guide to interference and other problems* (pp. 296-309). Cambridge: Cambridge University Press.

Vandergrift, L. (2003). Orchestrating strategy use: Toward a model of the skilled second language listener. *Language Learning, 53* (3), 463-496.

Vandergrift, L. (2007). Recent developments in second and foreign language listening comprehension research. *Language Teaching, 40*, 191-210.

Wagner, E. (2008). Video listening tests: What are they measuring? *Language Assessment Quarterly, 5* (3), 218-243.

Weil, S. A. (2001). *Foreign accented speech: Adaptation and generalization.* Unpublished master's thesis, the Ohio State University, USA.

Weir, C. (2005). *Language testing and validation: An evidence-based approach.* Hampshire; New York: Palgrave MacMillan.

Wells, J. C. (1982). *Accents of English.* Cambridge; New York: Cambridge University Press.

Widdowson, H. G. (1978). *Teaching language as communication.* Oxford: Oxford University Press.

Widdowson, H. G. (1994). The ownership of English. *TESOL Quarterly, 28*, 377-389.

Wilcox, G. K. (1978). The effect of accent on listening comprehension: A Singapore study. *English language teaching journal, 32*, 118-127.

Wu, Y. (1998). What do tests of listening comprehension test? – A retrospection study of EFL test-takers performing a multiple choice task. *Language Testing, 15* (1), 21-44.

Yule, G., Wetzel, S., & Kennedy, L. (1990). Listening perception accuracy of ESL learners as a function of speaker L1. *TESOL Quarterly, 24* (3), 519-523.

Zahn, C. J., & Hopper, R. (1985). Measuring language attitudes: The speech evaluation instrument. *Journal of Language and Social Psychology, 4* (2), 113-123.

Zielinski, B. (2006). The intelligibility cocktail: An interaction between speaker and listener ingredients. *Prospect, 21* (1), 22-45.

Zielinski, B. (2007). *Reduced intelligibility in L2 speakers of English.* Unpublished doctoral dissertation, La Trobe University, Australia.

Zumbo, B. D. (1999). *A handbook on the theory and methods of differential item functioning (DIF): Logistic regression modeling as a unitary framework for binary and Likert-type (ordinal) item scores*. Ottawa, ON: Directorate of Human Resources Research and Evaluation, Department of National Defense.

Zumbo, B. D. (2007). Three generations of DIF analyses: Considering where it has been, where it is now, and where it is going. *Language Assessment Quarterly, 4* (2), 223-233.

Appendix A

Intelligibility, Comprehensibility and Accent Rating Task (Speaker selection materials)

Appendix A contains (in the following order):

- Questionnaire on raters' biographical details
- Orthographic transcription task
- Comprehensibility rating task
- Accent rating task
- Forced choice accent identification task

Intelligibility, accentedness and comprehensibility (IAC) task

Name: _____

Email: _____

Gender: Female/Male (please circle)

L1: _____

Country of birth: _____

I speak to people from different L1 backgrounds (please circle):

        Never   Sometimes   Often   Everyday

I have _____ experience listening to these accents (please tick):

	little/no	some	extensive
Australian English	☐	☐	☐
British English	☐	☐	☐
American English	☐	☐	☐
Indian English	☐	☐	☐
Japanese English	☐	☐	☐
Chinese English	☐	☐	☐
Korean English	☐	☐	☐

Follow the instructions on the CD and complete the tasks in this booklet

1

- Listen to the following phrase and write down **exactly** what you hear.

- Now, rate the speaker's **comprehensibility** on the following scale (please circle one number)

Easy to understand								Extremely difficult to understand
1	2	3	4	5	6	7	8	9

2

- Listen to the following phrase and write down **exactly** what you hear.

- Now, rate the speaker's **comprehensibility** on the following scale (please circle one number)

Easy to understand								Extremely difficult to understand
1	2	3	4	5	6	7	8	9

3

- Listen to the following phrase and write down **exactly** what you hear.

- Now, rate the speaker's **comprehensibility** on the following scale (please circle one number)

Easy to understand								Extremely difficult to understand
1	2	3	4	5	6	7	8	9

1.
- Listen to the phrase and rate the speaker's accent on the following scale:

  No accent   Extremely strong accent

  1   2   3   4   5   6   7   8   9

- Now, identify the accent of the speaker (please circle one only):

  Australian English   British English   American English   Chinese English
  Korean English   Indian English   Japanese English   Don't know

2.
- Listen to the phrase and rate the speaker's accent on the following scale:

  No accent   Extremely strong accent

  1   2   3   4   5   6   7   8   9

- Now, identify the accent of the speaker (please circle one only):

  Australian English   British English   American English   Chinese English
  Korean English   Indian English   Japanese English   Don't know

3.
- Listen to the phrase and rate the speaker's accent on the following scale:

  No accent   Extremely strong accent

  1   2   3   4   5   6   7   8   9

- Now, identify the accent of the speaker (please circle one only):

  Australian English   British English   American English   Chinese English
  Korean English   Indian English   Japanese English   Don't know

Appendix B

Language Experience Questionnaire

1. General information

1a. Age: ....

1b. Gender: FEMALE ☐   MALE ☐

1c. Nationality: ....

1d. City/Local region(s) where you lived in your home country:
....

1e. First language(s):
....

1f. Other languages spoken fluently:
....

1g. How long have you been living in Australia?
....

1h. Have you ever lived for more than 3 months in another country? (excluding Australia)

YES ☐   NO ☐ (*If 'no', go to question 1i.*)

If "yes", where? ....

For how long? ....

1i. Have you studied at college or university before?

YES ☐   NO ☐ (*If 'no', go to question 2*)

If "yes", where? ....

What was your major? ....

2. Overall familiarity with specific accents

2a. In general, how familiar are you with English spoken with the following accents?
(*Please circle one number for each accent*)

	Not familiar				Very familiar
Australian accent	1	2	3	4	5
Japanese accent	1	2	3	4	5
Chinese accent	1	2	3	4	5

3. Contact with teachers

3a. What accents of English do your *current* teachers have? (tick ☑ all that apply)

Australian ☐
British ☐
American ☐
New Zealand ☐
Other ☐ *(please specify)*: ....
Don't know ☐

3b. In the past, what accents of English have your other teachers had?

(*For this question, think about **all** the English-speaking teachers you have had through your life, in Australia **and** in your home country. Include native and non-native accents*).

....
....
....
....
....

4. Contact with other students

4a. *In your classes*, how often have you had contact with other students speaking with the following accents when they speak English?

(*For this question, think about other students in your English classes in Australia, and in your home country*)

	No contact	Some contact	Regular contact
Australian	☐	☐	☐
British	☐	☐	☐
American	☐	☐	☐
New Zealand	☐	☐	☐
Korean	☐	☐	☐
Chinese	☐	☐	☐
Japanese	☐	☐	☐
Vietnamese	☐	☐	☐
Thai	☐	☐	☐
Indonesian	☐	☐	☐
Indian	☐	☐	☐
Arabic	☐	☐	☐
Spanish	☐	☐	☐
Italian	☐	☐	☐
German	☐	☐	☐

Other accents (*please add other accents below if required*)

....	☐	☐	☐
....	☐	☐	☐
....	☐	☐	☐
....	☐	☐	☐

Extra information (*please add extra information if you think it is necessary*):

5. Contact with people at home

5a. *In your home*, how often have you had contact with people speaking with the following accents when they speak English?

(*For this question, think about your family, home-stay family, house/flat-mates, and neighbours, in Australia and in your home country*)

	No contact	Some contact	Regular contact
Australian	☐	☐	☐
British	☐	☐	☐
American	☐	☐	☐
New Zealand	☐	☐	☐
Korean	☐	☐	☐
Chinese	☐	☐	☐
Japanese	☐	☐	☐
Vietnamese	☐	☐	☐
Thai	☐	☐	☐
Indonesian	☐	☐	☐
Indian	☐	☐	☐
Arabic	☐	☐	☐
Spanish	☐	☐	☐
Italian	☐	☐	☐
German	☐	☐	☐

Other accents (*please add other accents below if required*)

....	☐	☐	☐
....	☐	☐	☐
....	☐	☐	☐
....	☐	☐	☐

Extra information (*please add extra information if you think it is necessary*):

6. Contact with people at work

6a. *At work*, how often have you had contact with people speaking with the following accents when they speak English?

(*For this question, think about other employees, customers/clients, and other people you may deal with, e.g. on the telephone, in Australia and in your home country*)

	No contact	Some contact	Regular contact
Australian	☐	☐	☐
British	☐	☐	☐
American	☐	☐	☐
New Zealand	☐	☐	☐
Korean	☐	☐	☐
Chinese	☐	☐	☐
Japanese	☐	☐	☐
Vietnamese	☐	☐	☐
Thai	☐	☐	☐
Indonesian	☐	☐	☐
Indian	☐	☐	☐
Arabic	☐	☐	☐
Spanish	☐	☐	☐
Italian	☐	☐	☐
German	☐	☐	☐

Other accents (*please add other accents below if required*)

	No contact	Some contact	Regular contact
....	☐	☐	☐
....	☐	☐	☐
....	☐	☐	☐
....	☐	☐	☐

Extra information (*please add extra information if you think it is necessary*):

7. Contact with people in the community

7a. *In the community*, how often have you had contact with people speaking with the following accents when they speak English?

(*For this question, think about your contact with people in the community, in Australia and in your home country: for example: at a sports club, at a place of worship [church/mosque/temple], in your circle of friends*)

	No contact	Some contact	Regular contact
Australian	☐	☐	☐
British	☐	☐	☐
American	☐	☐	☐
New Zealand	☐	☐	☐
Korean	☐	☐	☐
Chinese	☐	☐	☐
Japanese	☐	☐	☐
Vietnamese	☐	☐	☐
Thai	☐	☐	☐
Indonesian	☐	☐	☐
Indian	☐	☐	☐
Arabic	☐	☐	☐
Spanish	☐	☐	☐
Italian	☐	☐	☐
German	☐	☐	☐

Other accents (*please add other accents below if required*)

....	☐	☐	☐
....	☐	☐	☐
....	☐	☐	☐
....	☐	☐	☐

Extra information (*please add extra information if you think it is necessary*):

Appendix C

Histograms

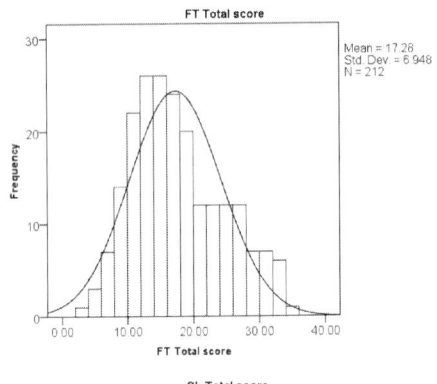

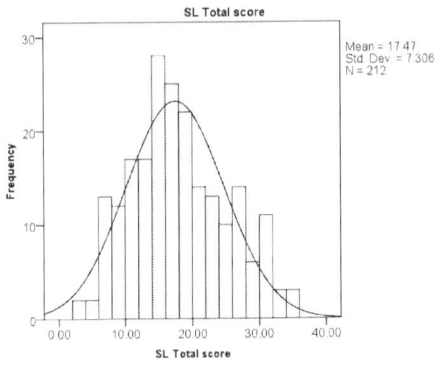

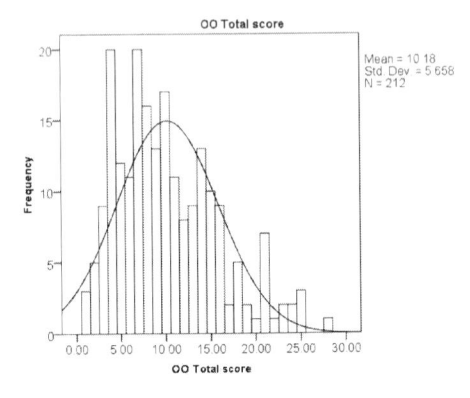

FT Total score — Mean = 17.28, Std. Dev. = 6.948, N = 212

SL Total score — Mean = 17.47, Std. Dev. = 7.306, N = 212

OO Total score — Mean = 10.18, Std. Dev. = 5.658, N = 212

Appendix D

DIF statistics (all items)

Appendix D contains (in the following order):

- Sleep test – DIF statistics for all items
    - Shared-L1 analysis
    - Familiarity analysis
- Oldest Old test – DIF statistics for all items
    - Shared-L1 analysis
    - Familiarity analysis

Sleep test		Japanese L1 (focal group) vs Other L1 (reference group)					
Item #	Q #	Estimate	ln(estimate)	Std. Error	Sig.	MH D-DIF	Dstd
1	1	2.546	.934	.496	.060	-2.195	-.088
2	2	.422	-.862	.361	.017	2.026	.163
3	3	1.570	.451	.404	.264	1.060	-.065
4		1.630	.489	.509	.337	-1.149	-.044
5		3.219	1.169	.935	.211	-2.747	-.041
6	4	2.725	1.003	.355	.005	-2.357	-.209
7	5	1.082	.079	.347	.819	-.186	-.026
8		.682	-.383	.479	.423	.900	.028
9	6	.657	-.420	.332	.206	.987	.087
10		.410	-.892	.327	.006	2.096	.198
11		.902	-.103	.333	.757	0.242	.024
12		.501	-.692	.339	.041	1.626	.146
13	7	.970	-.030	.341	.929	.071	.002
14	8	1.134	.126	.492	.798	-.296	-.011
15	9	.677	-.390	.535	.467	.917	.031
16	10	1.023	.023	.321	.942	-.054	-.003
18	11	.809	-.212	.332	.524	.498	.042
19		2.139	.760	.387	.050	-1.786	-.131
20	12	.896	-.109	.350	.755	.256	.027
21	13	1.351	.301	.318	.343	-.707	-.076
22	14	1.250	.223	.365	.541	-.524	-.046
23	15	1.258	.229	.404	.570	-.538	-.041
24	16	1.539	.431	.361	.232	-1.013	-.074
25	17	1.117	.111	.415	.789	-1.854	-.004
26	18	2.462	.901	.410	.028	-2.117	-.149
27	19	.408	-.897	.378	.018	-2.108	.149
28	20	1.043	.042	.389	.914	-.099	-.007
29	21	1.749	.559	.364	.124	-1.314	-.101
30	22	.545	-.607	.335	.070	1.426	.130
31	23(i)	.520	-.654	.349	.061	1.537	.137
32	23(ii)	.830	-.186	.314	.554	.437	.042
33	23(iii)	.594	-.520	.381	.172	1.222	.098
35	25	.746	-.293	.322	.361	.689	.070
36	26	.687	-.375	.355	.291	.881	.070
37		.888	-.119	.416	.775	.280	.022
38	27(i)	1.683	.521	.355	.143	-1.224	-.094
39	27(ii)	.808	-.213	.533	.689	.501	.015
40	28	1.121	.115	.450	.799	-.270	-.008

Sleep test		High familiarity with JA (focal group) vs Low familiarity with JA (reference group)					
Item	Q #	Estimate	ln(estimate)	Std. Error	Sig.	MH D-DIF	Dstd
1	1	.770	-.261	.474	.582	.613	.017
2	2	.446	-.807	.341	.018	1.896	.145
3	3	.646	-.437	.350	.211	1.027	.059
4		.334	-1.098	.465	.018	2.580	.103
5		.174	-1.750	.789	.027	4.113	.066
6	4	2.615	.961	.322	.003	-2.258	-.199
7	5	.970	-.031	.328	.926	.073	.006
8		.788	-.239	.448	.594	.562	.024
9	6	.855	-.157	.317	.620	.369	.023
10		.718	-.332	.303	.274	.780	.068
11		.915	-.089	.317	.779	.209	.011
12		.853	-.158	.310	.609	.371	.030
13	7	1.107	.101	.313	.746	-.237	-.016
14	8	1.540	.432	.456	.343	-1.015	-.042
15	9	.537	-.621	.510	.223	1.459	.051
16	10	.787	-.239	.301	.426	.562	.051
18	11	.628	-.465	.319	.146	1.093	.099
19		2.110	.747	.363	.040	-1.755	-.121
20	12	1.131	.123	.316	.697	-.289	-.030
21	13	1.169	.156	.295	.597	-.367	-.040
22	14	1.271	.240	.334	.472	-.564	-.045
23	15	1.714	.539	.376	.152	-1.267	-.076
24	16	1.709	.536	.329	.104	-1.260	-.103
25	17	.769	-.263	.400	.511	.618	.033
26	18	1.381	.323	.346	.350	-.759	-.062
27	19	.493	-.707	.371	.057	1.661	.105
28	20	1.866	.624	.346	.072	-1.466	-.097
29	21	1.489	.398	.319	.212	-.935	-.081
30	22	.755	-.280	.303	.354	.658	.065
31	23(i)	.812	-.208	.298	.485	.489	.058
32	23(ii)	.881	-.127	.280	.652	.298	.022
33	23(iii)	.699	-.358	.341	.293	.841	.063
35	25	1.037	.036	.291	.901	-.085	-.017
36	26	.985	-.015	.317	.963	.035	.011
37		1.031	.031	.353	.931	-.073	-.019
38	27(i)	1.241	.216	.335	.519	-.508	-.039
39	27(ii)	1.272	.241	.512	.638	-.566	-.015
40	28	1.390	.330	.419	.432	-.776	-.035

Oldest Old test		Chinese L1 (focal group) vs Other L1 (reference group)					
Item	Q #	Estimate	ln(estimate)	Std. Error	Sig.	MH D-DIF	Dstd
1	1	.318	-1.146	.364	.002	2.693	.235
2	2	.401	-.914	.371	.014	2.148	.166
3	3	.155	-1.866	.452	.000	4.385	.219
4	4	.770	-.261	.401	.516	.613	.042
5	5	.942	-.060	.354	.866	.141	.029
6	6	.773	-.257	.379	.497	.604	.064
7	7	.531	-.633	.392	.106	1.488	.109
8		.343	-1.071	.375	.004	2.517	.166
9	8i	.648	-.433	.383	.258	1.018	.096
10	8ii	.698	-.359	.338	.288	.844	.064
11	9	1.109	.103	.715	.885	-.242	-.005
12	10	.786	-.241	.438	.582	.566	.051
13		-	-	-	-	-	.071
14	11	.539	-.619	.408	.129	1.455	.099
15	12	.597	-.515	.837	.539	1.210	.037
16	13	.404	-.907	.466	.051	2.131	.093
17	14i	.333	-.1099	.450	.015	.258	.155
18	14iia	.814	-.206	.350	.557	.484	.038
19	14iib	.814	-.206	.350	.557	.484	.038
20	15	1.207	.188	.449	.676	-.442	-.007
21	16	.360	-1.020	1.001	.308	2.397	.033
22	17i	.309	-1.144	.540	.034	2.688	.104
23	17ii	.271	-1.307	.335	.000	3.071	.296
24	17iii	2.140	.761	.401	.058	-1.788	-.106
25	18	.351	-1.046	.342	.002	2.458	.193
26	19i	.503	-.687	.411	.095	1.614	.077
27	19ii	.157	-1.851	1.071	.084	4.350	.062
28	20	1.005	.005	.438	.991	-.012	.000
29	21	.629	-.464	.684	.498	1.090	.024
30		.444	-.813	.558	.145	1.911	.055
31	22	.884	-.124	.570	.828	.291	.018

Oldest Old test		High familiarity with Chinese accent (focal group) vs Low familiarity with Chinese accent (reference group)					
Item	Q #	Estimate	ln(estimate)	Std. Error	Sig.	MH D-DIF	Dstd
1	1	.507	-.679	.317	.032	1.596	.153
2	2	.587	-.532	.337	.114	1.250	.099
3	3	.225	-1.494	.432	.001	3.511	.183
4	4	.892	-.115	.378	.761	.270	.021
5	5	1.220	.198	.331	.549	-.465	-.029
6	6	1.060	.058	.350	.868	-.136	.002
7	7	.873	-.136	.341	.689	.320	.034
8		.444	-.811	.345	.019	1.906	.135
9	8i	.576	-.551	.368	.135	1.295	.097
10	8ii	.687	-.375	.316	.235	.881	.061
11	9	.727	-.319	.706	.651	.750	.019
12	10	.581	-.544	.406	.181	1.278	.083
13		.190	-1.660	1.181	.160	3.901	.043
14	11	.609	-.496	.390	.204	1.166	.076
15	12	.597	-.516	.845	.541	1.213	.031
16	13	.616	-.485	.438	.268	1.140	.049
17	14i	.421	-.864	.391	.027	2.030	.132
18	14iia	.641	-.445	.334	.183	1.046	.091
19	14iib	.641	-.445	.334	.183	1.046	.091
20	15	.872	-.137	.407	.737	.322	.023
21	16	.385	-.954	.983	.332	2.242	.028
22	17i	.808	-.213	.514	.678	.501	.021
23	17ii	.307	-1.180	.316	.000	2.773	.263
24	17iii	2.702	.994	.388	.010	-2.336	-.154
25	18	.494	-.706	.321	.028	1.659	.124
26	19i	.548	-.602	.413	.145	1.415	.069
27	19ii	.418	-.872	.931	.349	2.049	.026
28	20	1.250	.223	.414	.589	-.524	-.024
29	21	.428	-.849	.684	.215	1.995	.048
30		.383	-.959	.550	.081	2.254	.070
31	22	.921	-.082	.568	.885	.193	.014

Appendix E

Plots of exemplar DIF items

Appendix E contains (in the following order):

- Plots of Sleep item 2 (shared-L1 analysis and familiarity analysis)
- Plots of Sleep item 27 (shared-L1 analysis and familiarity analysis)
- Plots of Oldest Old item 1 (shared-L1 analysis and familiarity analysis)
- Plots of Oldest Old item 3 (shared-L1 analysis and familiarity analysis)
- Plots of Oldest Old item 8 (shared-L1 analysis and familiarity analysis)
- Plots of Oldest Old item 17 (shared-L1 analysis and familiarity analysis)
- Plots of Oldest Old item 23 (shared-L1 analysis and familiarity analysis)
- Plots of Oldest Old item 25 (shared-L1 analysis and familiarity analysis)

Sleep item 2

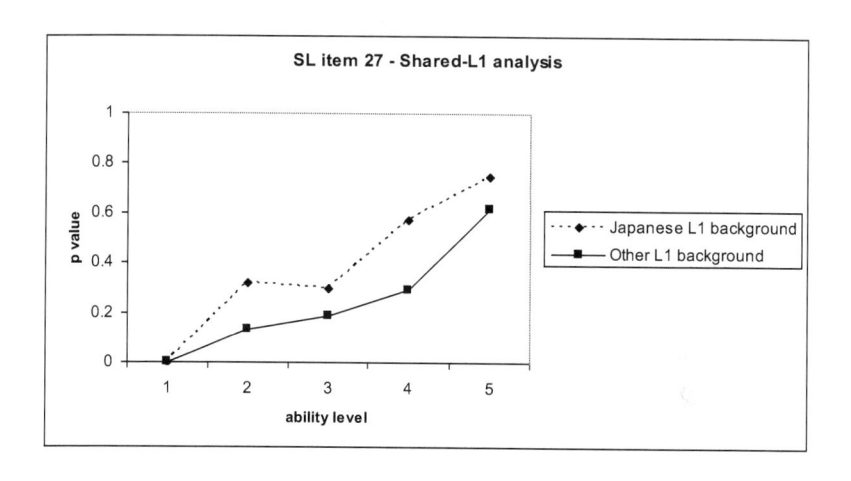

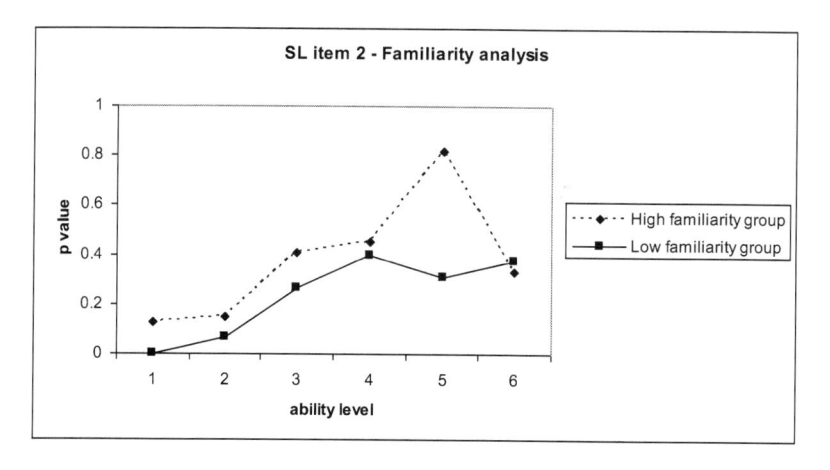

SL item 27 - Shared-L1 analysis

Japanese L1 background
Other L1 background

SL item 2 - Familiarity analysis

High familiarity group
Low familiarity group

Sleep item 27

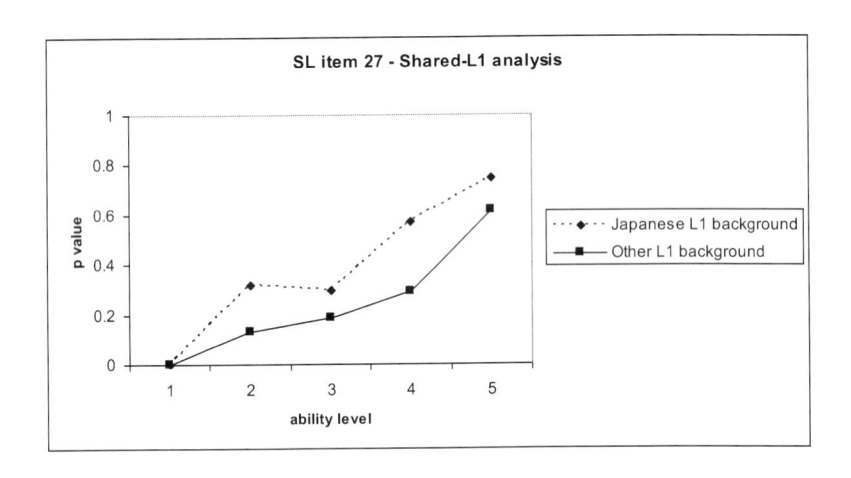

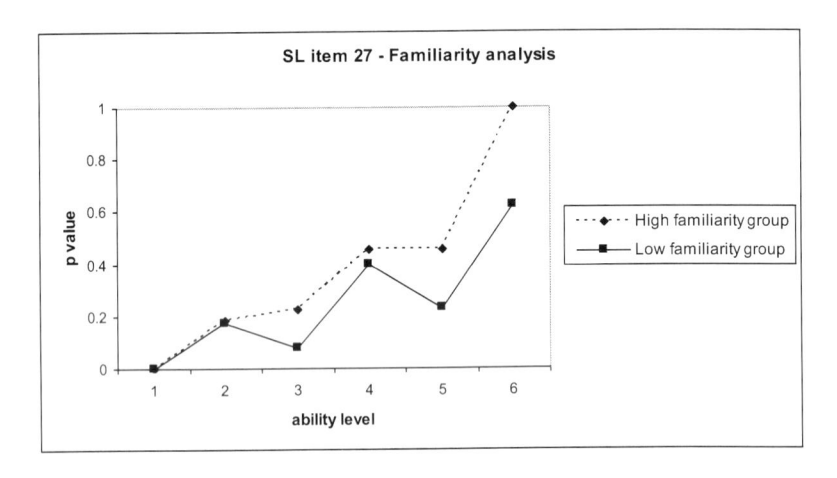

Oldest Old item 1

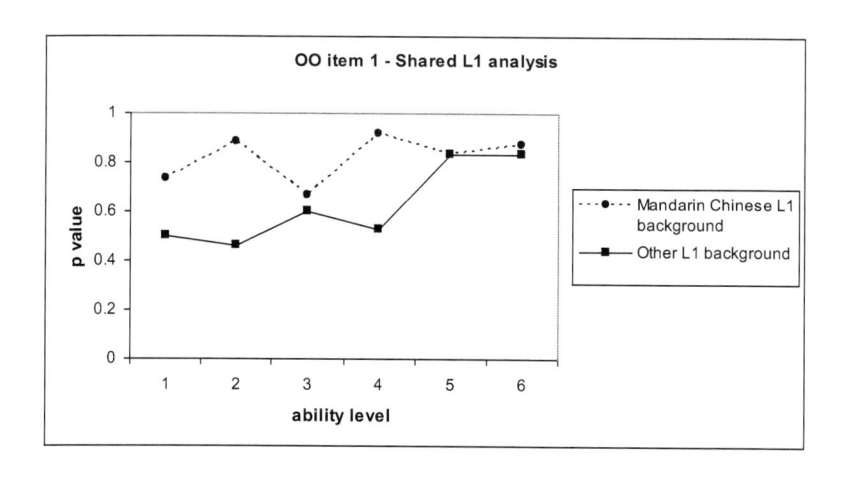

OO item 1 - Shared L1 analysis

- Mandarin Chinese L1 background
- Other L1 background

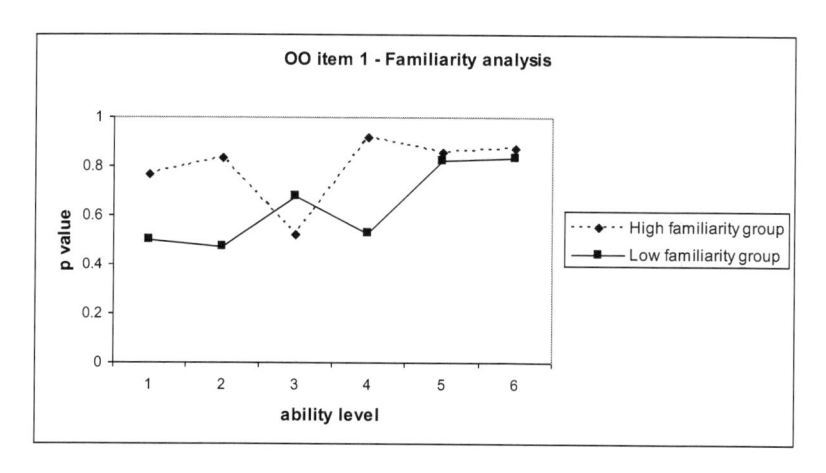

OO item 1 - Familiarity analysis

- High familiarity group
- Low familiarity group

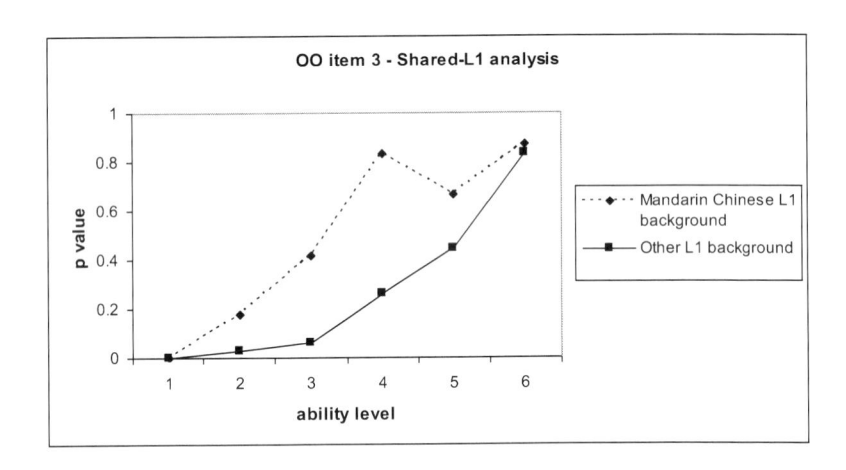

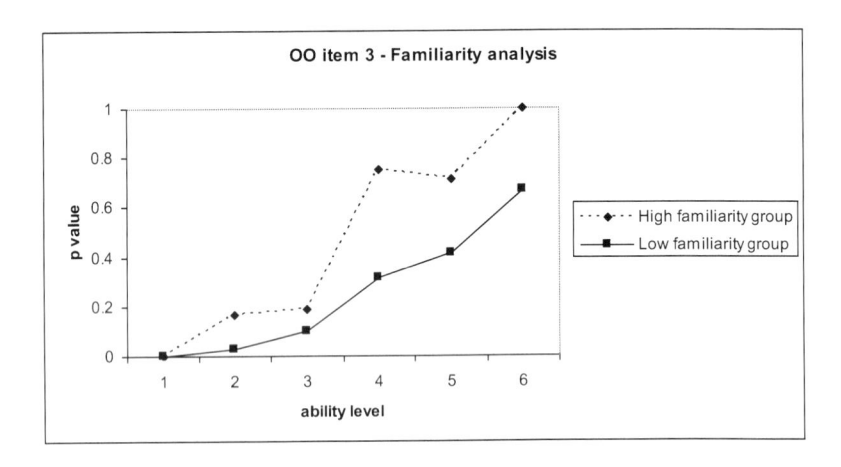

Oldest Old item 3

Oldest Old item 8

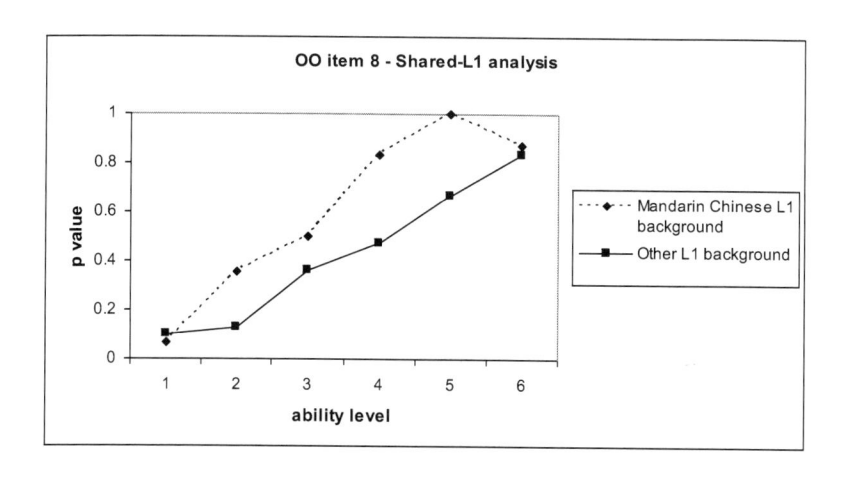

OO item 8 - Shared-L1 analysis

- Mandarin Chinese L1 background
- Other L1 background

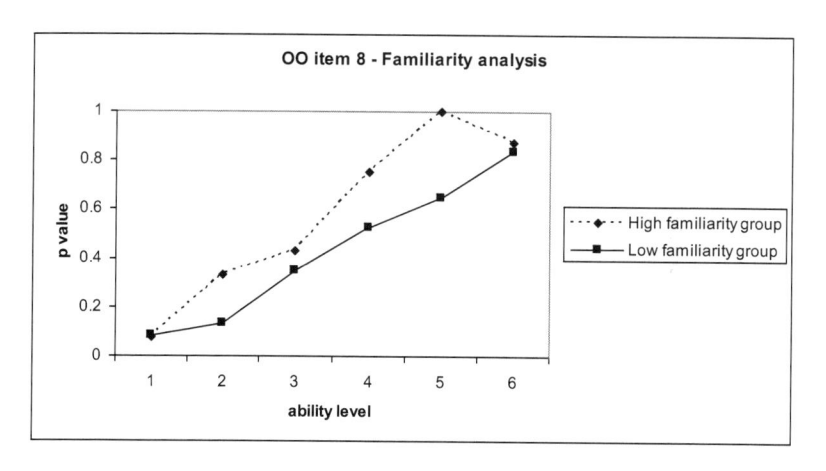

OO item 8 - Familiarity analysis

- High familiarity group
- Low familiarity group

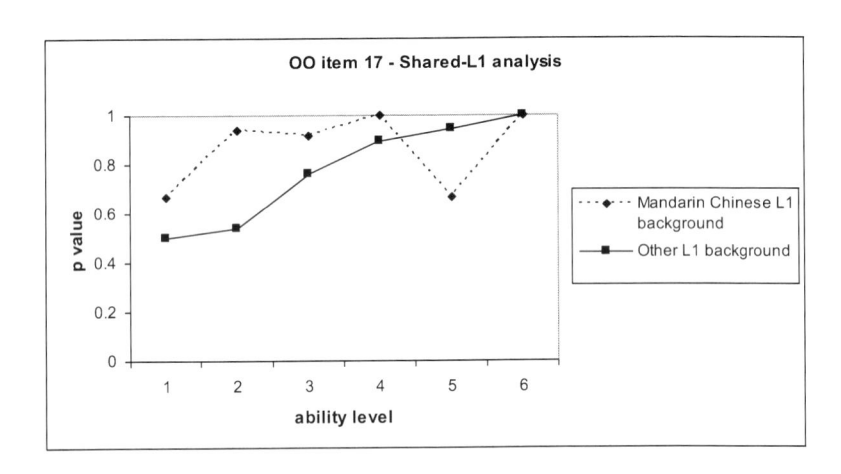

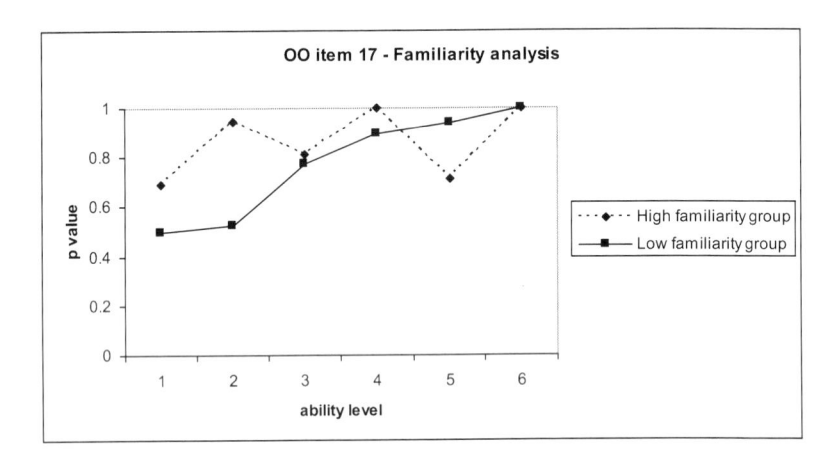

Oldest Old item 17

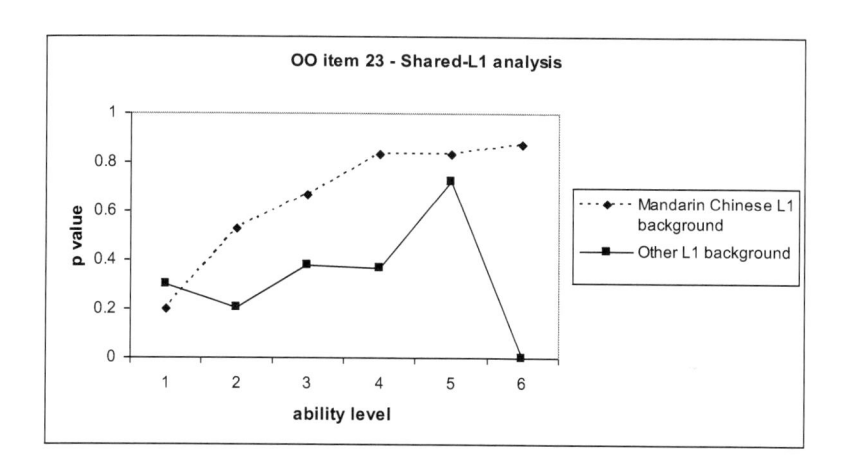

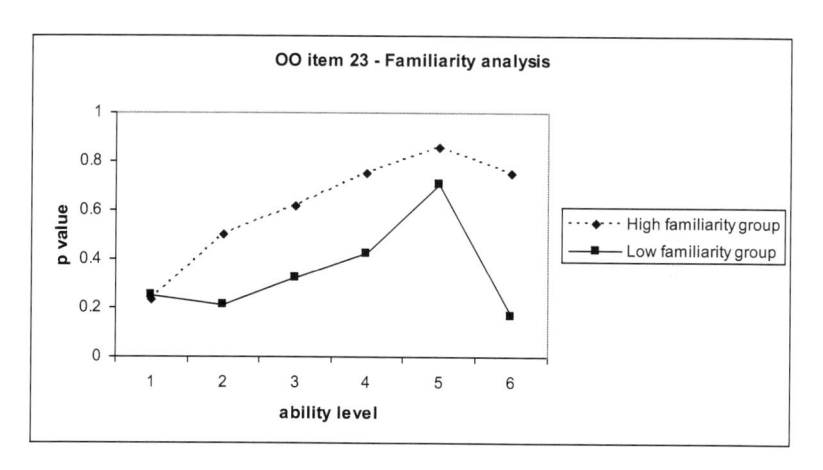

Oldest Old item 23

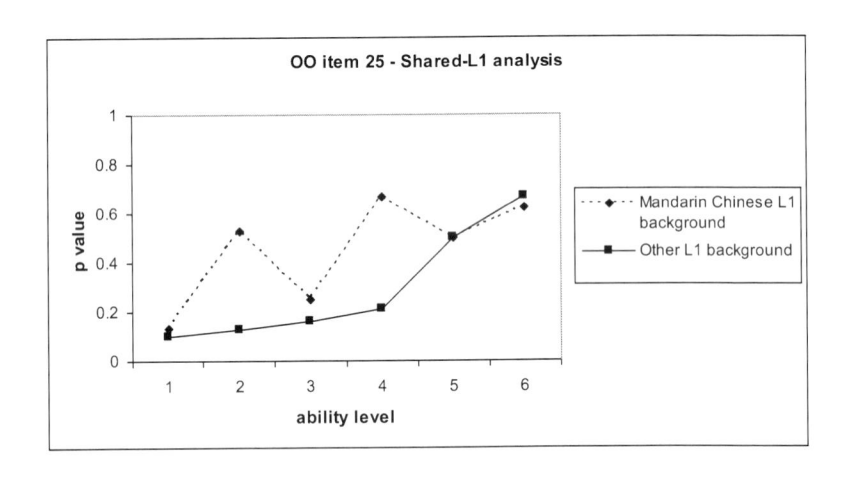

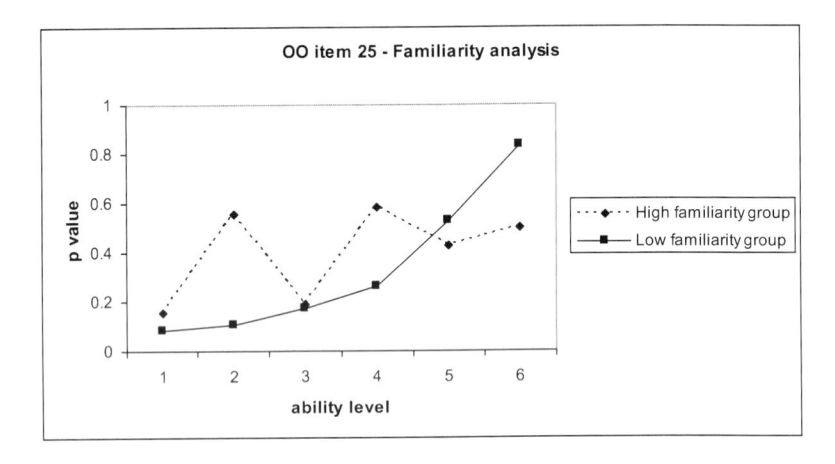

Oldest Old item 25

Appendix F

Speech Evaluation Instrument (original items)

1.	literate	—	—	—	—	—	—	—	illiterate
2.	educated	—	—	—	—	—	—	—	uneducated
3.	upper-class	—	—	—	—	—	—	—	lower-class
4.	rich	—	—	—	—	—	—	—	poor
5.	intelligent	—	—	—	—	—	—	—	unintelligent
6.	white-collar	—	—	—	—	—	—	—	blue-collar
7.	clear	—	—	—	—	—	—	—	unclear
8.	complete	—	—	—	—	—	—	—	incomplete
9.	fluent	—	—	—	—	—	—	—	disfluent
10.	organized	—	—	—	—	—	—	—	disorganized
11.	experienced	—	—	—	—	—	—	—	inexperienced
12.	advantaged	—	—	—	—	—	—	—	disadvantaged
13.	sweet	—	—	—	—	—	—	—	sour
14.	nice	—	—	—	—	—	—	—	awful
15.	good-natured	—	—	—	—	—	—	—	hostile
16.	kind	—	—	—	—	—	—	—	unkind
17.	warm	—	—	—	—	—	—	—	cold
18.	friendly	—	—	—	—	—	—	—	unfriendly
19.	likeable	—	—	—	—	—	—	—	unlikeable
20.	pleasant	—	—	—	—	—	—	—	unpleasant
21.	considerate	—	—	—	—	—	—	—	inconsiderate
22.	good	—	—	—	—	—	—	—	bad
23.	honest	—	—	—	—	—	—	—	dishonest
24.	active	—	—	—	—	—	—	—	passive
25.	talkative	—	—	—	—	—	—	—	shy
26.	aggressive	—	—	—	—	—	—	—	unaggressive
27.	enthusiastic	—	—	—	—	—	—	—	hesitant
28.	strong	—	—	—	—	—	—	—	weak
29.	confident	—	—	—	—	—	—	—	unsure
30.	energetic	—	—	—	—	—	—	—	lazy

(Developed by Zahn and Hopper, 1985)

Appendix G

Speaker Evaluation Task

Instructions

You will hear three different lecturers delivering the same excerpt from a lecture. Your task is to provide your evaluation of the lecturer's voice and speaking style by responding on the scales on the next two pages. (*Please look at the scales quickly now*).

The scales contain **seven-points**, and at the ends of each scale are two adjectives which are **exact opposites**. (*Please read through the adjectives now and make sure you understand the meaning of each word.*)

Respond on the scales by placing a cross (**x**) at one point on each of the scales to indicate your evaluation of the speaker on that trait.

For example:

If you think the speaker sounds *very* clear, you would place a cross near the word "clear" on the scale:

Example 1   clear   _x_ : ___ : ___ : ___ : ___ : ___   unclear

If you think the speaker sounds *very* unclear, you would place a cross near the word "unclear":

Example 2   clear   ___ : ___ : ___ : ___ : ___ : _x_   unclear

If you think the speaker sounds *fairly* clear, you might place you cross further towards the centre:

Example 3   clear   ___ : ___ : _x_ : ___ : ___ : ___   unclear

Remember that this is your opinion – there are no right or wrong answers.

Please be careful as you respond, because the **positive and negative adjectives are not all on one side of the scale**. Make sure you read each adjective carefully when you mark your response on the scale.

You may respond as you listen to each speaker, and you will be given **one minute** to complete your responses after you have heard each speaker. Try not to think about the content of the lecture; remember; you are rating each speaker on their voice and their speaking style.

- Read the adjectives on each scale carefully
- Place one cross (x) only on each scale
- Be sure you place one (x) on every scale
- Work quickly through the items
- Do not worry or puzzle over individual items. It is your first impressions that are wanted.

You will complete a practice task first, followed by the three real tasks.

PRACTICE TASK

The speaker sounds …

#	Left								Right
1.	clear	__	__	__	__	__	__	__	unclear
2.	cold	__	__	__	__	__	__	__	warm
3.	enthusiastic	__	__	__	__	__	__	__	unenthusiastic
4.	not fluent	__	__	__	__	__	__	__	fluent
5.	kind	__	__	__	__	__	__	__	unkind
6.	intelligent	__	__	__	__	__	__	__	unintelligent
7.	weak	__	__	__	__	__	__	__	strong
8.	friendly	__	__	__	__	__	__	__	unfriendly
9.	unsure	__	__	__	__	__	__	__	confident

The speaker has …

#	Left								Right
10.	good pronunciation	__	__	__	__	__	__	__	bad pronunciation

If this person was my lecturer, I would be …

#	Left								Right
11.	happy	__	__	__	__	__	__	__	unhappy

SPEAKER ONE

The speaker sounds …

#	Left								Right
1.	clear	__	__	__	__	__	__	__	unclear
2.	cold	__	__	__	__	__	__	__	warm
3.	enthusiastic	__	__	__	__	__	__	__	unenthusiastic
4.	not fluent	__	__	__	__	__	__	__	fluent
5.	kind	__	__	__	__	__	__	__	unkind
6.	intelligent	__	__	__	__	__	__	__	unintelligent
7.	weak	__	__	__	__	__	__	__	strong
8.	friendly	__	__	__	__	__	__	__	unfriendly
9.	unsure	__	__	__	__	__	__	__	confident

The speaker has …

#	Left								Right
10.	good pronunciation	__	__	__	__	__	__	__	bad pronunciation

If this person was my lecturer, I would be …

#	Left								Right
11.	happy	__	__	__	__	__	__	__	unhappy

SPEAKER TWO

The speaker sounds …

1.	clear	__	__	__	__	__	__	unclear
2.	cold	__	__	__	__	__	__	warm
3.	enthusiastic	__	__	__	__	__	__	unenthusiastic
4.	not fluent	__	__	__	__	__	__	fluent
5.	kind	__	__	__	__	__	__	unkind
6.	intelligent	__	__	__	__	__	__	unintelligent
7.	weak	__	__	__	__	__	__	strong
8.	friendly	__	__	__	__	__	__	unfriendly
9.	unsure	__	__	__	__	__	__	confident

The speaker has …

10.	good pronunciation	__	__	__	__	__	__	bad pronunciation

If this person was my lecturer, I would be …

11.	happy	__	__	__	__	__	__	unhappy

SPEAKER THREE

The speaker sounds …

1.	clear	__	__	__	__	__	__	unclear
2.	cold	__	__	__	__	__	__	warm
3.	enthusiastic	__	__	__	__	__	__	unenthusiastic
4.	not fluent	__	__	__	__	__	__	fluent
5.	kind	__	__	__	__	__	__	unkind
6.	intelligent	__	__	__	__	__	__	unintelligent
7.	weak	__	__	__	__	__	__	strong
8.	friendly	__	__	__	__	__	__	unfriendly
9.	unsure	__	__	__	__	__	__	confident

The speaker has …

10.	good pronunciation	__	__	__	__	__	__	bad pronunciation

If this person was my lecturer, I would be …

11.	happy	__	__	__	__	__	__	unhappy

Appendix H

Additional details of items

Appendix H contains (in the following order):

- Details of Sleep items 3-5
- Details of the Oldest Old item 12
- Details of the Oldest Old item 15
- Details of the Oldest Old item 22
- Details of the Oldest Old item 26

Details of Sleep items 3-5

Task (listing): *Three* activities the body carries out during sleep are: (i) .... (ii) .... (iii) .... **Key information in lecture:** Bodily activity continues during sleep. Certain chemicals, which encourage growth, are produced at the highest levels when we sleep. They are produced at other times, but their activity of production increases during sleep. Also, some waste products are removed from the body through the skin. The replacement of dying cells, which is a continuous process within the body, apparently becomes more intense during sleep. There is evidence as well that the body produces special proteins during sleep so that we feel rested when we awake. **Desired responses:** [any three of the following] chemicals produced (which encourage growth) **AND/OR** waste (products) removed (from body through skin) **AND/OR** replacement of dying cells **AND/OR** special proteins produced

Details of the Oldest Old item 12

> **Task (sentence completion):**
>
> *Complete this statement:*
>
> The 1991 study compared the number of people with Alzheimer's in the .... with ....
>
> **Key information in lecture:**
>
> We undertook a study in 1991 at the Boston Centre for the Aged and the aim of the study was to see if the occurrence of Alzheimer's disease among residents in the Centre matched the predictions of the previous surveys with regard to centenarians.
>
> **Desired responses:**
>
> Boston Centre/study **AND** (predictions of) previous surveys/research

Details of the Oldest Old item 15

> **Task (short answer question):**
>
> What *specific expression* is used to explain the good health of the oldest old?
> ....
>
> **Key information in lecture:**
>
> We've also found one aspect that's interesting in what may be called "selective survival" ...
>
> **Desired responses:**
>
> Selective survival

Details of the Oldest Old item 22

> **Task (table completion):**
>
> Complete the following table: [*relevant section of table shown below*]
>
> | (i) .... |
> |---|
> | Adaptive capacity |
>
> **Key information in lecture:**
>
> Obviously these factors interact in a complex way in determining our ability to maintain our good health. Perhaps the four main ones are the following: firstly, longevity genes; second, adaptive capacity ...
>
> **Desired responses:**
>
> Longevity genes

Details of the Oldest Old item 26

> **Task (sentence completion):**
>
> (i) 'Adaptive capacity' is the ability to
>
> ....
>
> **Key information in lecture:**
>
> We can define adaptive capacity as a person's ability to overcome a disease or injury.
>
> **Desired responses:**
>
> overcome disease/injury

Language Testing and Evaluation

Series editors: Rüdiger Grotjahn and Günther Sigott

Vol. 1 Günther Sigott: Towards Identifying the C-Test Construct. 2004.

Vol. 2 Carsten Röver. Testing ESL Pragmatics. Development and Validation of a Web-Based Assessment Battery. 2005.

Vol. 3 Tom Lumley: Assessing Second Language Writing. The Rater's Perspective. 2005.

Vol. 4 Annie Brown: Interviewer Variability in Oral Proficiency Interviews. 2005.

Vol. 5 Jianda Liu: Measuring Interlanguage Pragmatic Knowledge of EFL Learners. 2006.

Vol. 6 Rüdiger Grotjahn (Hrsg./ed.): Der C-Test: Theorie, Empirie, Anwendungen/The C-Test: Theory, Empirical Research, Applications. 2006.

Vol. 7 Vivien Berry: Personality Differences and Oral Test Performance. 2007.

Vol. 8 John O'Dwyer: Formative Evaluation for Organisational Learning. A Case Study of the Management of a Process of Curriculum Development. 2008.

Vol. 9 Aek Phakiti: Strategic Competence and EFL Reading Test Performance. A Structural Equation Modeling Approach. 2007.

Vol. 10 Gábor Szabó: Applying Item Response Theory in Language Test Item Bank Building. 2008.

Vol. 11 John M. Norris: Validity Evaluation in Language Assessment. 2008.

Vol. 12 Barry O'Sullivan: Modelling Performance in Tests of Spoken Language. 2008.

Vol. 13 Annie Brown / Kathryn Hill (eds.): Tasks and Criteria in Performance Assessment. Proceedings of the 28th Language Testing Research Colloquium. 2009.

Vol. 14 Ildikó Csépes: Measuring Oral Proficiency through Paired-Task Performance. 2009.

Vol. 15 Dina Tsagari: The Complexity of Test Washback. An Empirical Study. 2009.

Vol. 16 Spiros Papageorgiou: Setting Performance Standards in Europe. The Judges' Contribution to Relating Language Examinations to the Common European Framework of Reference. 2009.

Vol. 17 Ute Knoch: Diagnostic Writing Assessment. The Development and Validation of a Rating Scale. 2009.

Vol. 18 Rüdiger Grotjahn (Hrsg./ed.): Der C-Test: Beiträge aus der aktuellen Forschung/The C-Test: Contributions from Current Research. 2010.

Vol. 19 Fred Dervin / Eija Suomela-Salmi (eds./éds): New Approaches to Assessing Language and (Inter-)Cultural Competences in Higher Education / Nouvelles approches de l'évaluation des compétences langagières et (inter-)culturelles dans l'enseignement supérieur. 2010.

Vol. 20 Ana Maria Ducasse: Interaction in Paired Oral Proficiency Assessment in Spanish. Rater and Candidate Input into Evidence Based Scale Development and Construct Definition. 2010.

Vol. 21 Luke Harding: Accent and Listening Assessment. A Validation Study of the Use of Speakers with L2 Accents on an Academic English Listening Test. 2011.

www.peterlang.de